"I highly recommend that anyone who has questions about the issue of abortion read this book. I truly believe it was purposely written for the difficult time of decision about abortion that many people are facing.

Pastor Garuffi has written a book that expressly reveals God's heart about this controversial subject that is so relevant for all of us. Even if one does not accept the Bible as God's revelation of Himself and His will for us, the intellectual arguments about abortion are clearly presented. I especially would hope that any woman who is facing this life-changing decision about abortion would read this book. I certainly give "Your Body – God's Choice" a Five-Star rating."   REVEREND DONALD S. KRIGELMAN – *Church of God, Haleyville, NJ*

Your Body
God's Choice

Your Body
God's Choice
Abortion in 21ˢᵗ Century America

Melanie Jean Garuffi

A "God's Hand" Book

ISBN: 979-8-9853779-0-3

All scriptural quotations are from the New American Standard Bible (NASB) unless otherwise noted. Wherever I use the King James Version of the Bible (KJV), it is a result of a personal decision based on my love of the beautiful, poetic language found within its pages and because many people are already familiar with certain scriptures and passages as written in old English.

Scripture taken from the NEW AMERICAN STANDARD BIBLE®, Copyright © 1960,1962,1963,1968,1971,1972,1973,1975,1977,1995 by The Lockman Foundation. Used by permission. Lockman Foundation, Print.

Where possible, sources are credited in the Bibliography. In numerous cases, I relay the information I read or heard about many years ago, as this had been a subject long on my heart before I ever knew I would be writing a book. Most information is readily available and confirmable for anyone willing to do a quick internet search.

Email – agodshandbook@gmail.com

Disclaimer — Most names of organizations and politicians have been eliminated from this book. For privacy reasons, I have omitted or changed names to protect individuals' privacy.

Welcome!

Behold, children are a gift of the LORD, The fruit of the womb is a reward. — PSALM 127:3, NASB

I believe that you have picked up this book because you truly desire to know God's will concerning children, preborn babies, and the spiritual battle of the ages, which targets our youth. I believe that most people desire that every child should grow up safely in a loving and encouraging environment, having all the necessary tools to enable him or her to fulfill his or her divinely ordained purpose. You are welcome to join me in exploring what God's Word has to say about the importance of innocent preborn children and the beauty of life, love, forgiveness, and eternal destiny. I would like to share with you what God has been revealing to me about the spiritual nature of abortion, especially considering that children are gifts to us from Him.

Forgiveness

God is love. Please know that if you have had or have been part of an abortion, Jesus is waiting with open arms of forgiveness and love. Repent, and turn to Him. God wants you to be in His family. His mercy is wide. His forgiveness is a deep, deep, well of love.

We love, because He first loved us. — 1 JOHN 4:19

Dedication

This book is dedicated to our LORD and Savior, Jesus Christ, of whom Paul wrote:

For by him all things were created, both in the heavens and on the earth, visible and invisible, whether thrones or dominions or rulers or authorities — all things have been created through Him and for Him. — COLOSSIANS 1:16

It is also dedicated to the memory of every baby and every child whose life has been terminated or disrupted by the deadly agenda of the enemy of our souls and to those of you who have been called by God to work tirelessly to help save the lives of the innocent. Your larger reward is laid up in Heaven. Because you choose life, your blessings are assured:

> "I call heaven and earth to witness against you today, that I have set before you life and death, the blessing and the curse. So choose life in order that you may live, you and your descendants," — DEUTERONOMY 30:19

My primary purpose for writing this book is to share Scriptural confirmation of what the LORD has to say about the value of life and what He has shown me, personally, about this subject.

The number one reason that America will either rise in grace or fall in disgrace is the sin of abortion. We are killing our young and will face the severe judgment of God if we continue. This is our greatest national sin and the greatest human rights issue of our time. Still, we have a Hope in Jesus Christ!

> Therefore if any man be in Christ, he is a new creature: old things are passed away; behold, all things are become new. — 2 CORINTHIANS 5:17, KJV

Are You Considering an Abortion?

If you have found this book while considering an abortion, please do not think it is a coincidence. God is leading you to continue to give life to your baby who lives and breathes through you in your womb, which was designed for motherhood. He calls you to a life with Him as your Father in Heaven. He wants you to rely on Him for your own nurturing and provision.

We cannot always put our trust in the things that people tell us. Some people may try to steer you to end the life of your child and they may do this for their own priorities. Even if they appear to truly want to help, abortion counselors usually work for a monetary commission. That prejudices them in favor of ending the life of your child, even if they say that they are looking out for your best interests. If someone says that they "will be there for you" if you have an abortion but they do not say they will be there for you as a mother of an infant, then I can tell you with total assurance that they will never be people that you can fully trust. They do not have your best interest at heart, and they certainly have no concern for the life of your child.

It is hard to estimate the number of women who have been harmed by the cold and callous abortion industry's approach to conducting business. Abortion workers may seem warm and friendly, but they have often been misled by their industry and by our current culture. Abortion is never a quick fix for a woman's problems, as they would have you to believe. It does nothing to fix the underlying problems that might lead a woman to choose the unnatural route of aborting her baby.

As a pastor, I have talked to women who have suffered for years from guilt and shame and who suffer from post-traumatic stress. **Post-abortion syndrome** is a condition that many credible professionals suggest causes a severe psychiatric disorder. It is not surprising that abortion would take an emotional and spiritual toll on women. Because abortion clinics operate with a financial incentive, they do not offer the service of allowing clients to talk with those women who suffer from lifelong emotional and physical pain, from having had an abortion. Abortion workers will say what they need to in order to get your money.

Pro-life pregnancy care centers are free and will offer you the truth about what happens to many women who have abortions. Decisions made under intense fear and pressure often result in serious regrets. Pregnancy counseling centers will help you get through this tumultuous time in your life.

They have resources to guide you into making the best decision you could ever make — saving the life of your baby.

God gives us hope, and our HOPE is in Jesus Christ! The kind of hope He gives is an assurance that Jesus is with you when you accept Him as your Savior. Allow Jesus to guide you through the power of the Holy Spirit, which is the inward witness. The Spirit of God will only lead you into a decision for life for both you and your innocent baby. Rely on God to help you and He will lead the way. His way is the way of truth and love. Remember that God has the answers. People can help us, but it is God that will pull us through the difficult times. My prayer for you is:

> Now may the God of hope fill you with all joy and peace in believing, so that you will abound in hope by the power of the Holy Spirit. — ROMANS 15:13

If You Need Healing from Abortion, Jesus Awaits

If you have had an abortion, or have committed any other sin, and are truly repentant, you will find that God is waiting to receive you into His arms of love and grace. His grace is sufficient to correct any weakness:

> And He has said to me, "My grace is sufficient for you, for power is perfected in weakness." Most gladly, therefore, I will rather boast about my weaknesses, so that the power of Christ may dwell in me. — 2 CORINTHIANS 12:9

If you have repented, God forgives you, covers you in the blood of Jesus, and He does not see your sin! If you would like help in healing from the emotional pain of your abortion, there are many services available. Non-judgmental, post-abortion counseling is available at many pregnancy centers. Your age or the length of time since your abortion or abortion does not matter. I urge you to participate in whatever services you may find. You are not alone. Many of the counselors have also had abortions and understand the redemption found in Jesus Christ so do not let shame stand in the way of mental health and peace. Healing is available through Christ Jesus. He will take your burden. Jesus says:

> Come unto me, all ye that labour and are heavy laden, and I will give you rest. 29) Take my yoke upon you, and learn of me; for I am meek and lowly in heart: and ye shall find rest unto your souls. 30) For my yoke is easy, and my burden is light. — MATTHEW 11:28-30, KJV

The Church's Silent Horror

Secretly lurking in the church today is the pain and regret of abortion. With abortion so easily accessible, many young women, even churchgoers, turn to what may seem to be the easy way out of a very difficult situation. Statistics I have read show that by the age of forty-five, nearly one in four women in the United States has had an abortion. The guilt of abortion haunts many post-abortive women for life. Women may inwardly bury pain and shame that has been festering for decades until it comes out much later in life when they may have a breakdown or mental crisis. Many women resort to drugs or alcohol to cope when they find themselves in crisis and do not know where to turn. They lived in a time when little knowledge about abortions was available. Most church pulpits are silent on the subject and today, some churches say that abortion is a regrettable choice and, amazingly, many churches support the death of the preborn! These stands further advance shame upon women who regret their abortions. They are made to doubt themselves and their feelings when all around them are celebrating the misnomer — "right to choose."

God can only work with us after we have come to a place of utter remorse and regret for our sins. That is the place, in which we realize that we are helpless without Him. That is the place at which He can lift us up in love. He will strengthen us according to His Word and His riches in glory.

> And my God will supply all your needs according to His riches in glory in Christ Jesus. — PHILIPPIANS 4:19

Satan desires and delights to torture souls with taunting that leads to guilt, grief, worry, and anxiety. God wants the heart of every sinner to be healed. Acts 3:19, tells us, "Repent ye therefore, and be converted, that your sins may be blotted out when the times of refreshing shall come from the presence of the Lord" (KJV). Be refreshed through His love.

Table of Contents

Preface

Love . . . bears all things, believes all things, hopes all things, endures all things. — 1 Corinthians 13:7

Purpose of This Book

Please know that this book is written in love — love for mothers, fathers, and babies. We can do nothing in Christ without love. The love of God overcomes any hardship. This book is written prayerfully for all who are struggling with an unwanted pregnancy or guilt over having had an abortion, as well as those who are conflicted and hurting for any other reason. From conversations I have had, I have learned that many women considering abortion feel that they have no other option. Many are coerced. Much contained within these pages, especially Bible verses, is intentionally included to help others overcome a sense of helplessness. Empowered with Biblical knowledge, we can make more accurate decisions concerning issues of life.

Struggles are a part of living. We struggle with numerous difficulties, including broken families, poverty, death, addictions, and unplanned pregnancies. An unexpected pregnancy may be the greatest emotional and spiritual turmoil that a woman will ever face. The Bible teaches us how to be overcomers of worldly and spiritual concerns through Christ Jesus:

> And who is the one who overcomes the world, but he who believes that Jesus is the Son of God? — 1 JOHN 5:5

Like the old song says, "there is power in the blood" of Jesus, the Lamb of God.[1] Believers who give their lives to Christ to the very end will overcome even Satan.

And they overcame him by the blood of the Lamb, and by the word of their testimony; and they loved not their lives until the death. — REVELATION 12:11, KJV

This book is written for the seekers of truth, as well as for those in deep spiritual battles. The devil badgers us and seeks our souls. When we are unprepared spiritually for struggles, we may fall into sin. When we find our strength in Jesus Christ, we can do anything that is in God's will.[2] We must remember that, although Jesus died for all sins, His Word, applied to our lives, will keep us from all iniquity. We must also remember that God's love will pull us out of the pits of despair.

> We have come to know and have believed the love which God has for us. God is love, and the one who abides in love abides in God, and God abides in him. — 1 JOHN 4:16

Love

Since I preached my first sermon, God has shown me that the most important message I need to share is that God loves everyone. One of the calls that God has put on my life is to be a vocal advocate for the precious little lives, loved by God, that are yet to be born. I also believe that God wants me to show young women that God has a purpose for their lives, as well as for the lives of their babies. We cannot truly serve God unless we serve Him in love, just as this book is written in love. The most important purpose for anyone is to have a saving relationship with our loving God through His Son, Jesus Christ.

> And we know that all things work together for good to them that love God, to them who are the called according to his purpose. — ROMANS 8:28

Dads

The lives of the baby's fathers are every bit as important to God as those of the mothers and the babies. God's intentions and promises, truly, are always fulfilled with His love and righteousness. I hope to reach out with Bible truths to young men, who are also searching for answers. In response to God's love, our hearts should be bowed to Him, our Heavenly Father, as we consider what He ordains. The God of all Creation is concerned with each one of us. Considering the expanse of the universe, it is amazing how much He cares!

> When I consider Your heavens, the work of Your fingers, The moon and the stars, which You have ordained; What is man that You take thought of him, — PSALM 8:3-4a

Grace and Forgiveness

If you have already had an abortion, or even two or more, please consider the contents of these pages, especially Chapter 8, entitled "Hope and Forgiveness." I am thankful that God's nature includes immeasurable mercy, grace, and forgiveness. This includes forgiveness for repentant women and men who have aborted their children.

> For you, Lord, are good, and ready to forgive; abundant in loving kindness to all those who call on you. — PSALM 86:5

When we honestly repent of sin in our hearts, God is always quick to forgive. If you sincerely regret your abortion(s), lay your heart down at the foot of the Cross. Post-abortion counseling is often available at Christian pregnancy care centers. There is no need to continually suffer under the weight of the hurts and sins of your past. If you are suffering under the weight of any oppression and guilt, lay it all down at the foot of the Cross. Jesus said in Mark 1:15c, ". . . repent, and believe in the Gospel!" God's love and mercy are greater than all our sins. God's grace is larger than your abortion.

National Injustice and the Judgment of God

In the following pages, while leaning on the LORD, I will share with you what I believe God has shown me about the evil, spiritual nature of abortion, which is the destruction of a preborn baby. The stealing of the full promise of the lives of our precious little ones occurs through other means, as well, such as pedophilia, human trafficking, drug addiction, and now, so-called "after-birth abortion." These are all spiritual issues.

As a nation, we have gotten out of the will of God. We have abandoned Godly principles, ignoring the fact that God is righteous, as well as loving. He will ensure that we receive our just reward as a nation, either for the good or for the bad. In Jeremiah 30:11-17, God tells His people that He will bring them freedom from oppression but before that, He will chasten them for their sins. He warned, "And will by no means leave you unpunished."[3] Many people believe that we are already under national judgment and chastisement in America. Others believe that God is giving us time to repent and make things right, especially concerning the sin of abortion.

We can examine Bible history and compare our current situation to the past. The Jewish exiles, who had returned from Babylonian captivity to rebuild the temple in Jerusalem in 538 BC, compromised their position with God by marrying their heathen neighbors, thus raising new generations of pagan worshippers among God's chosen people. When they realized their spiritually fragile condition, caused by their disobedience, they "trembled at the words of God."[4] Ezra, the priest, who led the people in spiritual reforms, said,

> . . . O my God, I am ashamed and embarrassed to lift up my face to Thee, my God, for our iniquities have risen

above our heads, and our guilt has grown even to the heavens. — EZRA 9:6

I agree with Ezra. I am embarrassed that in congregations across America, the Christian church has married the world by allowing abortion to infiltrate the body of Christ. We should be humble and seek the face of the LORD in Heaven for the forgiveness of our grievous sins.[5] We have been lax in caring for the mothers of preborn babies. We need to repent of our great silence in the face of the great evil of allowing a nearly fifty-year, legally permitted holocaust.

The Spirit of Herod the Great

Abortion strongly influences our nation. Dark spirits, including the one that worked through Herod the Great, take orders from the top down, starting with the devil himself; they do not work independently. We know from Ephesians 6:12 that evil spiritual forces are orderly and work in a hierarchy with the main ruler, Satan, and his subordinates. The spirit of abortion is the same that is responsible for the deaths of all babies and young children, whether in the womb or after they are born into this world. This evil spirit is hungry for the blood of innocent life, just as the sweet baby hungers for his mother's milk and touch. The supernatural cause of legalized abortion in our country has roots that travel far and run deep all around this world. It is an ancient spiritual problem, and it is part of a plan for the destruction of destiny, hope, and promise for all people. The Apostle John saw part of this plan while on the Isle of Patmos:

> . . . and the dragon stood before the woman which was ready to be delivered, for to devour her child as soon as it was born. — REVELATION 12:4

The dragon symbolizes Satan. The above verse represents how Satan worked through King Herod to attempt to destroy the salvation plan of God through the Christ Child.[6]

It was over four years ago when the LORD God showed me the spiritual nature of this age-long war against children. This is a constant battle that rages between the forces of good and evil. It is the battle of righteousness versus the work of the devil, waged in the heavenlies and revealing itself in the moral and political battle we are witnessing here on earth. This war is more than about "women's rights," as you may have heard in the media. That is a deceptive term, created and used by the enemy of our souls to mislead our generation into ignoring the rights of preborn babies and the sovereignty of God. Pro-abortion activists call the movement to save the lives of innocent babies a "war on women" but legalized abortion and cultural affirmation of abortion is the real war on women. The devil always twists the truth to gain a foothold in our lives. He was a liar and a deceiver from the beginning. He, by his own choice, created the first rebellion against God in Heaven and he continues to do so. He uses unsuspecting people in his sinister tactical maneuvers. Many of his bases of operations in the United States are abortion clinics.

The truth of God's Word must not be neglected in this battle. The lives of all children depend on our human interventions of love and prayers as we stay grounded in the Word. John 1:1 tells us that Jesus is the Word. We know that Jesus came to present God's Word, which is truth.[7] Looking at Jesus, the bearer of eternal truth, Pilate said to Him,

> . . . What is truth? — JOHN 18:38a

The truth was not in Pilate that day, as he sentenced our LORD to be crucified, although Pilate's wife was being led by the Holy Spirit. She told him to have nothing to do with that man, meaning the crucifixion of Jesus.[8] Pilate had been warned of the truth. Abortionists and those who push abortion know the truth that abortion kills a human life, but they choose to ignore science and God. As members of the Christian community and the family of God, we are directed to share His Word and the truth that lies within the pages of the Bible.

Questions to Review to see if this book is for you.

1. Are you considering an abortion?

2. Is someone pressuring you to have an abortion?

3. Was someone you loved — a child, grandchild, niece, or nephew — aborted?

4. Have you had an abortion?

5. Are you against abortion but reason that it may be "okay" in certain circumstances?

6. Are you concerned with the prevalence of abortion? Are you concerned with the growing threat and prevalence of other sins, such as drug abuse and pedophilia?

7. Does your heart grieve at the mention of pedophilia, drug addiction, and/or abortion?

8. Have you considered stepping out in faith to serve the LORD by standing up for righteousness?

9. Are you learning to listen to the voice of God in discerning His call on your life and ministry?

10. Do you desire God's sovereign will above the wishes of man?

If you answered "yes" to any of these questions, this book is for you. I believe that everyone who wants to live out the will of God in his or her life will find much to consider within these pages. Living outside the will of God leads to confusion and, ultimately, spiritual death. If you want God to help with your decision-making on all matters of life, this book is for you!

Scripture

The focus of this work is to encourage us to think of the promise of life and blessings through the lens of scripture. Together we will explore what our Sovereign God has to say in the Bible about the sanctity of life. We will embark on a journey through God's written Word as we examine scriptures pertaining to the spiritual aspects of life and abortion. I believe that scripture is the inerrant Word of God. It is well-known that it was written by approximately forty men, over a span of about sixteen hundred years. Because it was inspired by the Holy Spirit, it fits perfectly and contextually together as our guidebook for life on this earth. The Bible also gives us a probing and educational look into eternity. If we keep our hearts open, as we study its divinely written pages, we may also learn how to please God and how to have an everlasting relationship with Him in Glory.

> All Scripture is inspired by God and profitable for teaching, for reproof, for correction, for training in righteousness; — 2 TIMOTHY 3:16

Personal Experiences

In addition to the Inspired Word of God, it is also important that I share what God has taught me through real-life experiences, both mine and of friends and acquaintances of mine, whose identities will remain private. I have lived and been in ministry long enough to have learned good practical skills and common-sense remedies to hand down to the upcoming generation. Examining how some have dealt with situations concerning surprise or unwanted pregnancies can give others facing the same issues an understanding that they are not alone in their problems. To deal with present problems and heartaches, we can often draw upon what others have learned. God has also gifted us with reason and intellect, along with free will. It would be foolish not to utilize all three of these tools, along with the lessons learned by others, so long as we ultimately rely on the wisdom that comes from above!

> For the LORD gives wisdom; From His mouth come knowledge and understanding. — PROVERBS 2:6

Leading of the Holy Spirit

There are supernatural experiences that I have had, in which the Spirit of God has given me revelation through either a dream, a word of knowledge, or a word of wisdom. This includes the revelation of the demon spirit that influenced King Herod. Although highly personal, I share these experiences because God has directed me to do so.

The revelation is not a "new revelation" because the Bible is complete in doctrine. It is, however, fresh in that God has also shown me certain situations while in the Spirit. We must always be discerning and careful to make sure that nothing contradicts scripture. There are sometimes experiences that we overlook or put aside for fear of ridicule. We must not fear man, however, but be obedient to God, as we listen for His voice. In Isaiah 41:10, we learn, "Do not fear, for I am with you; Do not anxiously look about you, for I am your God. I will strengthen you, surely I will help you, Surely I will uphold you with My righteous right hand." Of course, it is also important to "test the spirits, "[9] as there are many false prophets in the world. We must be discerning, relying on the Holy Spirit, who guides us "into all truth."[10]

> If we live in the Spirit, let us also walk in the Spirit. — GALATIANS 5:25

The Sermon on the Mount

We can learn a great deal about the issues of life by studying Christ's teachings on the "Sermon on the Mount," which many say is the most famous sermon ever preached. If the Christian believer learns the essential lessons of this great discourse, which is found in the Book of Matthew, Ch. 5-7, he or she will be greatly strengthened in the spirit. This is because this important sermon gives us a glimpse of God's mind on the affairs of this world and how we should behave towards others and before Him. God is concerned with the way we treat every person we encounter, including those who are preborn and still in the womb. Because God is love, He wants us to operate in love! With the Sermon on the Mount, Jesus Christ gave us instruction from on High on how to deal with a fallen world full of sin.

> When Jesus saw the crowds, He went up on the mountain; and after He sat down, His disciples came to Him. — MATTHEW 5:1

Salvation

Before Jesus delivered the Sermon on the Mount, He wanted people to be saved for eternity. His initial ministry began with a message of repentance and salvation.[11] Gathering disciples and traveling locally, He taught in Jewish synagogues all over the countryside, while also healing the sick and casting out demons. "Great crowds" followed Him.[12] They witnessed and experienced miracles of God. The message of repentance and salvation was foundational to His later teachings. The Sermon on the Mount, beginning in Matthew Ch. 5, became the center of our LORD's teaching. It was not immediately meant for the ears of the world but for those who were already prepared by having already repented and now believed in Him.

> Large crowds followed Him from Galilee and the Decapolis and Jerusalem and Judea and from beyond the Jordan. — MATTHEW 4:25

The Beatitudes

It is often said that, when Jesus came, He turned the world upside down. We can certainly see this at the beginning of the Sermon on the Mount as Jesus expounded upon "The Beatitudes." Preaching to His disciples and the crowds, Jesus taught His followers to love God and to love their neighbors. He addressed new believers with a deep level of spiritually practical teachings, equipping them with new spiritual tools. The lessons were profound and, surprisingly, were the opposite of common supposition, just as they are in today's world.

The Beatitudes are a series of eight blessings that Jesus promised to those who would adhere to these new lessons. The word "beatitude" refers to "a blessing." In these lessons, the followers of Jesus learn the rewards of placing others before themselves, in contrast to the common, worldly way of getting ahead by aggressively placing ourselves above others. Another way to express the word "blessing" is "to be happy."

The Westminster Dictionary of the Bible describes The Beatitudes as "an analysis of perfect spiritual well-being" correcting "all low and carnal views of human happiness."[13] The carnal, or the flesh, is always in a struggle against the Spirit of God. Believers who learn to live according to these essential teachings will move out of the carnal realm and into the Kingdom of God on earth. While we look forward to the future Kingdom of God, it is partially fulfilled here on earth as the Spirit of Christ lives within the believer.

> However, you are not in the flesh but in the Spirit, if indeed the Spirit of God dwells in you. But if anyone does not have the Spirit of Christ, he does not belong to Him. — ROMANS 8:9

Why I Have Included One Beatitude at the End of Each Chapter

The Beatitudes are wonderful, ethical, character-building teachings for the believer in Jesus Christ and God has impressed upon me to conclude the first eight chapters of this book with one Beatitude. Chapters 9 and 10 conclude with Jesus' admonition to be the salt and light of this world.[14]

Some say that considering how The Beatitudes collectively encompass an attitude of the heart, they can be called "The Be-Attitudes" (or the attitude of "how Christians should be"). They are:

1. "Blessed are the poor in spirit, for theirs is the kingdom of heaven" (Matthew 5:3).

2. "Blessed are they that mourn, for they shall be comforted" (Matt. 5:4).

3. "Blessed are the meek, for they shall inherit the earth" (Matt. 5:5).

4. "Blessed are those who hunger and thirst for righteousness, for they shall be satisfied" (Matt. 5:6).

5. "Blessed are the merciful, for they shall obtain mercy" (Matt 5:7).

6. "Blessed are the pure in heart, for they shall see God" (Matt. 5:8).

7. "Blessed are the peacemakers, for they shall be called sons of God" (Matt. 5:9).

8. "Blessed are those who are persecuted for righteousness' sake, for theirs is the kingdom of heaven" (Matt. 5:10).

I have also included:

9. "You are the salt of the earth; but if the salt has become tasteless, how will it be made salty again? It is good for nothing any more . . ." (Matt. 5:13).

10. "You are the light of the world. A city set on a hill cannot be hidden" (Matt. 5:14).

In this world, it is often assumed that aggressiveness is rewarded with power and that passivity causes powerlessness, so these ideals may seem surprising. To gain perspective on this, observe the competitive and combative habits of many in any city's rush-hour traffic. Jesus does not call His people to act obnoxiously but to act in love! Looking at the list of Beatitudes, we can see that Jesus really did challenge the world to turn its thought patterns upside down. God makes all things new!

> Therefore if any man be in Christ, he is a new creature: old things are passed away; behold, all things are become new. — 2 CORINTHIANS 5:17, KJV

A New Vision

Speaking of "new," it is significant that there are eight Beatitudes, which begin the Sermon on the Mount. In the Bible, the number eight represents a new beginning. For instance, there were eight people saved on the Ark, including Noah.[15] There are seven days in a week, and the eighth day begins a new week. Jesus was resurrected on the eighth day, which began a new Covenant between God and man. Unger's Bible Handbook explains, "Applied to the Scriptures the terms Old Testament and New Testament mean strictly Old and New Covenant."[16] We are made new when we are born again in Christ.

> Jesus answered and said to him, "Truly, truly, I say to you, unless one is born again he cannot see the kingdom of God." — JOHN 3:3

Notice, in the preceding verse, that, when we are born again, we receive new vision. When we get a glimpse into the kingdom of God, we can see anew and may appreciate more the importance of life. My hope is that those who believe in abortion, or who are on the fence, so to speak, will begin to look at preborn babies in a new light. It is also my hope that this book will give readers an expanded understanding of the scope of the spiritual battle that rages around us. Each of us engages in spiritual battles every day, whether we are aware of it or not. This book should at least ignite some introspection and will hopefully prepare you to deal with spiritual struggles.

The More the Merrier or A Quiver Full of Blessings

Scripture tells us that babies are blessings! It is interesting that "numerous progeny" are among many rewards that are listed in the Bible:

> Like arrows in the hand of a warrior, So are the children of one's youth. How blessed is the man whose quiver is full of them . . . — PSALM 127:4-5a

It makes me weary to hear people say that people in the past wanted to have many children because of their agricultural lifestyle. While that is true, God does not use the word "because" in the above-quoted verse. It simply states that having many children is a blessing. I believe the more children we have, the more love and joy we can share with others.

Abortion Breaks the Blessing

God's great and amazing love for each one of us also includes His love for every preborn child of His creation. All babies are His, regardless of the conditions of their conception. There are no mistakes. Because of sin, we are living in a fallen world, however, which encompasses all of creation until Jesus comes again. Consequently, we witness imperfections such as birth defects. Because of sin, babies are often born to unmarried parents. We cannot, however, take it upon ourselves to compound sin by taking innocent life.

Many consider abortion a tragic necessity and many do not see the serious harm it causes. They believe that snuffing out a baby's life may somehow advance the parent's life by not burdening them with parental responsibility. God's word says, however, that children are a blessing:

> Behold, children are a gift of the LORD, The fruit of the womb is a reward. — PSALM 127:3

Our Purpose and Destiny

Most parents are disappointed if their children do not fulfill the plans that they make for them because they have a sincere desire for their children to be blessed beyond measure. Our Father God is pleased when we live out our destinies, which He designed. He has a wide range of emotions. Imagine His heartbreak when we do not fulfill His plans for us and when babies die before the time that He allows. God's love is greater than all of ours. If someone tries to reason this away, saying that God cannot feel grief, then that one should be reminded that we are made in His image. When God's people stray, He grieves:

> Oh that my head were waters, And my eyes a fountain of tears, That I might weep day and night For the slain of the daughter of my people. — JEREMIAH 9:1

There is much to share about heartbreak, but there is, even more, to share about hope. Wherever you are right now, whoever you are, and no matter what point you are in life — God has an answer and a plan for you. There is nothing so big that God cannot handle if we put our trust in Him.

> Great is the LORD, and highly to be praised, And His greatness is unsearchable. — PSALM 145:3

My Experience

For the past eighteen years, I have served in Christian ministry in various capacities. I have served as Senior Pastor, Assistant Pastor, Associate Pastor, Bible study teacher, Worship Leader, guest preacher, Christian songwriter, and Christian radio show hostess. Through many years of preaching, teaching, and ministry, I have listened to the stories of many searching souls and have counseled many. A group of Spirit-led Christians and I are presently organizing a crisis pregnancy organization, Life Choice Pregnancy Center of Western North Carolina in our community. I also serve the LORD as Pastor of Christian ACTS Church at the Crossroads.

> Preach the word; be ready in season and out of season; reprove, rebuke, exhort, with great patience and instruction. — 2 TIMOTHY 4:2

The Big Picture

This world is the central scene of the largest battle of the universe. In the unseen realm, Satan's hatred of God and all life that He created, spurs the evil one on towards his destructive ends in every way possible. The Bible tells us that God created man for His pleasure.[17] God created life; the devil seeks to destroy life. This is because everything the devil does is opposite to the work and plan of God.

The battle for life that rages in America is the same battle that has gone on since the days of Adam and Eve. Cain was the first murderer. He killed his own innocent brother in a jealous rage. Satan seeks to destroy family bonds. The battle between good and evil, and life and death, has raged on through time and will not be over until Jesus returns as promised in victory over the final battle.[18] Destroying the family is the devil's mission because God calls us His family; this is one reason why the devil likes the savagery of abortion. When we take Jesus as our Savior, we can become the children of God and joint-heirs with Christ with a future in Glory.[19]

Lack of Biblical Teaching and Reading

American Christians are under-schooled and even unschooled in the Old Testament. We love our New Testament, but Old Testament teaching is sorely lacking. I once dreamed that I was desperately running around, trying to give everyone in sight a copy of the Old Testament. In my dream, I was very concerned that they only had New Testaments in their hands. The two Testaments work together. We cannot fully understand the New Testament without an understanding of the Old Testament lessons, prophets, prophecies, and law. Jesus said,

> Think not that I am come to destroy the law, or the prophets: I am not come to destroy, but to fulfill. — MATTHEW 5:17, KJV

Because there are churches that often neglect the full counsel of God by neglecting to teach scripture, we have lost a lot of our power to accomplish God's purposes both in the church and the culture. We need to fuel the power source of our faith:

> For faith comes by hearing and hearing by the word of God. — ROMANS 10:17

History of Pagan Sacrifice

We understand that murder is a sin. What is little known, but is written often in the Old Testament, is that the heathen people surrounding the children of Israel were practitioners of many sexual perversions and child sacrifice. This information is at our fingertips in the most popular book ever published, but we must open it to find out what it says!

The spirit of abortion and child murder is a shocking part of the Biblical narrative during the time of Moses, as it worked through Pharaoh to kill the Hebrew babies. After the birth of Jesus, it worked through Herod to kill the babies of Bethlehem. The "prince of the power of the air"[20] — Satan — is the "spirit that now worketh in the children of disobedience." All abortions, deaths of children, and every other sin had its beginning in the ancient rebellion in Heaven, through Lucifer, that we read about in Isaiah Ch. 14.

The LORD wants us to understand the spiritual dimensions of the blight of abortion and child murder in our society. Since churchgoers today are not as familiar with the Old Testament lessons and warnings as they would have been even one hundred years ago, we need to gain an understanding of the history of child sacrifice, which many cultures practiced. First-born children were often put into the foundation of a new building to appease the gods. Newborn babies were offered up to demonic gods to ensure a bountiful crop and for general provision. The pagan neighbors of our Old Testament patriarchs indulged in many repulsive rituals.

America's Spiritual Battle

Sadly, today America indulges in many of the same types of practices. Our babies are being lost to the tools (weapons) and medications of abortionists at a rate of approximately three thousand per day. These children have never had the opportunity to share their unique and individual calling with this world. Who knows what blessings these children may have been to humanity if they only had the blessing of life? Would any one of these preborn children, if given the choice, deny his or her own life? Abortion survivors testify again and again that they are thankful that they escaped execution. Preborn babies have no voice, so we must be their spokespersons:

> Open your mouth for the mute, For the rights of all the unfortunate. — PROVERBS 31:8

Satan requires the deaths of a nation's babies in to speed the annihilation of a God-honoring culture. In the United States of America, sadly, Satan has greatly influenced our land, which has slipped away from its original Biblical moorings. The promise of young life has literally been vacuumed and cut out of the mothers, thrown into waste buckets, and either burned or flushed into the septic systems of America.

The land is full of bloody crimes, and the city is full of violence. — EZEKIEL 7:23, KJV

Chapter One

God's Call

Trust in the LORD with all your heart And do not lean on your own understanding. — Proverbs 3:5

Message from the LORD in a Walmart Parking Lot

The word of God tells us to "pray without ceasing."[1] One afternoon, in a local Walmart, I was praying silently and seeking the LORD's will for this book. Stepping out in faith, I made some purchases, using what little money I had for packaging and mailing materials in expectation of one day mailing this book out to others. Leaving the checkout counter, I was still in prayer as I started walking out across the asphalt parking lot while pushing a shopping cart toward my truck. Then I unexpectedly had an overwhelming experience with the Holy Spirit. It was one of those uncommon, sweet, soul-penetrating times with the LORD that many of us have come to long for and cherish.

Speaking eternal truth into my spirit, the LORD stopped me in my tracks! **He said this — "The babies are fine; they are with me. It's the women that I want."** Often, when God speaks, it is a very short and direct message. I understood that He was telling me that it is the mothers of these aborted babies with whom God is truly concerned. I started to walk again to find my truck, but He was not done. He spoke into my spirit once more and again gave me complete assurance that all aborted babies are with Him in heaven. He allowed me to see that the young women are empty of a meaningful relationship with God at the time of their abortions. He wants to draw them into a close and comforting relationship with Him.

In my heart and in my spirit that day, I began to mourn for these lost young women who needed a Savior. I also mourned for those who believe there is a God but do not understand that they can have a personal relationship with Jesus. After I got into my truck, I could see, in my spirit, the sad faces of young women and girls lost in a hazy fog of misunderstanding of Who God really is. I could see hopeless and forlorn expressions on their faces and their sad eyes. He wants all the women who have aborted and abandoned their babies to know Him! This is His desire. He wants to reach every young woman who is considering abortion, as well as those who have already experienced and committed this grievous sin.

As the LORD gave me this word to share with others, I began to weep. What He was telling me, I was already familiar with from scripture, but to have this word of knowledge penetrate my very being was stunning at that moment. I marveled over this new, clear revelation of God's heart towards the women and girls caught in the mire of an abortion conundrum. I pondered over the spiritual situation of these, whom God desires to come to Him in true sorrow and repentance. To have an unrealized relationship with our LORD and Savior is to be alienated from God. Comparatively, it is much worse than being stranded in the Sahara Desert!

> My soul thirsts for God, for the living God; When shall I come and appear before God? — PSALM 42:2

When we are not walking in right relationship with God, it will feel like we are drowning in the deepest depths of the ocean. No matter how far out into the wilderness anyone wanders, however, or how low in life anyone can sink, or how despondent we may become, God knows where we are and will lay hold of anyone who welcomes His presence.

> If I dwell in the remotest part of the sea, Even there Your hand will lead me, And Your right hand will lay hold of me. — PSALM 139:9b-10

As I contemplated these things, my heart went out to these young women. I climbed into my truck and shed great tears of grief. Somehow their heartache and sorrow touched my spirit, and I had a renewed passion to finish this book so that those, whom God loves so much, would find the Hope in Jesus that they so desperately need. The young mothers and fathers who are rejecting their offspring all need Jesus.

Growing Awareness of My Call to Stand

About ten years ago, I was given two short dreams, on two separate mornings, just before I awoke in the darkness of the early dawn. At that time, I was serving as a Sunday morning Worship Leader and was preaching Sunday night services at a small local church. Teaching a weekly Bible study and hosting a weekly Christian radio program also kept me busy while two of my four children were still in school. Every morning, I took an hour's walk before work; that was my prayer time. I sought and received God's guidance on the prayer walks. God also used the following two dreams and others, to speak to me.

By the time God gave me the two dreams that I am about to describe, I had already learned to pay attention to specific dreams that were God-given. There are many dreams that are not from God, but because they had such a strong impact on me, I immediately sought the LORD in prayer for an interpretation of these two. He also gave me one more dream concerning abortion, which I will describe later in this book.

The First Dream — I Heard Crying Babies Being Painfully Aborted

The first dream was purely auditory. There was no image whatsoever. All that my spiritual eyes could see was complete darkness. It enveloped me as I slipped from sleep into the beginning of my day. From the midst of that darkness, I distinctly heard the sharp and mournful cries of a great number of babies in pain and distress. I did not see them, but I knew by the various sounds there were many babies crying. The LORD God allowed me to understand that what I was hearing was the sound of babies in the womb being killed during abortion procedures. The LORD was allowing me to literally hear their pain. It was an indescribably horrific and awful experience.

Although I have always strongly been on the "life" side of the abortion issue, advocating for babies' lives at every chance, it was not on my mind during the days preceding that dream. Many dreams originate because of thought processes that go through our minds during the day. They show up at night as remnants of life activities and thoughts. This dream was not one of those. It was entirely from the LORD. It seemed to me that He was making sure that I would absolutely think about abortion as I awoke that morning. I still carry the sounds of those innocent infant wails within my ears, and they are never far from me. At times I unexpectedly hit "playback" in my mind and heart and hear those sounds in my spirit all over again.

After this dream, I watched a video of a former abortionist describing unborn babies' "silent screams" as he showed ultrasounds of abortions. It was heartbreaking to watch the mouths of the babies opening wide in terror as their lives were about to end. They were obviously feeling both pain and fear. There are also videos of babies drawing away upward from the pain of the abortionists' metal tools. These videos are still available on the internet if you would like to search for them. For humanitarian reasons alone, we should not subject any baby to the pain of being torn apart limb from limb or the pain of having his or her spinal cord cut. I am sure that God allowed me to hear what those cries would sound like if only they could be heard. I will never forget their cries.

The Second Dream — The Unwanted Child

The LORD spoke to me directly, in this dream, as He showed me an image of a teenage boy who had been in my class the previous semester. I was working part-time as a horticulture teacher in the school of a special needs residential facility and knew this young man well. He was in one of my classes the previous year when I worked as a permanent substitute Fine Arts teacher. We had many conversations together. Like some difficult teenagers, this boy could be exasperating! Sometimes, he seemed to go out of his way to be obnoxious!

In this second dream, I heard the LORD say directly to me, "If you don't do something, he will die." That got my attention! As I awoke, I pondered over what that could possibly mean! At the time of the dream, the boy had already completed his time with us. After I asked the LORD for an interpretation, He showed me that the boy in the second dream was representative of all babies targeted for abortion. These are the unwanted and unloved members of our society. These are the kids whose very presence is a nuisance to their parents. God values every human life! If He knows every sparrow that falls to the ground,[2] He surely knows each aborted baby. He was showing me that no matter how unloved and unwanted someone may be in this earthly realm, that person is known in Heaven, and He still loves them. Jesus told us, "Thou shalt love thy neighbour as thyself."[3] Preborn babies are also our neighbors on this earth.

Somebody Has To!

I loved all my students dearly. Without the power of God working in me, I could not have loved them so much. In my natural flesh, it would not have been possible. Most came from difficult family backgrounds, and many had lived on the streets in inner cities across the state. Some had special emotional, developmental, and medical conditions such as Asperger's and other forms of autism. A few were gang members and others were "want-to-be" gang members. Many were there on court order. They could be difficult!

Love is different from pity. Pity recognizes a condition and involves sympathy and possibly empathy. Love can involve empathy but is also unconditional. That is God's love —

unconditional, even though there comes a point where He will turn us over to our sin, should we choose to live without repentance. Jesus loves us and He also has empathy with us because he endured the same temptations we face.[4] The Greek word "agape" is used for this love in the New Testament. It is one of the fruits of the Spirit listed in Galatians 5:22-23 (KJV). These "fruits" are the evidence of a changed life through Jesus Christ: love, joy, peace, longsuffering (patience), gentleness, goodness, faith, meekness, and temperance (self-control). All these fruits are helpful in influencing those we love and care for.

Loving these students meant wanting the best for them despite their behaviors and difficulties. Some of these students were "drug babies." One young teenager had a condition in which he was bound to regress mentally in the coming years. In other words, everything we taught him would be lost. There were some very sad stories there. Still, they were fed, taught, and given medical attention, and they shared many happy, warm (and some not-so-happy and warm) moments with the staff. They were given unconditional love even though many were incapable of returning it because of their life experiences. Jesus said:

> If you love those who love you, what credit is that to you? For even sinners love those who love them. — LUKE 6:32

My greatest joy came when I was able to lead some of the students to the LORD! This happened in various places, such as the school cafeteria, in the classroom before and after classes, and in the school chapel, when the Chaplain asked me to preach. As far as I knew, the student who was the subject of my short dream had not yet given his life to the LORD when I had him in my classes. Sadly, I heard he was incarcerated after he left us. I do not know where he is today, and I hope that he is not still in jail, but I pray that those of us who worked with this special-needs student had planted enough seeds to make him receptive to the watering of the Word of God. Hopefully, he has finally given his life to the LORD.

The point of all this explanation is to share that the young man in the dream was difficult to like, yet the other staff members and I loved him! One really had to search, however, to find something likable about him. Encouraging words from me, or any other teacher or aide, resulted in great negativity on his part of the conversation. It was evident that he spoke from a place of inner pain and hopelessness. If someone said "black," he would say, "white." It was very disheartening, yet we loved him as we loved any of our students — with God's love. The founder of the facility was a Christian minister. One day he stopped by to chat with me while I was outside gardening with some students. "I just love these kids!" I blurted out. "Somebody has to!" was his reply.

God loves those saved by faith in the LORD Jesus Christ, and He also loves the unsaved. Jesus said that He came that all might be saved.[5] Even if no one else ever loved and cared for the student that showed up in my dream, God did and still does! The LORD was showing me that, like this difficult teenager, the babies lost to abortions are also "the least of these"[6] — the unwanted and unloved by parents and by general society that are cast aside as societal "rejects." That is not how God wants us to treat anyone. That is not how we should treat preborn babies.

God showed me that all life is important to Him. He also is crystal clear about that in Scripture. He is the Creator and Sustainer. Every innocent baby is to be valued as we emulate our Savior Jesus and His concern for life and healing. Every baby that has a disability is precious to God. Which of us is perfect?

Reflection: What if the director and founder of the organization, of which I wrote, had never been born? How many kids with seemingly little or no hope would have been helped elsewhere? I watched many children gain the opportunity to have male leadership for the first time in their lives and many came to know the LORD. Many of our students would never have had the chance, otherwise, went on to graduate from high school. A preborn baby may be destined to help many others.

Discerning the Call

Both dreams that I have shared in this chapter were very disturbing and left me feeling unsettled. God was calling me to do something. But what? He was not specific. Someone must love difficult and handicapped children, both born and preborn. Someone must "do something." After these dreams, I started a blog but was limited in the amount of time that I could spend on it, and it did not make much of an impact. I also wrote three pro-life songs and a poem and was vocal about life issues wherever I went. It was not much, but whatever we do for God's kingdom is never wasted. Everything I wrote was inspired by God and is still valid. Do not think that anything you do for God is ever wasted. Even if you influence one woman to keep her baby from abortion, the impact is profound and immeasurable. This treasure is laid up in Heaven.

We must stay steady in sharing the true Word and allow the Holy Spirit to work. We may never know, on this side of eternity, how mightily God will use our faithfulness. Some people sit back and wait until they hear a booming voice from heaven. Sometimes He will speak that way! More often, though, God speaks in a still, small voice.[7] Sometimes we need to get moving in the area that we believe God may be calling us into before we understand our calling. Sometimes it means working in our natural gifts for His Kingdom while praying for anointing in that area.

While we have Biblical examples of being anointed with oil for healing and separation for service to the LORD, there is also an anointing that comes from above via the Holy Spirit of God. The word "anoint" means to set a believer apart in to authorize and equip that one supernaturally for God's Kingdom purposes. God always uses the willing vessel when that one is pure in spirit and intent. This is how we expand and grow in our gifts and callings.

God gave us a brain. He gave us the ability to reason. When we start ministering in our passion and God sees we are faithful to work for His kingdom, He then gives us a greater ability to serve and opens more doors for us in ministry. I have seen God anoint someone who already had a natural gift with a supernatural gift in the same area. If we step out in faith and then allow ourselves to yield to the Holy Spirit's anointing, God can use us greatly. However, if we are not called to a certain area of ministry, there will be no anointing, and there will be little true fruit for the Kingdom. We also must not allow Satan to distract us from our true calling.

Gifts of the Spirit

Sadly, many Christians are hindered from seeking true spiritual guidance from God outside of the Bible. They have been taught that God ceased to gift His followers with spiritual gifts after the New Testament was completed and after the death of the last New Testament apostle. This is called "cessationism." People that believe in cessationism have not experienced a spiritual gift and do not understand the validity of supernatural anointings. Christians that move in the Spirit of God in a Biblical gift are sometimes called "charismatic." Whether a cessationist or a charismatic, a Presbyterian or a Baptist, a Methodist, or a member of an independent nondenominational church, if we believe in the death, burial, and resurrection of our LORD Jesus Christ and the Gospel message, we are brothers and sisters in Christ. Jesus prayed that we would be in unity.[8]

There is sometimes the problem of certain people exhibiting manifestations that are not of God, but we must be wise in distinguishing between those that are of God and those that are of the flesh or the devil. That is why one gift given by the Holy Spirit is called "discerning of spirits." This is a spiritual gift that allows you to see into the supernatural world. Even if you do not usually operate in this gift, the Holy Spirit is your Guide. He will give you an inward witness in to discern what is real from that which is fake or counterfeit.

> Now there are various kinds of gifts, but the same Spirit. There are various kinds of service, and the same Lord. There are various kinds of workings, but the same God, who works all things in all. But to each one is given the manifestation of the Spirit for the profit of all. For to one is given through the Spirit the word of wisdom, and to another the word of knowledge, according to the same Spirit; to another faith, by the same Spirit; and to another gifts of healings, by the same Spirit; and to another workings of miracles; and to another prophecy; and to another discerning of spirits; to another different kinds of languages; and to another the interpretation of languages. But the one and the same Spirit works all of these, distributing to each one separately as he desires. — 1 CORINTHIANS 12:3-12

Even though I was raised in a church that did not believe in present-day spiritual gifts, I experienced them anyway! Perhaps, because I was a child, in that same church I did not even hear any teaching on sin or repentance. When my first job off the family farm (and my neighbor's farm) required that I work on Sundays, I sadly left that church. Later, as an adult, I gained an understanding of these important Biblical doctrines when I began searching out the truths of the Bible under the guidance and teaching of the Holy Spirit. Studying the Bible gave me the insight that I needed to understand both my salvation and my gifts. Years of ministry and study helped me to gain more knowledge and understanding. We should never underestimate or neglect the gift God gives us or the knowledge that He shares with us. Lives may depend upon it!

Our own walk with Jesus will be hampered if we overlook or put aside certain messages revealed in dreams, words of knowledge, or words of wisdom. They can be given to us to help in our own life situations, but the primary and most important application of any spiritual gift is to help others in the body of Christ. The gifts are given for the encouragement of Christians and to further the Kingdom of God. Through these gifts, we may be able to help others learn about and seek the true will of God. Because we are living in a world where the demonic is increasingly manifesting, we need to use the gifts that God has given us, along with the spiritual armor He has given us, to defend ourselves against the enemy of our souls.[9]

Our Teacher

Let us learn from His Word and not be like those of whom Paul spoke when he said, "Professing themselves wise, they became fools."[10] There is a lot of good information that we can learn from secular educators. When someone wants to learn eternal truth, however, there is no teacher like the Holy Spirit of God. In John 14:16-17, Jesus told His disciples that He would be leaving soon, referring to His upcoming death and resurrection, but He promised that after He left, He would send them a "Helper." In the King James Bible, this Helper is called the "Comforter" and the "Spirit of Truth." When we rely on the guidance of the Holy Spirit, He will comfort us with the Truth. In v. 26, Jesus says about the "Comforter," that "he shall teach you all things." It is the Holy Spirit, or as the King James Version says, "the Holy Ghost," that opens the revelation of the truth of the Bible to us. We simply cannot grasp the full depth and meaning of God's Word unless the Holy Spirit reveals it to us. That does not mean that we will not understand some of it, but to truly learn God's Word, we need to be born again. Every born-again believer is given the gift of the Spirit of God, but many do not draw on Him as a resource. He is a person — the Third Person of the Trinity — and if you are a true believer, you have the Holy Spirit living in you, giving you a spiritual understanding of the deep things of God. This is the same Spirit of Christ. Pray to God and ask Him to help you read and understand the Bible through His Spirit.

As the LORD drew me closer, in my early adult Christian walk, I knew that I needed a greater understanding of the Holy Spirit. I went to my knees and prayed. I said, "Dear LORD, please give me an understanding of Your Holy Spirit. Please fill me with Your Spirit. As I study Your Word, teach me what I need to know. I do not want to be in error, but I want to know the truth. I want to speak Your truth." That morning, knowing the usual "light" talk of the substitute layperson that was scheduled to speak that Sunday at my home church, I decided to visit another church in the hope of hearing a message with more Biblical weight. When I arrived at the other church, I checked my church bulletin and read that the topic of the day would be the Holy Spirit! Please keep in mind that this was also in a church of a mainline denomination that did not often speak on the Holy Spirit. It was quite a surprise!

Obviously, the LORD heard my prayer and sent me straight off to get my first lesson. That sermon was light on teaching, but it was a start as a Biblical outline was provided in the church bulletin. When I told the pastor that the Holy Spirit had sent me there in response to my prayer, he gave me a blank look. Apparently, he had endeavored to preach on something about which he had had little personal experience. Still, it was a good start for me in that I could see how God had answered my prayer immediately!

Holy Spirit Boldness and Power

Even though that pastor did not seem to be fully aware of the

the supernatural power of the Holy Spirit of God, my study of the Word became more intense after that prayer. It was as if the whole Bible was opening to me in a new way. I knew I was filled with the Holy Spirit, and I truly began to hate sin more passionately than ever. God began to open my mouth. I was usually very nervous in a crowd and often hid from large groups of people, but I was now emboldened to go on the radio with my own Christian program and was able to begin preaching in my church. I began teaching Bible Studies although I was once too shy even to attend adult Sunday school. God gave me the power to preach His Word. If you want to experience power in your ministry, go to your knees as I did and call upon the LORD for baptism with the Holy Spirit. Even if you have been filled before, ask Him for a fresh indwelling and a new anointing.

God always speaks to us through Scripture. Sometimes He may reveal something to us through another person or a sermon. I remember being in attendance when the pastor of a small church, years ago, preached on Matthew 28:19-20, known as the Great Commission. Ashamed that I was not out witnessing to the world, I flipped through my Bible while squirming in my seat. Being very shy back then, I could not imagine ever going out on the street to preach to people. God will, however, lead the willing vessel. In response to prayer, He has emboldened me and many others with His Spirit to speak His Word with "boldness."[11] Not long ago, with another Spirit-filled lady, I preached on the street through a bullhorn! After I was already preaching for a while, my friend mentioned to me that it was illegal! I continued in boldness. When two policemen walked by, I smiled at them and waved. They smiled and waved back!

The Spirit of the LORD will strengthen and embolden us with power when we request through prayer. For guidance and encouragement in your own walk and ministry with Jesus, read about the "Believer's Prayer for Boldness" in Acts 4:23-31:

> And when they had prayed, the place was shaken where they had assembled together; and they were filled with the Holy Ghost, and they spake the word of God with boldness —ACTS 4:31, KJV

God speaks to us in the way we will understand the best. At times, He may speak in a dream or vision. We are living in the days of which Joel prophesied:

> . . . I will pour out My Spirit on all mankind; And your sons and daughters will prophesy, Your old men will dream dreams, Your young men will see visions. "Even on the male and female servants I will pour out My Spirit in those days. — JOEL 2:28b-29

Satan would like nothing better than to curtail the ministry of our "sons and daughters." Who knows how many would-be preachers, missionaries, Sunday school teachers, servants to the needy, church builders, and more, have been aborted?

God Calls Us to Love

Perhaps God is also speaking to you? Put the matter to prayer, and God will lead the way. How can God use you in Kingdom work? One thing is certain: God always calls us to love. Whatever we do, we must do it in love, not in a jealous spirit. Do not envy others' gifts. We are all unique. God will use you according to your calling and your willingness. One may be called to be an international apostle. That same one may meet a martyr's death. I recently read that approximately one hundred and sixty thousand Christians are martyred annually. The heavenly reward of a martyr is great, but not everyone is willing to walk that road. We must, however, be willing to travel the road we are given, whatever the end.

> For whoever wishes to save his life will lose it, but whoever loses his life for My sake, he is the one who will save it. — LUKE 9:24

Not everyone is called to the more obvious ministries, such as preaching and leading worship. Some may be called to serve God behind the scenes in other, just as important, ministries. Encouraging and helping young mothers, before and after they give birth, is the most important place in pro-life ministry. Men and women are needed to minister to vulnerable young women and men who are in a crisis pregnancy situation. Some may be called to adopt a baby who needs stable parents. Some may be called to supply diapers or babysit. I knew a Christian lady who blessed a young, unmarried, pregnant woman with a washing machine. There are many avenues to ministry in pro-life work. We all must pray for guidance. It may be one of the most important prayers in any of our lives. Saving babies from death is monumental work and of great significance to God. We need to be still and listen to His divine voice. My prayer is that one or more, in reading this book, will be inspired, and encouraged to seek God in finding ministry guidance. Do you know yet where you may best serve the LORD?

> Call to Me and I will answer you, and I will tell you great and mighty things, which you do not know. — JEREMIAH 33:3

This is the message from the Cross: Christ died for all. He also can empower anyone at any time to bring the message of freedom in Christ Jesus to the masses. Whoever you are and wherever you come from, God has a purpose for your life. Any one of you may hear the voice of God calling you to stand up and be heard for your generation.

> There is neither Jew nor Greek, there is neither slave nor free man, there is neither male nor female; for you are all one in Christ Jesus. — GALATIANS 3:28

The Supernatural Reality of God

Our God is supernatural. He is not of this world. Neither are we Christians to be of this world, even though we live in His creation. We have the hope of a better, glorious home in a city "whose architect and builder is God."[12] We are not to cooperate with the world in its fallen, sin-laden condition. Jesus prayed to the Father:

> "I have given them Your word; and the world has hated them, because they are not of the world, even as I am not of the world. I do not ask You to take them out of the world, but to keep them from the evil one." — JOHN 17:14-15

Our God is triune. He is at once Father, Son, and Holy Ghost! He is above and beyond the natural order of this world. He lives outside of our time because time is a condition of the natural world. When God created our universe and our solar system, He also created time as a necessary part of creation. God does not operate on our clock! Time will be irrelevant to us as well once we finally leave this earth and enter the Kingdom of Glory. All supernaturally created beings are also not on our time clock. God and his angels, whom He created, live outside of our dimension. This is easy to understand if we grasp that time was created for man. Demons also live outside of our time. The spirit that influenced Herod was in existence before the actual life of Herod. Before we can understand the full spiritual nature of the abortion problem, and before we can even seriously begin to battle evil spirits, we need to understand what the Bible and Jesus have to say about the supernatural world.

Biblically, a supernatural world with a hierarchy of spiritual beings, both good and evil, is very real. In the Bible, we read about powers and principalities.[13] This is a world that we usually cannot see or touch, which exists beyond our time and our understanding of space. Some people have the gift of discerning of spirits and can see into the spiritual realm, but most of us are unaware of the spiritual world all around us.

Angels were created before man. From the Genesis account of creation, we know that man was created on the sixth day after plants and animals were already introduced. In Job Ch. 38, we read God's words to Job, when He asked him, "Where were you when I laid the foundations of the earth? Declare, if you have understanding . . . when the morning stars sang together, and all the sons of God shouted for joy? [14] The "sons of God" in this verse, refer to the created host of Heaven. The Apostle Paul speaks of the creative power of Jesus. Jesus Christ was not created, but, along with the Holy Spirit and the Father, was part of the creation process:

> All things were made by him; and without him was not any thing made that was made. — JOHN 1:3

The heavenly angels are included in the phrase, "all things." Therefore, men and angels were both created, and, according to the Genesis Creation account and the Book of Job, it was at different times. We are not the same kind of creation, and a person cannot become an angel. We will always be as God created us and our resurrected bodies will be a perfect version of our earthly bodies. It is not in the natural order of God's creation to exchange one kind of created being with another.

One major difference between angels and human beings is the fact that an angel cannot be saved! They love and glorify God, but they cannot know the joy generated by the knowledge of salvation by Jesus Christ. 1 Corinthians 6:3 tells us that, one day, we will even be the judge of angels!

For some, it is hard to believe that there are supernatural beings living in a supernatural realm beyond our experience. We must remember, however, that the Bible tells us that there are powers and principalities in the unseen world. We even may entertain "angels without knowing it."[15] God is supernatural, but so is Satan. The good news is that, in the spiritual realm, God's loyal angels outnumber the fallen angels two to one.[16] God has already given us the victory, and this will be fully manifest to our eyes in the future. When we have earthly struggles, we just need to learn to walk victoriously with our spiritual eyes focused on the final victory. God has us engraved on the palms of His hands.[17]

Is Satan Real? What Are False Gods?

Satan, the devil, is certainly real. Jesus taught us to pray the LORD's Prayer, saying, "deliver us from evil." As expressed in the New American Standard Bible, those words are better translated, as "deliver us from the evil one."[18] The "evil one" is a real entity. He is "a roaring lion seeking to devour" us and our families. He never rests from his only occupation. Look at his job description:

> Be of sober spirit, be on the alert. Your adversary, the devil, prowls about like a roaring lion, seeking someone to devour. — 1 PETER 5:8

If we are Christians, we believe that the Bible is God's true Word. The whole of scripture applies to our Christian walk, and we must not leave out the parts with which we may not agree. If you are not a Christian, or if you believe you are but do not agree with the entirety of Scripture, I hope that by the end of this book, you will have learned about the real forces of good and evil in the universe. Christians that are fully walking in the Spirit of the LORD know the battle that rages against our lives. Jesus never promised us "a bed of roses." He did promise us trouble. The King James Bible calls it "tribulation." We have no need to fear, however, because Jesus also promises us a final resolution to all troubles at the end of the age, and He keeps His promises.

> These things I have spoken to you, so that in Me you may have peace. In the world you have tribulation but take courage; I have overcome the world. — JOHN 16:33

Years ago, we learned about false gods in Sunday School, especially when we learned about the Ten Commandments. I thought "false" meant that they were not real and did not exist. I think a lot of people are under that impression. However, I grew to understand that the false gods, although their representations are often carved stone and wood idols, are very real spiritual entities and are part of Satan's army. That is why God says, empirically:

> Thou shalt have no other gods before me. — EXODUS 20:3, KJV

In our American culture, we do not have as much of a problem with wood and stone idols, except for those who are practicing New Age religions. Attaching power to runes, crystals, and gems and worshipping nature is all occultism. We also tend to attach power to musicians and even our own appearance. Narcissistic self-adulation seems to have taken over part of our culture. That is idol worship. Obsessions with perfect bodies and tattoos are examples of idol worship as is anything that takes our focus away from God.

There are many false idols in America. Cars, fashion, houses, secular music and movies, drugs, bars, nightclubs, and casinos are all often idolized. The television set can be considered a false god. All over America, night after night, many more hours are spent at the altar of TV worship than at the sinner's bench at the front of the church in repentance. We need to repent for ignoring the thousands of casualties of preborn babies being aborted each day.

How I Came to Understand the Reality of the Devil

There was a time I was not sure if there was an actual devil. When I first went back to church after being away for many years, I mentioned my uncertainty while attending an adult Sunday school class. A wonderful man named Bob cleared it up for me. I had observed that Bob was a man of character as he was a good and loving husband and father. I will never forget the earnest look on his face and his exact words in response to my uncertainty. He said, "All you have to do is look at what is happening in the schools and on television to know that there is a real Satan."

That was a "light bulb" moment for me! It was as if everything came together and became much clearer to me at that moment. I never understood evil. I never understood why people would hurt other people. I just did not "get" meanness! God, through His Holy Spirit, had used this man to reveal to me that Satan is the root cause of all evil.

I had two sons in school at the time, and I was very upset about many things that were going on in the world. I had already been severely limiting my kids as to what programs they could watch on TV and had sometimes (fruitlessly) contacted television stations with complaints about their smutty programs. I soon got rid of our television.

Studying the Bible on my own, I began to see the real threat of Satan in this world, and that we also battle our inherited sin nature. When Eve allowed Satan to beguile her in the Garden of Eden and she ate the forbidden fruit, with Adam following suit, sin entered the world. In Romans 5:12, we read, ". . . By one man sin entered the world, and death by sin; and so death passed upon all men . . ." Our flesh is now forever tainted.

Our hearts can never truly be known, except by God. He tests us and rewards us accordingly:

> I, the LORD, search the heart, I test the mind, Even to give to each man according to his ways, According to the results of his deeds. — JEREMIAH 17:10

When we are not born again in the Spirit, we are apt to be Satan's tools. Even believers can be deceived if they are not walking with God and allowing Him to renew them daily.[19] The spirit of Herod, or any other spirit, can influence those walking hand in hand with the world. Remember that Satan is the god of this world[20] and therefore is a major part of the decision-making process of those that do not follow God, although most are unaware of it. The devil is our adversary, and that is exactly what his name means. Careful study of the scriptures in Isaiah Ch. 14 and Ezekiel Ch. 28 reveals him to be God's highest created cherubim, which is part of the angelic realm.

In Matthew 4:1-10, we read of the temptation of Jesus by the devil in the wilderness, just before He began His earthly ministry. Jesus preached against that old liar who had recited twisted scripture to Him. The devil will do that to us. Be aware of people that seem to know the scriptures but twist around the Word of God to suit their own selfish agendas. That is why we must study the Word daily and be on our guard. There are pastors that will tell us that abortion is a Christian act. They do not know Jesus. Luke spoke of the Christians in Berea when he said:

> Now these were more noble-minded than those in Thessaloniki, for they received the word with great eagerness, examining the scriptures daily to see whether these things were so. — ACTS 17:11

We need to be Bereans.

God Prepares and Equips Us for the Battle of the Ages

He gives us everything we need.

> Finally, my brethren, be strong in the Lord, and in the power of his might. 11) Put on the whole armour of God, that ye may be able to stand against the wiles of the devil. 12) For we wrestle not against flesh and blood, but against principalities, against powers, against the rulers of the darkness of this world, against spiritual wickedness in high places. 13) Wherefore take unto you the whole armour of God, that ye may be able to withstand in the evil day, and having done all, to stand. 14) Stand therefore, having your loins girt about with

truth, and having on the breastplate of righteousness; 15) And your feet shod with the preparation of the gospel of peace; 16) Above all, taking the shield of faith, wherewith ye shall be able to quench all the fiery darts of the wicked. 17) And take the helmet of salvation, and the sword of the Spirit, which is the word of God: — EPHESIANS 6:10-17, KJV

Reflection: Jeremiah 1:5 says that God singled the prophet out while he was still in the womb. God said, "Before I fashioned you in the womb I knew you" (KJV). He made us. He knew us before conception. Who is to say what baby has been singled out and for which purpose? God gives all of us something to share with humanity. Only God has the answer.

Beatitude 1: "Blessed are the poor in spirit, for theirs is the kingdom of heaven" (Matt. 5:3).

Life suggestion: Love everyone! This should be our response to God and everyone we meet regardless of the evil that is present in this world. (This does not mean to live with true abuse.) This cannot be done without God. Having poverty of spirit, or being "poor in spirit," means to know that we are nothing without Jesus Christ. This knowledge brings us the reward of a Heavenly eternity when we commit our lives to Him. King Herod suffered from intense pride, which caused him to create a large swath of destruction across his lifetime. He may have had an earthly kingdom, but his lack of poverty of spirit most likely caused him to lose any chance of being a part of the Kingdom of Heaven forever.

". . . every spirit that does not confess Jesus is not from God; this is the spirit of antichrist, of which you have heard that it is coming, and now it is already in the world. You are from God, little children, and have overcome them; because greater is He who is in you than he who is in the world. — 1 JOHN 4:3-4

Chapter Two

An Evil King

*But Jesus said, Suffer little children, and forbid them not, to come unto me: for of such is the kingdom of heaven. —
Matthew 19:14, KJV*

The Evil Spirit of Abortion

Once upon a time, there was an evil king, who ordered every child under the age of two to be massacred, began no fairy tale in the history of childhood bedtime stories. Even a genre that imaginatively transports children to far-off lands of nightmarish, evil stepmothers, trolls, poisoned apples, and old witches that eat children, would not dare to embrace the concept of a real village filled with dead babies. Yet, in America today and in countries around the world, there are villages and large cities filled with the precious remains and memories of children that have been killed in an ongoing slaughter of nightmarish proportions. Speaking of this tragedy is unfit for the ears of children, depending on age, but adults must discuss it because abortion affects each one of us greatly because it is so common.

It is not likely that King Herod intended on becoming a pawn of Satan, but history records him doing just that. Anyone who deliberately kills an innocent child is in league with the devil. In Herod's case, he allowed a murderous spirit to rule his thoughts and desires. His heart, with its fleshly pride and arrogance, as well as its extreme lust for power, became a gateway for a loathsome, demonic spiritual entity to take up residence. This was the spirit of Herod.

The same spirit that operated through Herod the Great, who was responsible for the slaying of the babies of Bethlehem, is still extremely active in the world today — even more so knowing that, along with his master, Satan, his time is short and his final destination is in the lake of fire.[1] This spirit is the same as Molech, the ancient god of Baal, and has many demons working with and beneath him in the dark spiritual hierarchy of Satan's kingdom. God has revealed to me how the many demons in Satan's army are responsible for all abortions today. They deceive many into wrongly justifying the untimely deaths of the innocent.

The devil has waged a war against the Kingdom of God, and we are engaged in a spiritual battle.[2] We should not directly rebuke the devil in our own authority. Even the archangel Michael would not do that.[3] Like Michael, instead of directly rebuking the devil, we can say, "The LORD rebuke you, Satan." We must rely on the LORD's authority and judgment as we battle for the people of God's Kingdom. (For further study, you may also read Zechariah 3:2.)

The devil is only capable of being in one place at a time, and when we see evil, we are most likely dealing with the sinful flesh of man or a demon. Because Satan, however, is at the root of man's sinful flesh and instituted evil on the earth, we should resist him, and he will flee.[4] We have authority to fight the demons that wage direct war against us, as they work through other people. The evil demon, Molech, that influenced King Herod the Great, is one of Satan's top commandos. He works under the demon god Baal and is among our greatest enemies. It seeks to crush the promises that will manifest in the future if left unhindered. It does this by seeking to destroy the lives of those who will populate our future.

War has been declared on each baby from the moment of conception. This spirit of Herod is prospering through the multitude of murders all around the world. In the United States of America, vile, pre-birth murder has been given the deceptively sterile name of "abortion" and currently acts under the authority of our government, as well as Satan.

The Slippery Slope of Acceptance of Premature Death

What is unknown to most people is that full-term abortion has been occurring regularly in the United States. For many years, babies that survive abortion attempts have often been left to die, unloved and uncared for, until their little hearts pump their last beats. Abortion clinic workers who have come out of the abortion business testify to many types of atrocities concerning the deaths of the babies that survive abortion. While many states are heroically passing bills that effectively curtail abortions at the six-week gestational age, and even declaring all abortions illegal, others are boldly declaring that we may legally kill babies that have health issues or birth defects — even after birth — if they are born alive during an abortion. Now we are blurring the lines between euthanasia and abortion. Remember that the babies in Bethlehem were also killed legally, under the authority of King Herod.

When God first revealed the atrocities of the spirit of Herod to me, I was slightly confused. Herod, as far as I know, did not order the murders of preborn babies. His crime was the death of children who had already been born. Now that "after-birth abortion" is on the table of discussion, we can see how the cruel lies of this spirit have been advancing down the "slippery slope" of the growing acceptance of the murder of preborn children in this country. Some are now accepting the murder of newborns who have survived abortion. Next on the plate of acceptance will be the euthanasia of disabled and depressed children. It has already begun overseas. Recently, a teenager in England was legally allowed to starve herself to death.

How I Received the Revelation

One sunny Sunday morning, I visited a church I loved very much. I was sitting in the pew, awaiting the services, and praying as usual, when suddenly a strong anointing of the Spirit of our LORD came over me. Usually, when I feel the LORD's anointing, I am either preaching, preparing a Bible study lesson, conversing with a fellow Christian, or heavily praying and meditating on heavenly matters. The LORD led me to Matthew Ch. 2 and the story of the evil King Herod and the Wise Men.

We were not in the Christmas season, so I had not been thinking about this chapter in Matthew at all. Obediently, I read the verses opened before me. As I read, the LORD gave me one of the strongest revelations that I had in a very long time. He began to show me that King Herod was under the influence of a dark, evil spirit — the very spirit responsible for all abortions throughout time. It is a spirit sent straight from Satan, and it wants the promise of the new life of each baby obliterated from the face of the earth.

The LORD told me that we can call this spirit "the spirit of Herod" because it is the same one that urged Herod to try to kill the Baby Jesus over two thousand years ago. He ordered every male child, under the age of two, to be massacred in Bethlehem. This evil spirit existed before the arrival of the Christ Child. Sadly, it will also affect all those abortions that are yet to occur — unless we pull down the strongholds of greed, laziness, murder, and vanity, and rebuke this spirit in spiritual warfare. While Herod may not be its actual name, it is an evil spirit that corrupts through greed, avarice, and lust for power. He is a spirit of murder and mayhem in the chain of command that starts with Satan at the top, Baal, the demon-god Molech, and many evil spirits working under him.

As I sat there, deep in the Spirit, God spoke into my heart about the verses in the book of Matthew and the scorn that King Herod had for Baby Jesus. I reflected on his murderous intentions toward the innocent child. I was silent as God revealed to me how Herod allowed this spirit to control his evil heart and is still running rampant throughout the world today, killing all the babies of promise — for each baby in the womb is a promise for the future. Even as the Baby Jesus carried with Him the promise of a future Kingdom of Peace and salvation for the lost, each baby that is born today carries a promise of something worthwhile that will benefit humanity in some way. God showed me that we must engage in true spiritual warfare against this spiritual enemy of every baby.

The verses, which the Lord showed me, begin after the Magi departed from their visit with the two-year-old Jesus:

> Now when they had gone, behold, an angel of the Lord appeared to Joseph in a dream and said, "Get up! Take the Child and His mother and flee to Egypt, and remain there until I tell you; for Herod is going to search for the Child to destroy." — MATTHEW 2:13

As God continued to speak into my spirit, and as I continued to read while under the LORD's anointing, I began to weep under the power of God that was falling so heavily upon me. God made it clear to me that I would have to share the revelation. My natural flesh began to argue with my spirit. "Nooooo . . . I can't tell people this!" I thought. Then I reasoned with God (even though I knew that was futile), saying, "They will think I'm crazy!" Long ago, though, I learned the necessity of obedience to His call and have been enjoying the blessings that follow obedience. Even if we never receive a reward, we should be open to anything He directs us to do simply because of Who He is! I remained open to receiving what He had to say about this evil and malicious spirit.

God wants everyone to know the reason for the problem of abortion and to be informed and equipped to do the spiritual warfare necessary to overcome it. Many churches today are negligent in teaching the Biblical truth of the real spiritual war in our atmosphere and world. I hope to open spiritual eyes to this reality and to the fact that God equips us, Biblically, with the means to overcome. Christians are overcomers. We have the "shield of faith" by which we may "quench all of the fiery darts of the wicked."[5]

For whatever is born of God overcomes the world; and this is the victory that has overcome the world — our faith. Who is the one who overcomes the world, but he who believes that Jesus is the Son of God? — 1 JOHN 5:4-5

The Enemy of Our Hope

Let us take a step back and look at the birth of the precious Son of God. As we examine the beautiful verses that tell us of the birth of our Savior, I hope that we will grow in our joy and appreciation of the Christmas story. Every year at Christmas time, most churches read the prophetic words of the book of Isaiah. The prophet promises Hope for the future, which will be fulfilled in Jesus. Part of Isaiah's prophecy of the coming Messiah is as follows:

> For unto us a child is born, unto us a son is given: and the government shall be upon his shoulder: and his name shall be called Wonderful, Counselor, The mighty God, The everlasting Father, The Prince of Peace. Of the increase of his government and peace there shall be no end, upon the throne of David, and upon his kingdom, to order it, and to establish it with judgment and with justice from henceforth even for ever. The zeal of the LORD of hosts will perform this. — ISAIAH 9:6-7, KJV

This prophecy was partially fulfilled at the birth of Jesus but will be totally fulfilled after Jesus comes again! This is one of the Messianic prophecies that King Herod feared. We see the essence of royalty in these verses. Herod did not understand that Jesus would not be coming in the fullness of His Kingship when He came as a baby. His Kingship will be fully manifested later when He comes as the Lion of Judah.[6] He came as a baby to live a humble servant's life and to sacrifice His pure and perfect life by a humiliating death on a wooden cross. Herod, in his prideful ignorance and envy, wanted no competition for his rule. History reveals this by the violent aggression he showed both the real and imagined contenders to his throne.

Born in Edom, Herod the Great was by birth an Arab of Idumean descent.[7] "Herod" was the family name of his line and was used as we use a surname today. There were six "Herods" named in the New Testament, but in this book, we are concerned with only two: Herod the Great and Herod Antipas, also known as the Tetrarch. According to Unger's Bible Dictionary, Idumeans were descended from the Edomites and had converted to Judaism by conquest in the year 130 BC. They were the descendants of Esau, the brother of Jacob/Israel, and the son of Isaac, the son of Abraham, the patriarch of the Jews. They were "regarded with considerable suspicion and prejudice" by the Jews 'calling the Idumeans but "half-Jews."'[8] Herod the Great was a heathen. As descendants of Abraham, the Edomites had started out worshipping the true God, Yahweh, but over the years they had begun to worship other, false gods. Herod's father had political alliances in Rome that ruled the world at that time. Thus, Herod was placed, first, in the position of Governor of Galilee from 47-37 BC and then, second, as King of the Jews from 37-4 BC. He conquered Jerusalem in 37 BC. Marc Antony was the one who placed him on the throne as king, and Herod's "coronation by Caesar was made an occasion of great magnificence."[9] His allegiance was more with Roman officials than the people over whom he was ruling. He erected pagan temples in other areas.[10]

He became known as Herod the Great because he was a talented builder of magnificent examples of architecture, which may still be visited today. He was responsible for the beauty of the Jerusalem temple, which existed in the time of Jesus. He reconstructed the original temple, as perhaps a conciliatory act, to appease the Jews who were disgusted by his "cruelties." He may have done this only with the underlying "sinister motive" to gain access to the priestly genealogies and then destroy any connection he could find concerning the "expected Messiah." His passion for building was then passed down through "his ruling descendants after him."[11] Another legacy he left behind was a twisted, gnarled, and ghastly family heritage.

Herod's Wicked and Dysfunctional Family Tree

The ancient Jewish historian, Josephus, wrote much about King Herod. From his writings, we learn that Herod was filled with multiple fears about losing his kingdom, which resulted in him ordering the murders of anyone he feared might cross him or usurp his power. This included many members of his close and extended family. He had first married Doris, by whom he had a son, but both wife and son were banished when an opportunity came to strengthen political ties, which Herod realized by marrying the beautiful Mariamme I, one of the last heirs to the Hasmonean dynasty of Judea. He feared losing power to this important Jewish family; his marriage to her connected him to real Jewish royalty.[12]

Altogether, Herod had ten wives. Besides murdering the mother of four of his children and the love of his life, Mariamme, because of jealousy, he also had her grandfather Hyrcanus, her mother, Alexandra, and her seventeen-year-old brother, Aristobulus, killed. He then had two of his grown sons by Mariamme — Alexander and Aristobulus — strangled to death because of false rumors.[13] They were accused of planning espionage against him.[14] One of their accusers was a jealous older brother and political rival, Antipater.[15] Another was Herod's sister, Salome, a manipulative and distrusted woman who hated them.[16] At least one of Herod's wives was a niece.[17] Inappropriate relations and strangulation infiltrated Herod's family. This influenced Herod the Great's son, Herod Antipas, who offered his wife's young daughter, also named Salome, any gift she wanted in response to her provocative dance. At the prompting of her mother, Herodias, she asked for the head of John the Baptist on a large platter. John had called out Herodias and Herod for their improper marriage because she was his brother's wife.[18] It is no coincidence that abortion proponents use incest and other inappropriate relationships as a reason for abortion, and, according to testimonies of former abortion workers, strangulation is one of the ways that legally sanctioned abortionists illegally use to kill babies that survive abortions.

Intrigue and danger ruled the royal palace during the time of Herod the Great. Days before he died of illness, Herod had his son, Antipater, executed after plans came to light of this son's intentions to kill him.[19] Herod's body was laid to rest in all the splendor befitting a king. With a gold crown on his head, adorned in purple robes, and a scepter by his side, he was placed in a gold bier "studded with precious stones." His remaining sons walked in the funeral procession.[20] It is difficult to imagine what they thought of their father, who had murdered so many, including their own half-brothers. The family dysfunction is almost incomprehensible. As Augustus claimed, "It is better to be Herod's hog than to be his son!"[21]

In Satan's army, spirits often work in the same deadly capacity. Another evil spirit that many believe is associated with abortion is that of Queen Jezebel. A Phoenician princess who brought Baal worship into Israel when she married King Ahab, she sacrificed the lives of babies to the false god, Molech. I believe that the spirit behind Queen Jezebel was of the false goddess Astarte, and it also influenced King Herod and his sinister sister, Salome. History records that both Herod the Great and Salome were schemers and heartless manipulators, which puts into question whether their conversion to Judaism through their father's conversion was authentic.

We can contrast Herod's conversion with that found in the Bible story of Ruth, which tells us about a young widow from nearby Moab. Ruth converted from the heathen gods of her homeland to the God of her mother-in-law, Naomi, because of love and a real heart change. Through her faithfulness, she went on to join the ancestral line of Jesus, through the line of David.[22] We must remember in our evangelism that we cannot force anyone to love God. Ruth's sister-in-law, Orpah, chose to return to her people.[23] We always have a choice. There were two thieves who were crucified with Jesus. One chose the Heavenly way, while the other chose the path to Hell.[24]

The Christmas Story

In stark contrast to the dark, depressing, and evil reality of the Herodian dynasty is the simplicity and beauty of the Christ Child's family. Let us look at the Christmas Story as it is told in Luke 1:26-56 in the King James Bible. In a beautiful depiction of surrendering one's life to God, we first see Mary submitting to His will after the angel Gabriel tells her of God's plans for her, as well as for the world:

> And in the sixth month the angel Gabriel was sent from God unto a city of Galilee, named Nazareth, 27) to a virgin espoused to a man whose name was Joseph, of the house of David; and the virgin's name was Mary. 28) And the angel came in unto her, and said, Hail, thou that art highly favored, the Lord is with thee: blessed art thou among women. 29) And when she saw him, she was troubled at his saying, and cast in her mind what manner of salutation this should be. 30) And the angel said unto her, Fear not, Mary: for thou hast found favor with God. 31) And, behold, thou shalt conceive in thy womb, and bring forth a son, and shalt call his name JESUS. 32) He shall be great, and shall be called the Son of the Highest; and the Lord God shall give unto him the throne of his father David: 33) and he shall reign over the house of Jacob for ever; and of his kingdom there shall be no end. 34) Then said Mary unto the angel, How shall this be, seeing I know not a man? 35) And the angel answered and said unto her, The Holy Ghost shall come upon thee, and the power of

the Highest shall overshadow thee: therefore also that holy thing which shall be born of thee shall be called the Son of God. 36) And, behold, thy cousin Elisabeth, she hath also conceived a son in her old age; and this is the sixth month with her, who was called barren. 37) For with God nothing shall be impossible. 38) And Mary said, Behold the handmaid of the Lord; be it unto me according to thy word. And the angel departed from her.

39) And Mary arose in those days, and went into the hill country with haste, into a city of Judah; 40) and entered into the house of Zechariah, and saluted Elisabeth. 41) And it came to pass, that, when Elisabeth heard the salutation of Mary, the babe leaped in her womb; and Elisabeth was filled with the Holy Ghost: 42) and she spake out with a loud voice, and said, Blessed art thou among women, and blessed is the fruit of thy womb. 43) And whence is this to me, that the mother of my Lord should come to me? 44) For, lo, as soon as the voice of thy salutation sounded in mine ears, the babe leaped in my womb for joy. 45) And blessed is she that believed: for there shall be a performance of those things which were told her from the Lord. — LUKE 1:26-45, KJV

Notice that here we have an account of Elisabeth (Elizabeth, in modern English) being filled with the Holy Spirit (Holy Ghost), and we also see her preborn infant operating in the realm of spiritual awareness. Elizabeth's baby, later known as John the Baptist, was already filled with the Holy Ghost. She recounted, "the babe leaped in my womb for joy." This baby, who was the cousin of Jesus, recognized the Savior of all mankind while both were in the womb. Later, when he was grown and had already become an important teacher to the Jews, he announced to the world and to the ages, "Behold the

Lamb of God, which taketh away the sins of the world."[25] He then baptized Jesus in the Jordan River.

In the preceding verses of Luke 1:39-45, as we read along, we may almost feel as if we are right there witnessing the joy of two women expecting the birth of their children. Compare that to the bitterness of young women who carry signs proclaiming that babies are parasites. As Christians and as a nation, we must tackle the root of this bitterness in order to heal the brokenness of these young women. They need to hear the Gospel of Jesus Christ and of the love that one baby brought to all the world.

Whose Body?

A common cry from abortion supporters is "My body - my choice." Even though they are connected by an umbilical cord, the child in the womb of a pregnant woman is a separate entity from the mother. That baby has its own head, body parts, heart, and other organs. He or she is a person. Personhood and identity are not determined by the level of care needed. Babies need love and nurturing and at some level, we all do. That baby, however, will never use any part of the mother to physically survive, other than breast milk, if the mother chooses to nurse. The mother's body nurtures the baby while in her womb, but a baby is a separate person. The creation of a baby is God's choice because He created the baby-making process! The abortion of a baby aborts the plan of God. Abortion destroys a real person. To any mother, I would say, **"It is your body that is carrying the baby, but it is always God's choice to create life or take life. Abortion usurps the authority of God."**

The Magnificat

Mary's song, also known as the Magnificat, was an echo of the old prophetic song of Hannah in Samuel 2:1-10. Hannah had prayed intensely to be blessed with a child, and her prayer was answered. She gave birth to a child who grew up to become a great man of God: the prophet, Samuel. Both women prophesied of the future glory and salvation of Israel through the Messiah. We see that, during her discourse with Elisabeth, Mary is exultant:

> And Mary said, My soul doth magnify the Lord, 47) and my spirit hath rejoiced in God my Saviour. 48) For he hath regarded the low estate of his handmaiden: for, behold, from henceforth all generations shall call me blessed. 49) For he that is mighty hath done to me great things; and holy is his name. 50) And his mercy is on them that fear him from generation to generation. 51) He hath showed strength with his arm; he hath scattered the proud in the imagination of their hearts. 52) He hath put down the mighty from their seats, and exalted them of low degree. 53) He hath filled the hungry with good things; and the rich he hath sent empty away. 54) He hath holpen his servant Israel, in remembrance of his mercy; 55) as he spake to our fathers, to Abraham, and to his seed for ever. — LUKE 1:46-55, KJV

The Bethlehem Birth Announcement

The miraculous and humble birth of our Savior is recorded for all time:

> And it came to pass in those days, that there went out a decree from Caesar Augustus, that all the world should be taxed. 2) (And this taxing was first made when Cyre'ni-us was governor of Syria.) 3) And all went to be taxed, every one into his own city. 4) And Joseph also went up from Galilee, out of the city of Nazareth, into Judea, unto the city of David, which is called Bethlehem, (because he was of the house and lineage of David,) 5) to be taxed with Mary his espoused wife, being great with child. 6) And so it was, that, while they

were there, the days were accomplished that she should be delivered. 7) And she brought forth her firstborn son, and wrapped him in swaddling clothes, and laid him in a manger; because there was no room for them in the inn. — LUKE 2:1-7, KJV

Next, we read about the witness of the shepherds. On a hill just outside old Bethlehem, in approximately the year 3 BC, these lowly shepherds stood watch over their sheep one night as they normally would. To their amazement, instead of a quiet night in the darkened pasture, a brilliant heavenly host surrounded them and gave them an astounding message! Angels announced the birth of the most adored Child to ever live. Notice that God ordained the angels to proclaim to shepherds — some of the most common people of the ancient world — the heavenly news that the promised Good Shepherd and Savior of the world had been born.

> And there were in the same country shepherds abiding in the field, keeping watch over their flock by night. 9) And, lo, the angel of the Lord came upon them, and the glory of the Lord shone round about them; and they were sore afraid. 10) And the angel said unto them, Fear not: for, behold, I bring you good tidings of great joy, which shall be to all people. 11) For unto you is born this day in the city of David a Saviour, which is Christ the Lord. 12) And this shall be a sign unto you; Ye shall find the babe wrapped in swaddling clothes, lying in a manger. 13) And suddenly there was with the angel a multitude of the heavenly host praising God, and saying, 14) Glory to God in the highest, and on earth peace, good will toward men. 15) And it came to pass, as the angels were gone away from them into heaven, the shepherds said one to another, Let us now go even unto Bethlehem, and see this thing which is come to pass, which the Lord hath made known unto us. 16) And they came with haste, and found Mary and Joseph, and the

babe lying in a manger. 17) And when they had seen it, they made known abroad the saying which was told them concerning this child. 18) And all they that heard it wondered at those things which were told them by the shepherds. 19) But Mary kept all these things, and pondered them in her heart. 20) And the shepherds returned, glorifying and praising God for all the things that they had heard and seen, as it was told unto them. — LUKE 2:8-20, KJV

The Story of the Magi — Wise Men Invest in the Future

Herod was born during an interesting time in history and in an interesting place. The Messiah was born during Herod's reign over Judea. Unlike Herod and even many in the world, wise men, following a star, came to give honor to the child King from the line of David, whose birth fulfilled ancient prophecies. They had already determined that the King of the Jews had appeared on the world scene. We can determine that it was a long journey because they did not arrive until Jesus was about two years old. They brought valuable gifts, fit for a king, to present to the Baby Jesus. They understood that their studies proved this Child would be the King of all kings. They traveled from the East, which is in the direction of Babylon from Israel. In Babylon, the Jewish prophet Daniel had lived, led, and taught six hundred years before, during the Babylonian captivity of the Jewish people. These learned kings were most likely familiar with the ancient, prophetic Hebrew scriptures. Daniel 2:48 says, "Then the king promoted Daniel and gave him many great gifts, and he made him ruler over the whole province of Babylon and chief prefect over all the wise men of Babylon." That Daniel was an influential Jewish leader in a pagan land illustrates how God wants all people drawn into His family. He wants the whole world to know His love!

Now after Jesus was born in Bethlehem of Judea in the days of Herod the king, magi from the east arrived in

Jerusalem, saying, 2) "Where is He who has been born King of the Jews? For we saw His star in the east and have come to worship Him." — MATTHEW 2:1-2

Wise investments are crucial to our security and even our health, especially when our lives are long. Many years ago, these wise men of wealth, intelligence, and spiritual awareness trekked across the desert to invest in the future of their people. These men were Gentile leaders visiting a Jewish baby. (Some speculate that they may have been descended from the Jews in Babylon from the time of the Babylonian captivity, but there is no record.) This was more than just an incredibly unusual event. As far as history records, it was a one-time event.

The wise men had a three-fold purpose! They confirmed prophecy, invested in the future of this Child by bringing Him expensive presents, and protected His life! Let us continue with this amazing story:

> And when Herod the king heard it, he was troubled, and all Jerusalem with him. 4) And gathering together all the chief priests and scribes of the people, he began to inquire of them where the Christ was to be born. 5) And they said to him, "In Bethlehem of Judea; for so it has been written by the prophet,
>
> 6) 'AND YOU, BETHLEHEM, LAND OF JUDAH,
>
> ARE BY NO MEANS LEAST AMONG THE LEADERS OF JUDAH;
>
> FOR OUT OF YOU SHALL COME FORTH A RULER
>
> WHO WILL SHEPHERD MY PEOPLE ISRAEL.'
> — MATTHEW 2:3-6

These verses reflect and confirm the prophecy found in the Old Testament prophetic book of Micah, which claims that the future ruler of Israel would come from the little town of

Bethlehem. We then read how the magi visited Jesus and His family. They brought the finest of gifts, seeking nothing in return. Their visit was remarkable. Now we continue in the King James Version:

> Then Herod, when he had privily called the wise men, inquired of them diligently what time the star appeared. 8) And he sent them to Bethlehem, and said, Go and search diligently for the young child; and when ye have found him, bring me word again, that I may come and worship him also. 9) When they had heard the king, they departed; and, lo, the star, which they saw in the east, went before them, till it came and stood over where the young child was. 10) When they saw the star, they rejoiced with exceeding great joy. 11) And when they were come into the house, they saw the young child with Mary his mother, and fell down, and worshipped him: and when they had opened their treasures, they presented unto him gifts; gold, and frankincense, and myrrh. 12) And being warned of God in a dream that they should not return to Herod, they departed into their own country another way. — MATTHEW 2:7-12, KJV

The Bible does not tell us how many wise men there actually were. Based on the number of gifts, tradition holds that there were only three, but there may have been many more. The prophetic implications of the gifts are notable. Gold represented purity and kingship. Myrrh, a fragrant, medicinal gum resin from certain trees, represented affliction and death as it was used in embalming and was also put as a pain reliever into Jesus' wine while he was on the cross. Frankincense was used as an incense offering in the temple and so represented both a "sacrificial offering" and the priesthood. These were all gifts of hope and signified the satisfaction of a promise answered. These gifts all honored the birth of this uniquely special child. Likewise, we give parents gifts because their newborns are all promised blessings of God and are therefore worthy of our honor and recognition.

Since the magi were considered Gentiles, it showed the world that Jesus came not only as the King of the Jews but also as the Lord of all lords and the King of all kings, to be fully revealed in the future.[26] His lordship covers the entire earth and all people — Jews and Gentiles — and this will be fully revealed at His Second Coming. The magi invested time, worship, and gifts. It is possible that these costly gifts may have even helped finance the young family's escape from Herod into Egypt. Our lesson from the wise men is that our investment of time, worship, gifts, and offerings to the LORD are important, and our investments in babies are always well-placed.

Possibilities and Potential

We should learn from the wise men, or the magi, that it is always wise to invest in the future of our young ones. Just as God had plans for the birth of the Christ Child, He has a plan for every child. Perhaps a newly conceived baby may grow up to change a standard medical procedure for the better or perhaps to be a teacher or mentor to someone who will in turn do the same for others. There is no way to know what lives could have been touched and blessed by a life unjustly ended in the womb.

It is a heinous sin to destroy the plan that God has for any life. He shows us individual purpose throughout the pages of scripture. It is evident that the Bible figures Moses, Ruth, John the Baptist, and so many others were all born with tremendous purpose. God invests in life. Only Satan invests in death.

Much good can come from any child's life when he or she is nurtured to his or her full potential. We are each created with a purpose. The possibilities present in each preborn child are endless and unknowable to us. The possibilities in the children of their children are unknowable to human minds, but God knows! I once read that, when a mother carries a baby girl in her womb, she is also carrying the egg that will one day potentially create her grandchild, because a preborn girl develops all her eggs before she is born!

Promiscuity and Abortion

Too often, people use abortion as birth control. Obviously, these people are living in disregard for God. Promiscuous behavior has visible repercussions when a baby is conceived. Both men and women may find abortion to be a dark cloak to cover up their sin.

A young unmarried pregnant female is in a very precarious place. She is often too young to support herself, or if she is married, she may have other children to support. If she is unmarried, she may not know who the father is, if she has been living a promiscuous lifestyle. Perhaps her boyfriend is pressuring her to end the life of the baby. Then she may fear losing his love if she does not have an abortion. If her emotional state is such that she craves the love of this young man, then she may be willing to do anything to keep his affection, even sacrificing the life of her child. The aftermath will then affect this young woman for the rest of her life. She may eventually lose her love for her boyfriend, but she will never lose the memory of her abortion. She will never lose the memory of the promise of life she once nurtured in her womb.

Herod Desired the Death of the Righteous King

The LORD revealed to me that the spirit of Herod, under Satan in the hierarchy of the demonic realm, desired to destroy the promise of the Righteous King — Jesus Christ. As King of Judea, Herod could not bear the thought of having his power and wealth usurped by this mere Child, whether He was promised to Israel through the prophets, or not. Herod did not walk with God, and so he did not understand the nature of this Child who was, in fact, born to be King of kings and LORD of Lords. Rather than being guided by the Holy Spirit, Herod was influenced by at least one, and probably more, demonic spirits. The Baby Jesus was not safe until Herod was dead.

> So Joseph got up and took the Child and His mother while it was still night, and left for Egypt. He remained there until the death of Herod. This was to fulfill what had been spoken by the Lord through the prophet: "OUT OF EGYPT I CALLED MY SON." — MATTHEW 2:14-15

The spirit of Herod leaves no room for chance. Lacking patience, King Herod did not want to waste the time that it would take to discover which child was the One born to be King. Although Jesus was his only perceived threat, the Bible records that he ordered the deaths of every child in Bethlehem that was two years old and under. He took no chances that the Baby Jesus might escape death.

Rachel Weeps

We continue further along in Matthew and learn of a mother's grief:

> Then when Herod saw that he had been tricked by the magi, he became very enraged, and sent and slew all the male children who were in Bethlehem and in all its environs, from two years old and under, according to the time which he had ascertained from the magi. 17) Then that which was spoken through Jeremiah the prophet was fulfilled, saying,

> 18) "A VOICE WAS HEARD IN RAMAH, WEEPING AND GREAT MOURNING, RACHEL WEEPING FOR HER CHILDREN; AND SHE REFUSED TO BE COMFORTED, BECAUSE THEY WERE NO MORE." — MATTHEW 2:16-18

Are there any scriptural words more haunting to a mother's heart than these? This passage portrays a womb that once was full but is now barren, with no living child as evidence of the life that was once nourished there. As is often said, there is nothing more grievous than losing a child, no matter his or her age. As a mother, I never want to experience that grief that knows no equal. Many mothers today grieve the child they aborted. Only God can bring them healing and transforming love. Later in this book, we will talk about why God allows the death of babies.

Why Was Rachel Weeping?

The sad and poetic picture of a mother's tears for the generations of her children through the years was prophesied by Jeremiah. His description evokes tremendous and painful emotions. Biblical prophecy is often layered. Rachel's cries span the ages. She was the beautiful wife of Jacob[27] and one of the original mothers of the nation of Israel. There are historical reasons for this mother's spiritual tears to have fallen during various eras of her nation's history. Matthew 2:18 draws upon the ancient prophecy of Jeremiah 31:15, which tells us that Rachel refused to be comforted.

First, we may see her pain during the Hebrew's time in Egypt, during a time of suffering and slavery when Pharaoh ordered the killing of newborns. Next, her tears would fall during the time of the Babylonian captivity. In Jeremiah 40:1, we learn that Ramah was a gathering point from which the people of Israel were sent into exile "bound in chains." This was also a period of a great slaughter of God's people. Spanning across the years then to Bethlehem, approximately in the year 1 BC, we see the foretold grief of the Hebrew matriarch, Rachel, as Herod's army attacked the unsuspecting families of two-year-old babies.

If we may intentionally still our minds for a moment, we may be able to hear the wails of the Bethlehem mothers and fathers through time. We may be able to imagine their anguish, sense of loss, and helplessness as the Roman soldiers slaughtered their dear, innocent babies in Herod's quest to silence the prophecies and to keep Jesus from fulfilling His destiny. Over the centuries, Satan has been expending tremendous energy, through people, on killing the descendants of the patriarchs of our faith. Many Bible teachers claim that there was a continued attempt by Satan to keep the promise of the Christ child from being fulfilled. The most well-known times of attempted Hebrew and Jewish annihilation are:

1. Under the rule of Persian King Ahasuerus, which we learn about in the Book of Esther.

2. In flight from the Egyptian Pharaoh, as they were chased to the Red Sea, which we learn about in Exodus 10.

3. The Holocaust under Adolf Hitler. (Even though the Christ child had already been born, many believe that the Holocaust and all anti-Semitism was an attempt to keep the Biblical prophecies concerning the return of God's chosen people to the land of Israel from being fulfilled.)

4. Anti-Semitism has been growing in Europe, the US, and around the world, having roots in Socialism and Communism. An increase in anti-Jewish rhetoric, vandalism, and terrorist attacks prove that Satan is not yet done attacking "the apple" of God's eye.[28]

Rachel died after the birth of her son, Benjamin, while she was traveling along the road to Bethlehem. She never arrived in the town of the future birthplace of the Baby Jesus and was buried at Ramah, but her descendants lived in Bethlehem, the place of our Savior's birth.

The Importance of Family in God's Word

When Rachel's husband died, the Bible speaks of him returning to his ancestors.

When Jacob finished charging his sons, he drew his feet into the bed and breathed his last, and was gathered to his people. — GENESIS 49:33

The theme of marriage and family runs strongly throughout the Bible. When we accept Jesus Christ as our LORD and Savior, we then have the right to be called the children of God.[29] If we share in the sufferings of Christ on earth as we stand for Jesus Christ, we become heirs and will be glorified with Him.[30] We may not be heirs to material wealth on this planet, but God has eternal splendor reserved for us in Heaven! With faith in the Messiah, the Hebrew patriarchs died looking forward to leaving this earth and entering a heavenly country and "a city which has foundations, whose builder and maker is God."[31] Heaven is not made with the hands of men. Rachel passed away while in this state of expectation, and her body was buried in a tomb in Ramah.[32]

Children were extremely important to Rachel, for she battled with infertility for much of her young life. God finally did bless her with two sons — Joseph and Benjamin — whom she and Jacob (whom God later named Israel) loved very much. Joseph was the famous Joseph, who had been gifted by his father with a coat of many colors and was then sold into slavery (by his brothers) in Egypt. As he had God's hand on him, His Godly wisdom and obedience helped him to rise to the second-highest position in Egypt. He is an example of a child who rose to great worldly heights to save the Hebrew nation. He saved his own family that had sold him into slavery from starvation during a time of severe famine. God had a great plan for his life. Part of that plan was revealed to him in dreams when he was a young man.

Grief Over the Death of Murdered Babies

Following are the actual verses (Jeremiah 31:15,16) where we see Rachel weeping over the future loss of her descendants during the Babylonian captivity, which began in 586 BC.

Jeremiah foresaw this through the LORD. Verse 16 promises a brighter hope for the future:

> Thus saith the LORD; A voice was heard in Ramah, lamentation, and bitter weeping; Rahel weeping for her children refused to be comforted for her children, because they were not. 16) Thus saith the LORD; Refrain thy voice from weeping, and thine eyes from tears: for thy work shall be rewarded, saith the LORD. . . — JEREMIAH 31:15,16 KJV

Indeed, hope is promised throughout scripture as the LORD promises Israel a bright and glorious restoration. Even today, we see glimpses of that future as we did when Israel was restored as a country in 1948. Jeremiah's prophecy, however, is a promise for the millennial age — when there will be many Jewish believers in Jesus Christ and a millennial reign of peace. This prophecy also anticipates a glorious future in which evil will be forever vanquished, as noted in many places in Scripture.

Comparison of Abortion and the Weapons of Death in Bethlehem

The spirit of Herod is a spirit of death that especially wants to kill all babies because they are bright with the hope of life. Like the murdered innocents in Bethlehem, babies brutally killed in the womb have also had their lives cut short. I once read somewhere that Herod's soldiers most likely killed the male toddlers of the little town with broad axes or spears, and either of these seems likely.

Many babies in today's legal abortion clinics are killed with sharp instruments or dismembered limb from limb. Many babies have had the backs of their heads pierced with sharp scissors. Although the Bible does not record it, we can suppose that large soldiers attacking tiny little boys with large weapons most likely resulted in dismemberments and beheadings, just as aborted babies suffer now. In many hours of studying about abortions, I learned that cutting and dismemberment occur in these types of suction abortions: D&C and D&E. (A further brief, discussion of these methods can be found in chapter 5.) We need to remember that these preborn babies, while not fully mature, are still babies. Just as there are physical similarities between the death of the babies in Bethlehem and abortion procedures, there are also spiritual similarities. (This includes so-called "abortion pills.") Not only were physical lives cut off in Bethlehem; whatever good that could have come from their young lives was also cut off. Whatever influences they were destined to create in God's plan for them could never be realized. Herod's attack on the babies of Bethlehem pales in comparison to the number of babies that have been killed under the auspices of legal abortion. Imagine the talents, the inventions, and the cures for disease that could have been realized without the loss of one billion children worldwide.

Today, those who approve of and vehemently argue for the right to kill a preborn baby are also under the influence of the evil spirit that drove Herod into his depravity. The abortionist's tools are as bloody as the swords Herod's soldiers used to kill. They are weapons of death. I picture the mouth of the spirit of Herod being crammed with many long thin swords in the place of teeth because this is a spirit that is ravenous for the blood of infants. Most abortionists are content for millions of babies to be killed because it lines their pockets with unending income. We learn from personal testimonies that even the receptionists who take the first calls of pregnant women gain a sales commission for each completed abortion.

There are female as well as male abortionists because this spirit can operate in males and females. The Good News is that Christ died for all. He came to set the captives free. Every woman who has experienced abortion can be set free from the guilt and pain of abortion by renouncing her sin and turning to the LORD of all. Every abortionist, parent, boyfriend, and husband who caused, pressured or coerced abortion may also be saved. The spirit of Herod can be bound and cast out, and the Holy Spirit will fill the heart of every believer in Christ. Redemption is real when we repent and reform. Jesus lives today. Herod tried to kill the Hope of Salvation, but the devil will never win. God had and has a plan. His Way is always higher than the ways of man; in Christ, we have power over the ways of demonic forces.

Reflection: If Joseph had never been born, Egypt and the surrounding nations, including the Hebrews, would have suffered and died of starvation.

The Bible contains story after story of tremendous problems from which God delivered His people because of the obedience of a man or woman called by Him. The Greatest Savior of all, we know, was Jesus incarnate, who was fully man, yet fully God. He was the Word made flesh.[33]

> For in Him all the fullness of Deity dwells in bodily form. — COLOSSIANS 2:9

Beatitude 2: "Blessed are those who mourn, for they shall be comforted" (Matt. 5:4).

Life suggestion: Hate no one! We may mourn over the sin of abortion, yet we know that God has an answer. Jesus is the answer to every sin. We should recognize that sin is part of every life that is lived without God, but that forgiveness through Jesus' work on the Cross is available for the repentant. God extends His wondrous grace and is merciful. We must always act in love, but we cannot accept sin.

Chapter Three

The Loss of the Promise of the Future

I will pour my Spirit upon thy seed, and my blessing upon thine offspring . . . — Isaiah 44:3 c,d

How Many Children are "Too Many"?

I once knew a woman who had twenty-one children. She lived in the backwoods, and I played with her grandchildren. My great-grandfather had an artesian well that must have dried up at some point because I remember her walking up the dirt road, in her old boots, to bring him a bucket of water when she was in her seventies. He was in his nineties. She was tough! One summer, I ran into an elderly retired preacher who had driven back to visit her after he had moved away. He told me that he found her up on the roof of her old wooden house — when she was in her seventies — fixing the roof!

Do you think twenty-one children is too many? Students of John Wesley's teachings may recall that his mother, Susanna Wesley, bore twenty-one children, although twelve did not grow to adulthood. She was an excellent home-schooling mother to the nine that lived. Recently I saw a photograph of a woman in Russia who had one-hundred and sixty-nine children, including many twins, triplets, and quadruplets! Most women would probably say that their bodies could not have handled so many children. I am glad that the grandmother with twenty-one children never aborted, or I would never have had hours of fun playing with her grandchildren, one of whom I counted as a friend for some time before life brought us separate ways. Incidentally, they also taught me how to swim overhand!

God is in control. He is our Jehovah Jireh, meaning "Yahweh will provide." **Whether we have twenty-one children or**

one child, when we walk with the LORD and follow Godly, Biblical principles, He will provide the resources we need. We have been hearing about the overpopulation of the world for many years, but I disagree. Our directive from God is to populate the earth.[1] Man often thinks he knows better than God.

Infants Who Have "Never Seen the Light" and Loss of Blessings

It is well-known that approximately sixty-three million babies in the United States of America alone have lost their chance at life since abortion was legalized by the court case of Roe vs. Wade in 1973.[2] These babies never had a chance to develop and thrive according to God's unique plan for them. Neither were they allowed to discover their calling in life to explore their talents. These babies' lives were cut short before they were ever even allowed to breathe outside of the womb. Job 3:16 (KJV) says that babies who die before they are born are, "infants that never saw light." They were never allowed to be the blessing that God says they were meant to be. We are also meant to be a blessing to our children. It goes both ways:

> Children's children are the crown of old men; and the glory of children are their fathers. — PROVERBS 17:6, KJV

As a nation, America is robbing her own future of God's promises and has disrespected His authority. We have robbed ourselves of God's blessings. The total cost of the lost lives of America's babies is unknowable to us, but God knows what is lost when mothers give their babies over to the hands and authority of abortionists. It is time to give control of innocent lives back over to the Creator of the Universe. Isaiah 44:24 specifically says that God, the Creator of all, formed the prophet in the womb.

God Blesses Us with Children

Children are a blessing from the LORD. A blessing of children was voiced to Ruth.[3] It was also the blessing given to Rebekah, the wife of Isaac — ". . . Thou art our sister, be thou the mother of thousands of millions."[4] We know that blessing was honored, as Rebekah's descendants now encircle the earth. As one who enjoys genealogy, I am aware that many are surprised that their DNA tests reveal some Jewish roots.

In one Biblical case, God closed the wombs of the women in Abimelech's household as a punishment. Prayer to God, however, restored their fertility.[5] Children are a gift. Without children, many people feel that a marriage loses its blessing. Hannah, grief-stricken over her barrenness, was given a son after she cried out to the LORD in emotional prayer.[6] God ordered us to procreate when He told Adam and Eve, "Be fruitful and multiply."[7]

When babies are aborted, blessings are broken for both parents. Rewards will be found, however, in fighting the battle against the wickedness of the death of preborn babies. We do this by praying and engaging in spiritual warfare. My prayer is that we will all be encouraged to walk in the light of Biblical wisdom and God's love as we seek His will and direction in ending abortion in America and throughout the world. America will reap many blessings when we stop deliberately killing the preborn. How can any country be fully rewarded with goodness when it aids and abets the devil?

Loss and Honor

Any time we get out of the will of God, we suffer loss. Since God knows every detail about us before we are born, He also knows the plans that were made ahead of time for families and for each baby's purpose. When a child is killed before he realizes God's expectations, the whole family suffers loss. We should remember that every child is wanted by God.

Oftentimes, loss occurs because of other people's sins (as when Herod had the babies in Bethlehem murdered).

As mentioned in the previous chapter, the Bible focuses on family. From Adam and Eve in Genesis, and forward through the Bible, we learn that descendants are important to God. The Ten Commandments show the important relationship between children and their parents. In Commandment number five, children are promised the blessing of long life if they honor their parents:

> Honor your father and your mother, that your days may be prolonged in the land which the LORD your God gives you. — EXODUS 20:12

Sometimes, however, the devil gets in the way, through no fault of the children. As we just discussed in the last chapter, Rachel's descendants, the children of Israel, were destroyed by the sword for greed, lust, and power in the little village of Bethlehem. This killing was propelled by the spirit of abortion or the spirit of Herod. It is the killing of the promise of youth, strength, beauty, and vitality. It is the destruction of new life or birth. It is the destruction of the blessings of God.

The Spirit of Herod in Egypt

God also showed me that it was the same spirit of Herod that influenced the Egyptian Pharaoh eighty years before Moses led his people out of bondage. In those days, Pharaoh gave the order to kill the Hebrew male babies by throwing them into the river.[8] Satan was attempting to kill the promise of the prophesied Savior by trying to circumvent the Old Testament prophecies. Through Pharaoh, He sent the evil spirit to destroy any chance of Hope for God's people. You may remember from sermons or Sunday school lessons that the promised Messiah was to come from the Hebrews. Satan did his best, throughout the history of God's people, to destroy that promise. We can see the spirit of fear but also the lust for power and greed in the next verses about Pharaoh speaking of the Hebrews, who had occupied land in Egypt for approximately four hundred years:

> He said to his people, "Behold, the people of the sons of Israel are more and mightier than we. "Come, let us deal wisely with them, or else they will multiply and in the event of war, they will also join themselves to those who hate us, and fight against us and depart from the land." — EXODUS 1:9-10

Despite being worked hard under difficult conditions and treated harshly, the Hebrew slaves still "multiplied."[9] They must have been very strong and healthy people. Pharaoh decided to instigate a process of keeping the numbers of the Hebrews down by killing the male children. This was another satanic war against the male Hebrew bloodline. The spirit of Herod tried to eliminate the future possibility of the Messiah being born:

> Then the king of Egypt spoke to the Hebrew midwives, one of whom was named Shiphrah and the other was named Puah; and he said, "When you are helping the Hebrew women to give birth and see them upon the birthstool, if it is a son, then you shall put him to death; but if it is a daughter, then she shall live." But the midwives feared God, and did not do as the king of Egypt had commanded them, but let the boys live. So the king of Egypt called for the midwives and said to them, "Why have you done this thing, and let the boys live?" The midwives said to Pharaoh, "Because the Hebrew women are not as the Egyptian women; for they are vigorous and give birth before the midwife can get to them." So God was good to the midwives, and the people multiplied, and became very mighty. Because the midwives feared God, He established households for them. Then Pharaoh commanded all his people, saying, "Every son who is born you are to cast into the

Nile, and every daughter you are to keep alive. —
EXODUS 1:15-22

God's Favor on Those Who Honor Life; Moses' Mother Paid to Nurse Her Own Child

The Hebrew midwives and mothers who were disobedient to the orders of man, but obedient to the will of God, saved the prophet, Moses.[10] They also saved many other babies.[11] We must always be obedient to God. In speaking to a governmental authority, prolife workers can be the modern equivalent of the Hebrew midwives. Just as those midwives were literally in council with Pharaoh, we need to maintain a voice professionally and proactively in government circles so that we may save babies' lives. Pharaoh obviously had respect for these women because he listened to and spoke with them. For their obedience, God ensured that the midwives were provided with homes! [12]

God even took care of Moses' mother:

> Now a man from the house of Levi went and married a daughter of Levi. 2) The woman conceived and bore a son; and when she saw that he was beautiful, she hid him for three months. 3) But when she could hide him no longer, she got him a wicker basket and covered it over with tar and pitch. Then she put the child into it and set it among the reeds by the bank of the Nile. 4) His sister stood at a distance to find out what would happen to him. 5) The daughter of Pharaoh came down to bathe at the Nile, with her maidens walking alongside the Nile; and she saw the basket among the reeds and sent her maid, and she brought it to her. 6) When she opened it, she saw the child, and behold, the boy was crying. And she had pity on him and said, "This is one of the Hebrews' children." 7) Then his sister said to Pharaoh's daughter, "Shall I go and call a nurse for you from the Hebrew women that she may nurse the

child for you?" 8) Pharaoh's daughter said to her, "Go ahead." So the girl went and called the child's mother. 9) Then Pharaoh's daughter said to her, "Take this child away and nurse him for me and I will give you your wages." So the woman took the child and nursed him. — EXODUS 2:1-9

Remarkably, Moses' mother was paid to nurse her own beautiful infant son! God not only saved her son but also moved her into the palace as she was elevated into a position she probably never could have imagined. She was following God's agenda when she directed her daughter to place the baby Moses in a homemade waterproof ark in the river for safety. God is so very good! He certainly honored her commitment to saving her baby's life. **He blessed both her and the Hebrew midwives for refusing to compromise with the government agencies when the matter of life was at stake. Today, doctors, nurses, and pharmacists will be blessed when they refuse to be complicit in government-authorized abortion!**

Whoever receives one child like this in My name, receives Me . . . — MARK 9:37a

Reflection: If Moses had been killed by the midwives, millions of people may never have been freed from Egyptian bondage. The plan for God's people to return to the Promised Land would have been forfeited because of their fear and Pharaoh's greed. Pharaoh enjoyed the benefits of Hebrew slave labor.

Financial Impact of Abortion

There is also a financial aspect of abortion. Proponents of abortion often say that abortion is an economic necessity. The same argument was made for slavery in our country at one time. A former president's daughter somehow came up with the idea that abortion is a Christian practice and even said it has been an economic boon to the country because the practice has enabled women to work. She also somehow tallied up a figure of three and a half trillion dollars that she said legal abortion added to our economy between the years 1973 and 2009. Many verses in the Bible prove her first statement wrong. As for the second, there is no way to fathom how anyone could speak of financial gain from the death of babies. Her logic is skewed and sickening. It is impossible to measure the financial loss from lives that were not permitted to live out their God-given destinies, let alone any kind of supposed gain. She later backtracked on the second statement due to heavy criticism.

There is a wide consensus that our Social Security system has been in financial danger for many years because of abortion. This is because, many believe, legalizing abortion has led to fewer workers that would have grown up to add to the economy and the Social Security program. **The abortion-minded baby boomers have killed off their support system! A civilization cannot continue to murder its young without severe consequences — spiritually or practically.**

If a child is destroyed in the womb, we can never know what that child may have been born to specifically accomplish! Abortion is a deadly assault against the work of God on this earth. Abortion cuts off the promise of the future. When we are living close to God, we feel deeply in our hearts that God would never want one of His babies, created in the image of God,[13] to die uselessly. How painful it is to know that a child has never had the chance, or the choice, to live out his or her destiny.

God has a purpose and plan for each one of us, including each innocent preborn baby. All of us have something to share with humanity. There are some preachers that are actively disputing this, but they are preaching a message of death, not life. Life can be an adventure when we discover our unique purposes. We each have a call on our lives, whether we acknowledge it or not. God does not create waste! Even today, not every baby that this murderous spirit seeks to kill, dies. Some babies survive abortion attempts, but most do not. Those that survive have a story to tell.

The Thief of Youth

The spirit of Herod seeks to kill off the promise of the youth, strength, beauty, and vitality found in a new birth. It hates the promise of hope brought through each baby. Just one person can make a huge difference in the life of another person. That baby may carry a promise of hope that benefits many, even a large population of people. A handicapped child that some would deem not worthy to live because of being a potential physical and financial burden may be a blessing to his mother, or perhaps even a neighbor. That handicapped child may invoke love in a heart that may have never known a great, deep, and sacrificial love. Beautiful personal and spiritual growth can happen in the lives of some who, at first, may doubt they are able to cope with a difficult situation.

This spirit of Herod is a minion of his master, Satan, who is the great deceiver. Just as Herod the Great sent soldiers to kill the Christ Child, this spirit sends orders to kill through his unseen demonic spirits in a great aggressive web around the world. Jesus champions life and life everlasting.[14] Satan's realm is the realm of death and destruction.

> The thief comes only to steal and kill and destroy; I came that they may have life, and have it abundantly. — JOHN 10:10

Satan tried to rob us of the promise of everlasting life when he tried to kill the line of the prophesied Savior through King Herod just as he also tried to destroy the ancestral line of Jesus through the Egyptian Pharaoh.

The Promise is in the Seed — The Battle Began in Genesis

Satan knows scripture. He took scripture and twisted it around to try to tempt Jesus before He began His earthly ministry.[15] He knew the Messianic prophecy given below because God had spoken these words to him:

> And I will put enmity Between you and the woman, And between your seed and her seed; He shall bruise you on the head, And you shall bruise him on the heel. — GENESIS 3:15

This is considered, by many, to be the first prophecy of the Messiah in the Bible. It brings all mankind the message that contains the first hint of the Virgin Birth. Because a woman does not naturally produce seed, this describes a very unusual birth. In it, we also see that Satan would hurt Jesus badly (on the heel), but that Satan would be defeated because Jesus would harm his head. The head is a more vital area than the heel and so would mean a more serious wound. Being hurt in the area of the foot will impede motion and will certainly slow one down, but it will not destroy one's life. Satan also knew the prophecy that all nations would be blessed through the Hebrew people:

> Now the LORD had said unto Abram, Get thee out of thy country, and from thy kindred, and from thy father's house, unto a land that I will show thee: 2) And I will make of thee a great nation, and I will bless thee, and make thy name great; and thou shalt be a blessing: 3) And I will bless them that bless thee, and curse him that curseth thee: and in thee shall all families of the earth be blessed. — GENESIS 12:1-3, KJV

We also see the importance of obedience to receive God's blessings. We know that, when God called Abraham into a foreign land, he willingly obeyed:

And in thy seed shall all the nations of the earth be blessed; because thou hast obeyed my voice. — GENESIS 22:18, KJV

The entire world would be blessed through Abraham because through his descendants would be born the King of all kings — Jesus Christ. This is what is overlooked in Christian circles that actively promote abortion. All of God's promises were answered in the miracle birth. The answer to the abortion question is simple and is expressed throughout the pages of the Bible because we see how God promotes life. The Promised Savior was in the seed of the Hebrew people. Jesus is promised to us from cover to cover in God's Holy Book. There are many prophetic passages concerning Jesus, His birth, and his second advent, for which He tells us to be prepared. He is The Promise. He is our only Hope. All the families of the earth may be blessed through the promise the LORD gave to Abraham:

> Now the promises were spoken to Abraham and to his seed. — GALATIANS 3:16

God Plans Our Days Before We are Born

The Bible tells us that God thinks numerous, amazing thoughts about us. His creation of each one of us is indescribably wonderful. A very profound truth can be found in Psalm 139, where David speaks of his creation by God:

> 13) For You formed my inward parts; You wove me in my mother's womb, I will give thanks to You, for I am fearfully and wonderfully made; Wonderful are Your works; And my soul knows it very well. My frame was not hidden from You, When I was made in secret, And skillfully wrought in the depths of the earth; Your eyes have seen my unformed substance; And in Your book were all written The days that were ordained for me, When as yet there was not one of them. — PSALM 139:13-16

God thinks of each of us all day long and is involved in each of our lives. **His Word tells us that He ordained our days before we were born.** Our destiny is very important to Him. Each baby is a special creation of God. He knows the hidden gifts of each child. He, as our Maker, knows what unique talent He has put into each of us. He knit together each of us with His great love, instilling, in each, an ability that enables us to serve Him and others.

How deeply do we grieve the Holy Spirit, who was also present at Creation, when a baby of God's promise is murdered in cold blood like the babies in Bethlehem two thousand years ago? When King Herod ordered his henchmen to murder the babies of Bethlehem, he killed part of the promise of the future for that Judean community. Who knows what was lost in that fateful escapade? Those babies and generations of potential descendants may have had a wonderful influence, not only on their immediate community but also on all mankind.

The spirit of Herod sought to murder the Baby that held the promise of salvation for all, but he failed. King Herod thought that, by murdering the baby who was born to be king of all Judea, he would be saving the kingdom for himself. He did not have the spiritual discernment to understand God's greater plan. Jesus Christ was anointed to be the King of all kings and the LORD of all lords.[16] God had planned that Jesus would be the Savior for all mankind who would be the Way of Salvation for whoever would believe. This was a plan that existed from the foundation of the universe.[17] Only God knows what precious gifts and promises were lost in the murder of the innocents of Bethlehem.

Devalued Human Life in the "All About Me" Culture

It is difficult to understand why there are otherwise nice people who fail to see the value of a preborn baby. Even more important is that we fail to see God's hurt and anger over the murder of His babies! We must consider the heart of God. So often, we place our personal needs above His sovereignty. We need to consider God's love for the baby and His will for the baby. Too many would rather let selfish practicality and economy rule the thought process in determining the value of the preborn child's life. In these ungodly thoughts, the baby is thought of as something to be disposed of at will, as if that is a wise and practical decision.

Is it any wonder that we have so many mass shootings, pornographic movies, pedophiles, and terrorists when the culture is on a progressively downward spiral of minimizing the value of human life? Abortion has created a lack of empathy and complacency, even among Christians. Many people do not even attempt to understand that God values all life. Remember that King Herod the Great also saw no value in life even in the lives of his own children. As the spirit that seeks the lives of one's own children and those of others, its influence is felt nationwide. We especially see it in centers of influence, such as Washington, DC, New York City, Los Angeles, and Hollywood. Hollywood had moved much of its entertainment business to Atlanta, GA, and there is a stronghold there as well. Child trafficking is also very large in these areas because of a demonic stronghold made easy by the culture of death. As states are beginning to pass "the heartbeat bill," meaning that babies are not allowed to be aborted after a heartbeat can be heard, outrage has erupted. Those in the sports world and the Hollywood set have boycotted Georgia for that state's stand on Life. The outrage of these actors, directors, and others is against God and the people seeking to do God's will.

The rich and famous like to "rub shoulders" with politicians and vice versa. Many prominent performers and politicians act as if they have a complete understanding and the answer to all concerns of life and death. Their confidence is much greater than their knowledge. Many have a narcissistic belief that they have the answers to everything, yet they often say wild, contradictory things! For instance, a well-known television personality agrees with her contemporaries that abortion is "a right." That same woman said recently that she thinks a baby in the womb can "feel" if it is male or female. Why does she think it is alright to kill a human being if it is that self-aware while still in the womb? How can she defend her stance without condoning murder? She is very wise, in her own mind, and many people listen to her. Many famous people are publicly displaying such foolishness. "For the wisdom of this world is foolishness with God."[18]

As human beings, we can quickly and easily make a mess of things. We take what is lovely and of God and turn it upside down and misinterpret it, somehow making it ugly. We take the miracle of life and trample upon it and call it abortion, and we call that a right! Isn't it better to strive to stay in God's perfect will and respect life, which He created, whether we fully comprehend it or not? Isn't it better to leave what we may not fully understand in the hands of God who is all-knowing? It is not only the fault of politicians that we have babies being killed up to their nine-month gestational age. They are representing some of their constituents who have no Biblical moorings. Unfortunately, playing to the progressive, liberal base has ended up costing innocent preborn babies their very lives, which makes them all accomplices to murder. The only way to bring America back to a place where life is valued is to bring those who are spiritually lost back to the God who made us.

After a woman has an abortion, a crisis of guilt will often arise in both the mother and the father. It is normal to question the consequences of having killed one's young. Sometimes, a woman may find that she cannot have another child because of a complication of abortion. Some women reach the age of sixty before they go into a deep depression over the loss of their child and the knowledge of their own responsibility in that child's death. Sometimes, deep wounds form when siblings find out that another sibling was aborted. The living children may wonder about how and why their mother could have killed a baby. "It could have been me," they may say. To have been raised in such a home may lower their level of empathy and ability to think of life as being other than meaningless and valueless.

Reflection: As a nation, we seem to lack overall empathy with God's heart about the lives of the preborn. We place what we think are the best choices for ourselves and society above God's sovereignty. What does this say about us as a society?

Abortion and the Empty Womb

Since abortion became legal on a federal level, we have seen unprecedented cultural changes as a nation, a loss of the voice of the church, and easier access to abortion clinics. The sad reality is that the lost babies of abortion have never been held and have never been loved by a mommy or a daddy. They have never been tucked into bed or read a bedtime story. They have never learned a nursery rhyme and have never gotten to sing "Jesus Loves Me." They have never eaten a peanut butter and jelly sandwich or had their pudgy little fingers wiped clean by a doting grandmother or aunt. They never got to go fishing with a grandpa or had a chance to participate in any of the many loving family outings that most of us take for granted.

Maternity clothing lines and baby outfitting shops cater to those planning new additions to the family. Cheerful and bright colors dominate the store displays, trying to catch the eyes of the buyers of gifts for these little ones, who are yet to be born. On the darker side, there are unborn babies traveling in wombs to seedier destinations. These are babies who will never see a bright color or hear a new musical toy. Their first and only taste of the outside world will be an abortionist's gruesome killing tools or chemicals.

There is a profound emptiness on this earth because of lives that have never been lived. Instead, these precious little ones have been attacked and stripped of all humanity and opportunities for life, while they should have been protected in the warmth and safety of their mother's womb. God designed a woman's womb with utmost precision to support the life of each baby. **The mother's womb should be the safest place on earth for a baby**, whether the gestational age is one day or nine months. Every baby that was ever born first takes up residence there, where he or she can be nurtured and fed in safety and peace. The environment in the womb is perfectly planned for maximum comfort, security, and health. It is supposed to be "home" for a baby for a full nine months. The entire purpose of the special and beautiful design of a woman's body is reproduction — childbearing. That is reality. There are even health benefits to the mother who has carried an infant in the womb. For instance, it is believed that protection against breast cancer and Alzheimer's disease is a benefit of a full-term pregnancy.

Why Does God Allow Abortion?

People wonder why God even allows abortion, as well as all the other hideous sins and crimes of humanity. God does not ordain abortion, but He gives us free will — the choice to sin or to follow Jesus. That choice is a supernatural decision because we cannot choose Jesus without the Holy Spirit drawing us to Him.[19] He draws all to Him, but the devil tries to keep every one of us from making Jesus our choice. Since we are each given free will, some problems are our own causing.

Our sin always touches someone else. A "little leaven leaveneth the whole lump" means that sin contaminates everything it touches.[20] It is like a snowball rolling downhill, gathering more snow, and becoming larger in the process. When promiscuous sex results in the conception of a baby and a woman decides to take the life of that baby, she is perpetuating the sin. The one who pays for and encourages or even forces that abortion is also in sin. Everyone involved in that abortion decision is in sin, except the baby!

People that are considering abortion need to understand how seriously God takes their decision. Further on in this book, we will see how aborting a baby is the equivalent of sacrificing that baby at the altar of Satan. Spiritually, aborted babies are offered as sacrifices as payments for the cost of the sins of pre-marital sex and rape. Those sins cannot be covered by the sacrifice of a baby. Blood pays the price of sin, but Jesus is the one Who made the blood donation. He did it for every sin, but it is faith in the power of His blood that sets us free from sin.

Dare we question our Maker as to the viability of any preborn child? We face the wrath of God when we take the life and death of an innocent baby into our own hands. Just as all violence is a choice, the taking of the life of a preborn baby is a choice that God gives us. That does not mean that we should not expect His condemnation. He allows evil, but woe to the one who partakes in it! The taking of any human life is an open confrontation with God. Taking the life of a baby is robbing, not only the child of his life but also God because He suffers the loss of that child's life. Who knows the plans He may have had for that little one? Who knows whose lives that child may have impacted?

> But whoso shall offend one of these little ones which believe in me, it were better for him that a millstone were hanged about his neck, and that he were drowned in the depth of the sea. — MATTHEW 18:6, KJV

The age-old question, "Why does God allow sin?" I cannot fully answer. I can try to explain by posing this rhetorical question, however: "If we do not see the ugliness of sin, could we still appreciate the beauty of holiness and anticipate Heaven as much?" One thing is certain. Like the old song says, "We'll understand it by and by."[21]

Playing God

Everything we have belongs to God. Abortion-minded people are not focusing on honoring Him or what is His. Conversely, they are replacing God with their own feelings and intellect. In the Bible, the word "fear," when used in reference to God, means a true reverence for Him. It means having a strong respect and acknowledgment of His awesome power. When a child is aborted anywhere in this country or the world, there is a mother, an abortionist, and perhaps the father, parents, and even grandparents, standing in open defiance of our Maker. There may be friends, included in this group, who exert pressure upon a young woman to destroy the life of the child she is carrying. I fear for them on the day they must stand before the LORD. By the time that day comes, they will have exhausted every choice. We can pray that instead of choosing abortion, they will choose Jesus before it is too late.

Working under Satan, the spirit of Herod, in his strong influence over these people's lives, moves into areas where there are already strongholds. The thoughts, "How can I pay the bills?" or "My boyfriend will leave me" are extremely strong motivators. If we do not cast down the strongholds right away, we leave the door open for the destructive spirits of fear and abortion to come in.

Satan moves quickly, allowing little time to think or pray. The spirit of Herod uses stealth as there is a relatively short period of time to get his job done. An abortion that is delayed is harder to accomplish. Demons will hunt that baby down — even until the due date. If they win, they leave women (except those who give their sins and grief to Jesus) to deal with lifelong repercussions in the memory of their selfish and violent acts.

In seeking to kill Baby Jesus, Herod believed that he was saving his political position. He was operating in fear that he would lose his kingdom to another king. Along with a loss of power, often comes a loss of finances. He was not about to let that happen! In both modern-day abortions and in the killing of Bethlehem's babies, spirits of greed and fear are, and were, operating. Abortion clinics are a multi-million-dollar business in the United States. Taxpayers have unwittingly been funding some of the largest abortion businesses. While our tax money is not supposed to go directly to support abortions because of a 1976 ruling called the Hyde Amendment, the main way abortion clinics keep their doors open is through government funding. Ex-abortion workers have said that, even though clinics claim the money goes to other services, the money is shuffled around on paper to make it look like they are following the law. In the end, the money goes to fund abortions. In some states, we even pay for full-term abortions with state-funded Medicaid money. Many of us do not want to help contribute to the loss of these innocent lives. We do not want to be responsible for the loss of what these babies may have contributed to society. More importantly, we do not want to offend God.

Satan's plot to kill young children is horrendous. Only a black heart could tolerate the thought of a baby in a casket. The "casket" of an aborted baby is often a medical waste bin, a trash can, or a toilet. Its little body ends up in a landfill, incinerator, or sewage plant. Afraid that the baby Jesus would somehow usurp his power, King Herod ordered his soldiers to murder every male child under the age of two; it was a black heart that gave the command. It was a heart that had no respect for God as Creator. It was a deceived heart that only considered selfish greed and feared losing worldly power. A heart that prideful is an open door for demons to come in and do their dirty work on this earth. I am sure that Herod never intended to be Satan's tool, just as most of us do not intentionally consider dishonoring God in our personal plans. We become the willing vessel for either Satan or God, however, by the choices we make.

Pedophilia, Pornography, Alcohol, and Drug Abuse, and Other Hidden Ways to Satisfy Satan

The sinister spirit of Herod works with spirits of pedophilia, pornography, alcohol, drug abuse, and other unhealthy spirits. They attack any weakness to interrupt the healthy upbringing of children. Abortion is the easiest way for Satan to rid the world of children. Satan is sneaky and God's design for families is often thwarted in many ways because Satan's satanic lust for blood and sex can never be satisfied. The devil's goal is to find ways to destroy your children and mine.

Many pervasions have a stronghold on America and are becoming normalized in the eyes of society, but the crimes associated with them are usually hidden in the dark. We need to pray for God to expose and uproot the evil spirits. Our children need deliverance from the darkness.

Abortions are often done in private, without the knowledge of friends or relatives. **The last thing Satan wants is a praying grandmother!** A praying grandmother has brought many a child out of many kinds of evil circumstances. If the devil can kill the child without the grandmother even knowing that the child ever existed, then he has gotten quite the victory. That child's greater, God-ordained purpose has then been eliminated.

Children that are born to drug-abusing parents are sometimes necessarily separated from their families for safety, but the children still suffer the pain of separation. We cannot let demonic powers, which work to further Satan's agenda, continue to steal our children's future. Thankfully, many volunteers and law enforcement personnel work tirelessly to put an end to perverse vices. Prayers for these warriors and for our country are our greatest defense.

A generation has been raised up under Satan's lie that abortion is a choice without eternal consequences. The future for our children on Earth looks very grim in many places.

Jesus is our only Hope! Just as abortion kills the physical life of a child, criminal pedophiles who either mentally, or physically, commit atrocities against unsuspecting children are guilty of greatly harming their spirits. This abuse often gives the innocent over to a lifetime of fear, insecurity, and sexual confusion. Judgment awaits! Pedophiles or parents who are using children to push their own sexual agendas will not go unpunished; even if they do not pay for their crimes during their lifetimes, they will meet Christ at the Judgment Seat.[22]

Abortion and Infanticide Are Against God's Purposes

The Bible does not directly use the word "abortion," but it does state that the taking of any innocent life is a grievous sin. God hates hands that shed innocent blood.[23] While the Israelites were taught and understood that God's laws honored life, their pagan neighbors practiced infanticide through child sacrifice. Ancient Rome also did not honor the lives of infants. An unwanted baby was often barbarically left out in the elements to die, in a practice called "exposure." Children born alive during a botched abortion today are sometimes laid out on a shelf to die in the same way. In the Roman Empire, when a baby was born, he was laid at the feet of the father. The father would then determine whether the baby was to live or die. Some believe that the cause of the fall of the Roman Empire was God's judgment on their loose and immoral culture. We may experience the same fate.

Children Are of the Kingdom of Heaven

God is love, and He loves all little children, including the preborn. Isaiah 64:8 says, "Yet you, LORD, are our Father. We are the clay, you are the potter; we are all the work of your hand" (KJV). We were all created for His pleasure. Ephesians 1:4-5a says, "just as He chose us in Him before the foundation of the world, that we would be holy and blameless before him. In love, He predestined us as sons through Jesus Christ to

Himself . . ." God cares for the preborn babies because they are His creation.

Jesus gave honor to little children:

> And He called a child to Himself and set him before them, 3) and said, "Truly I say to you, unless you are converted and become like children, you will not enter the kingdom of heaven. 4) "Whoever then humbles himself as this child, he is the greatest in the kingdom of heaven. 5) And whoever receives one such child in My name receives Me; —MATTHEW 18:2-5

We must never keep children from the knowledge of Jesus Christ. He is concerned with the innocent. While abusers will be dealt with by God, those who are abused are able to be healed by the love of Jesus:

> "You know of Jesus of Nazareth, how God anointed Him with the Holy Spirit and with power, and how He went about doing good and healing all who were oppressed by the devil, for God was with Him." — ACTS 10:38

The spirit of Herod is a rebellious spirit. God honors and blesses obedience:

> Now it shall be, if you diligently obey the LORD your God, being careful to do all His commandments which I command you today, the LORD your God will set you high above all the nations of the earth . . . Blessed shall be the offspring of your body . . . — DEUTERONOMY 28:1,4a

God places a high value on offspring and life! Children are precious. Life is precious.

When we take our focus off God and place it on the things of this world, we open ourselves up to satanic influences. I once saw a documentary that featured felons who were convicted of murder. It showed how, although they were criminals, they all believed they were basically "good people." Most of us have good thoughts and want to help others. Most of us think we are decent, but we need to look at ourselves as God sees us. Isaiah 64:6 says, "All our righteousness is as filthy rags . . ." Since the filthiness of the rags spoken of in this verse refers to the pollution of menstrual blood when we look at the original language, we can see just how despicable our pretense of goodness appears to God. Truly, we are unworthy to call ourselves "good." There is no amount of "goodness," that will cover any sin, including abortion. Our own attempts at covering up unrighteousness with self-righteousness (without Christ) hinder us.

God has a way out for us. He sent us His Son. Only the blood of Jesus can cover us so that God cannot see our sin:

> . . . we have redemption through his blood, the forgiveness of sins, according to the riches of his grace
> — EPHESIANS 1:7

The Strength of Meekness

The King James Version uses the word "meek" in the third Beatitude, while the New American Standard Bible uses "gentle." To be meek is to be humble, which requires great strength of character. This supernatural strength can only be found through God. Pride was Satan's sin. Pride can be so easily displayed by us when we walk in the flesh. The male peacock puts on quite a show but if you were to ask him why he does it, he would not be able to give you an answer. Prideful people are like that. That is because they are not considering the results of their shameless displays. The male peacock gets good results with his display because the female peahen is just as clueless. These birds are operating on instinct. God has created us to have a deeper understanding than does a fowl. He has created us with a spirit.

To be spiritually minded is the only way to temper the pride of the flesh and to walk in the humility of understanding of who we would be without Christ. Hebrews 12:1 speaks of us running a race with patience, laying aside the sin that, "so easily beset(s) us" (KJV). This speaks of not allowing our feet to get tangled up in this Christian journey that the Apostle Paul likens to a race. When we get tangled up in sinful pride, we are hindered in our attempts to reach the finish line. We stumble and fall. As stated in Galatians 5:23, we should not defend ourselves when we are attacked. We need to let go of natural pride. Instead, when attacked, we should remember that, when Jesus walked up Calvary's Hill, He willingly offered Himself up as a sacrifice for our sins, and He offered no response in defense of Himself. While Jesus suffered on a Roman cross for a crime he did not commit, He never answered His oppressors. He exhibited Godly meekness. His strength was in His obedience and knowledge that He was following the will of His Father. As we follow the will of God, let us be gentle in the strength of our knowledge of the truth of God's Word.

Beatitude 3: "Blessed are the gentle, for they shall inherit the earth" (Matt. 5:5).

Life suggestion: Bless everyone. Walking in peaceful obedience to God not only blesses your friends and family but also blesses God. We must understand that those who promote abortion are lost and do not have the truth. Women who have had abortions have often been coerced or misled. We need to point them gently to Jesus. We need to love these women to God. Love is an action word.

Chapter Four

The Value and Beauty of Life

"Before I formed you in the womb I knew you, And before you were born I consecrated you; I have appointed you a prophet to the nations." — Jeremiah 1:5

God Knew Us Before We Were Conceived

Before I knew that I was pregnant with my daughter, God showed her to me in a dream. As I was sleeping, I had a vision of the night. In this dream vision, I was in the yard of my grandparents' house. It was a place I had spent many happy childhood days. The house was a big, late Victorian-style home built by my great-grandfather and considered the family homestead.

In the dream, I was facing the sandy driveway at the old homestead, and there stood a little girl about nine years of age. She was very pretty and slender, and her hair was long and blonde. She just stood there silently looking at me. Upon awakening, I wondered if I was pregnant. Less than nine months later, my beautiful little girl was born. Initially, her hair was on the reddish side, but it quickly became a beautiful mass of pure blonde tresses. It is somewhat remarkable that I always thought that if I had a daughter, she would look like me with curly brown hair, green eyes, and light olive skin. While we do resemble each other a bit, my daughter is a blue-eyed, natural blonde, just as in my dream.

Interestingly, soon after my pregnancy had been confirmed, I had another prophetic dream. This one took me around twenty years to understand and confirm! It was very similar in mood to the first dream about my daughter, so I truly believed it was from God; however, there were two little girls! In this dream, I was on a street near a school, and there were two little, slender girls skipping along the sidewalk, moving ahead of me. What I saw, I did not understand at first. One of the girls had blonde hair, but the other's hair was a bit darker — not red or brown, but not quite blonde, either. Because of the words God spoke to Jeremiah in quoted scripture from chapter one, we know that God knew us before we were born. He knows all! He knows the end from the beginning.[1] That little girl in my second dream was my darling granddaughter. While she resembles my daughter very much, her hair is a light honey brown — the same as the second little girl in my dream. We are close as I spend a lot of time with my grandchildren. Before my daughter was born, God graciously allowed me to see my daughter in her spirit and my future granddaughter! I do not understand all of it, but God's ways are not our ways.

The Reality of Our Creation

Every baby is important to God because He created each one of us. Unlike the angels, whom He created before He laid the foundation of the earth, we human beings were created later, starting with Adam and Eve. God spoke to Job, saying:

> "Where were you when I laid the foundation of the earth? Tell Me, if you have understanding, — JOB 38:4

Rightly so, God challenges us to examine our position before him. We are the created ones; He is the Creator. Scientists are trying to experiment with manipulating DNA so that we can select our offspring's hair colors, eye colors, and even intellectual abilities. Challenging God places us in a dangerous position. The story of the tower of Babel shows us that when we try to usurp God's authority, it will not work out very well.[2]

God also spoke of our creation in the womb through the prophet, Isaiah:

> Thus says the LORD, your Redeemer, and the one who formed you from the womb, "I, the LORD, am the maker of all things, Stretching out the heavens by

Myself And spreading out the earth all alone, — ISAIAH 44:24

In verse 3b of the very well-known Psalm 100, we read, ". . . it is he that hath made us, and not we ourselves (KJV)."

While God has created all things, from babies in the womb to the heavens above, Satan, our adversary, is always trying to counter the magnificence and omnipotence of our Creator. While God promotes life, the devil and his agents promote death. The whole of the Bible shows us that our eternal God was, and is, and ever will be:

God is omnipotent, which means "all-powerful."

> For with God nothing shall be impossible. — LUKE 1:37, KJV

God is omniscient, which means "all-knowing."

> Great is our Lord, and of great power: his understanding is infinite. — PSALM 147:5, KJV

God is omnipresent, which means that "He is everywhere."

> Can any hide himself in secret places that I shall not see him? saith the LORD. Do not I fill heaven and earth? saith the LORD. — JEREMIAH 23:24, KJV

God is love. He created us and works through us in His love:

> for it is God who is at work in you, both to will and to work for His good pleasure. — PHILIPPIANS 2:13

Because He gave us the Bible, which is a love letter full of instruction and wisdom, Christians have access to the truth of the universe.

> So God created man in his own image, in the image of God created he him; male and female created he them." 28a) And God blessed them . . ." — GENESIS 1:27,28

The following verse explains the personal interest that God takes in each one of us from the moment of our creation. Job also speaks of his own creation as he lamented his grievous circumstances before God delivered him and blessed him. He said:

> Let the day perish on which I was to be born, And the night which said, 'A boy is conceived.' — JOB 3:3

At conception, a human being is already in existence. Job knew that he was completely formed at conception in that he had all the components of his masculinity. He was conceived as a boy. Science tells us that the DNA of a human being is already determined before birth. Here we see one of the many times where modern science confirms the Bible. Job knew that when he was conceived, his gender was already determined. God authored the Bible and created us. He also created science.

Every individual not only has unique DNA but also a unique set of fingerprints and footprints! Each baby is a specially formed, unique individual full of promise for the future, and ready to walk his or her unique trail. Those who fight for the right of "choice" to kill the preborn need to reconsider the choice of God, who creates each baby in His divine image. Many call a pro-life stand a "war on women." The real war is being fought in the spiritual realm against our Creator God. The real war is also against the babies and the mothers who are misled to believe that abortion could ever possibly be a good choice.

Throughout the pages of scripture, our Father God shows us that He gives His children individual purpose. It is evident that Moses, Ruth, John the Baptist, and so many others all allowed themselves to be used by God for specific reasons. In the book of Jeremiah, we learn that God singled the prophet out for a specific purpose long before he was ever born.

Reflection: How does it feel to know that God knew everything about you even before your conception? Does it make you consider or reconsider your purpose in life?

The Importance of the Womb, which Is Mentioned 73 Times in the Bible

The womb of a woman is very important to God because this is where one of the most beautiful examples of the evidence of His creation occurs. Often, we speak of "birthing" a project or idea. We speak of giving birth in a positive light, and every birth begins in the nurturing environment of the womb. I counted how many times the word "womb," and the plural "wombs," occurs in my King James Bible. The womb is mentioned seventy-three times. Here is one example in which Jesus tells Nicodemus that He must be born again of the Spirit:

> Nicodemus saith unto him, How can a man be born when he is old? can he enter the second time into his mother's womb, and be born? — JOHN 3:4, KJV

Here is an example of God's loving care for us and our praise for Him at every stage of life:

> By You I have been sustained from my birth; You are He who took me from my mother's womb; My praise is continually of You. — PSALM 71:6

As we read previously, John the Baptist was filled with the Holy Ghost as a preborn. The angel Gabriel told His father, Zacharias:

> For he will be great in the sight of the Lord; and he will drink no wine or liquor, and he will be filled with the Holy Spirit while yet in his mother's womb. — LUKE 1:15

The Bible Calls Both a Born Baby and a Preborn Baby "Brephos" in the Original Greek

The New Testament was originally written in the common Greek language that was used in Judea at the time of Christ. Interestingly, the NT does not differentiate between the value of the life of a preborn, an infant, or a toddler. Luke, who was a doctor, used the Greek word, "brephos," when he mentioned a baby ("babe" in the KJV), whether the baby had already been born or was still in the womb. It made no difference to Luke. It is apparent that he considered the baby a person, whether he was in or out of the womb. In the following passage, the word "brephos" is used for a preborn baby:

> . . . when Elizabeth heard Mary's greeting, the baby (brephos) leaped in her womb; and Elizabeth was filled with the Holy Spirit. 42) And she cried out with a loud voice and said, "Blessed are you among women, and blessed is the fruit of your womb! 43) "And how has it happened to me, that the mother of my Lord would come to me? 44) "For behold, when the sound of your greeting reached my ears, the baby (brephos) leaped in my womb for joy!" — LUKE 1:41-44

In the following passage, Luke used the same word, "brephos," to depict the Christ child, who was now born:

> This will be a sign for you: you will find a baby (brephos) wrapped in cloths and lying in a manger." 13) And suddenly there appeared with the angel a multitude of the heavenly host praising God and saying, 14) "Glory to God in the highest, And on earth peace among men with whom He is pleased." 15) When the angels had gone away from them into heaven, the shepherds began saying to one another, "Let us go straight to Bethlehem then, and see this thing that has happened which the Lord has made known to us." 16) So they came in a hurry and found their way to Mary

and Joseph, and the baby (brephos) as He lay in the manger. — LUKE 2:12-16

The apostle Peter also used the same word "brephos" for "infant" in 1 Peter 2:2. Other places where Luke used "brephos" was for the word "infant" in Luke 18:15 and Acts 7:19. The first Christian martyr, Stephen, said this about Pharaoh:

> It was He who took shrewd advantage of our race and mistreated our fathers so that they would expose their infants (brephos) and they would not survive. — ACTS 7:19

Reflection: There is no distinction between a preborn baby and an already-born child in the New Testament Greek language! If God calls them all by the same name, shouldn't we? A baby is a baby.

Breath of Life

Each child deserves to take his first breath of life, just as Adam was given life the very day that God breathed life into him. Acts 17:25b tells us that God is the One who "gives to all life, breath, and all things." Every preborn baby requires oxygen in the womb. Those who argue that babies are not considered people because they do not breathe on their own are simply reaching into an empty hole to find a reason to back their pro-abortion argument. We must be loving but truthful. We cannot accept abortion simply because many people want it. God created life; we thwart the plan of Creation by allowing the blessings of innocent babies — the "fruit of the womb" — to be murdered before they take their first breath of life outside the womb. The Word tells us that God is the Giver of Life.[3] We usurp His authority when we put authority into the hands of abortionists.

When Does Life Begin?

Life starts at conception. This is a scientific fact based on simple high school-level biology and is not an opinion up for debate. Science backs up the Bible. When a sperm fertilizes an egg, they are no longer a singular egg and a singular sperm. They are now joined into a newly created life that carries all the genetic material that distinguishes this baby as a unique individual. Human life begins with the fertilization of a single cell. What would make someone deny this? Let us go back to the father of all lies. The devil is a liar and a murderer.[4] If someone wants to debate that a preborn baby of any age or stage is not a real person and a real human being, then that one is not dealing with science but in speculation and is relying on his own false belief system.

At conception, the baby has all the genetic coding for eye, hair, skin color, propensity for a certain height and weight, and even if the baby will potentially have a dimple in the chin. Even with scientific knowledge and an understanding of biology, we still witness the miracle of life every time a baby is born. What is mysterious, beautiful, and wondrous is the miracle of God's love in His creation of all life. Even with modern scientific explanations, we are still in awe over many of the great mysteries of our universe, including the birth of a beautiful newborn. God understands what we do not about the miracles behind the science, as King Solomon wrote:

> As you do not know the path of the wind, or how the body is formed in a mother's womb, so you cannot understand the work of God, the Maker of all things. — ECCLESIASTES 11:15

Women Were Created to Create

God designed motherhood. Did you know that Adam called the woman that God created for him "Eve" because "she was designated the "mother of all living?"[5] If you think deeply about it, you will realize there is something unnatural about women, formed by our Creator God to be mothers, passionately fighting for the "right" to end the life of an innocent baby. Even a mama bear will defend her young — to the death if need be.

God has included women in the magnificence of the creative process. It is a gift and an honor. Imagine God's love when He looked upon his newly created man and woman, Adam and Eve. Before sin entered the world, He lovingly took time with them, physically walking and talking with them in the Garden. Even today, he takes special time with us and invites us to communicate with Him in prayer. He created us for His good pleasure:

> Thou art worthy, O Lord, to receive glory and honour and power: for thou hast created all things, and for thy pleasure they are and were created. — REVELATION 4:11, KJV

Mothers of newborns look at their babies with love and hold them, cooing to them as they admire the beautiful new addition to the family. Many mothers will tell you how their hearts burst with joyous love as their newborns were handed to them. There are women, however, whose motherly bonds are broken. Something has damaged their maternal instincts. Even though they may have children of their own and may appear to outsiders to be kind and loving mothers, something must have happened at some point in their lives to make them devalue motherhood. As an artist and a creative person, I would never deliberately destroy a product of my creation and certainly not my baby.

Those Endless Genealogies and Our Importance to God

The Bible is specific in recounting certain lines of marriages and families. How many of us skip over the genealogical records? We do it, perhaps while guilt creeps in around us because we do not quite understand the importance of them.

We often stumble over them in our pronunciation, and quite frankly, we often miss the point of their inclusion. So then, why does God include these long lists of names in Scripture?

There are two possible reasons:

1. They were written as historical records to prove legal descent while confirming prophecy. The entire Bible predicts and confirms the birth of, records the life of, and declares the Kingship of Jesus. The book of Luke provides Jesus' genealogy through Mary, telling us of His human descent and His bloodline from King David. Joseph, Jesus' earthly father, is legally descended from David, as chronicled in the book of Matthew. This proves the prophecy that Jesus would be born of the house of David. Other important messianic prophecies are given through the birth order of generations.

2. Each name in the seemingly endless lists of names is of importance to our Creator. We are all united in His creation. We break that unity when we deny our faith in Him and deny Him as Creator. However, every one of us is important to God. After all, he sent His only begotten Son that "the world" might be saved through faith in Him.[6] Although we are unworthy because of our sins, He still pays attention to every detail about us. He knows the number of hairs on each of our heads.[7]

There are also some Bible scholars that believe the purity of the line of Noah had to be proven through genealogy because his ancestors did not intermarry with the descendants of the children of angels and the women of earth.[8]

Reflection: *If God knows every hair on our heads, doesn't He also know every detail of each conceived child?*

> Are not two sparrows sold for a cent? And yet not one of them shall fall on the ground without your Father. — MATTHEW 1:29

Each preborn child has the right to learn about life on this earth and the privilege to make a choice for Jesus to be the Lord of his or her life. Each child deserves the chance to grow in a relationship with Jesus. Each one deserves the chance to grow and take his or her place as a rightful heir of our Father God. We become members of the family of God by faith in His Son.[9] Every child, since Adam and Eve had children, has been important to God. Thus, we are given endless genealogies. Incidentally, the people in the genealogies were not perfect; all were sinners in need of a Savior!

Who are we to believe that we have the right to cut these lists short by the unnatural termination of pregnancies? God has given us the gift of life. These lives are not ours to kill. They are God's, so we must allow these little ones to live. We need to let God be God; we must acknowledge His authority.

Racism

Racism and eugenics are the roots of the large promotion of legal abortion in this country. A well-known abortion chain has placed most of its clinics in Black neighborhoods. Black, preborn babies have been killed legally since 1973, in a shockingly disproportionate amount as compared to Whites and Hispanics, and yet not one mainstream media outlet that I know of has reported these scandalous facts. [10]

Margaret Sanger was the main proponent of eugenics in the United States in the early part of the last century. Eugenics seeks to create a supposedly better class of people through selective breeding. Adolph Hitler was a fan of eugenics. Sanger opened the first family planning center in Harlem, NY to promote birth control and is said to have purposely put family planning clinics in Black neighborhoods to discourage the birth of Black children. She is supposed to have said that they had to get the "Colored pastors" on board with her plan, to drum up Black customers at these businesses. This is often quoted.

Amazingly, a popular presidential candidate admitted her admiration for Margaret Sanger. Sanger's philosophies have been put into practice. The truth will eventually be better known. Without apology, she addressed the ladies of the Ku Klux Klan at Silver Lake, NJ, in 1926.

Some of the things I have read about her beliefs make sense, such as the need to be able to afford the children that one has, but she did not understand the tenets of the Bible. From some of her writings, we can determine that she knew something about Jesus and called Him the Great Teacher. It is clear, however, that she had no understanding that He is our only Savior. Her ideas of population control were very frightening. How can any man or woman determine who is truly fit to bear a child? As I go through the final editing of this book, there is a disturbing, nationwide news story concerning a famous young woman who is forced by her conservator to wear an IUD, a birth-control device (which causes dangerous side effects). That kind of control needs to be thoroughly scrutinized. Both Sanger and Hitler thought they had good motives to control the birth of a population.

Today, the abortion industry, especially the largest abortion provider in the US, operates with billions of dollars with the CEOs earning tremendously more money than most of us. Our tax dollars have been massively funding this abortion enterprise. This organization, in turn, uses millions of tax dollars that we give them to lobby politicians to influence their abortion votes. The information is publicly available. You can research how much money is given to your various state representatives as well as those running for the office of President of the United States. Our past President defunded this abortion provider whose profits largely came from abortions, but the present President reinstated these payments. A certain governor received over one million dollars from the largest abortion provider a few years ago. Many political candidates are given donations by this abortion company. Is it any wonder that many unethical politicians favor abortion until the ninth month of pregnancy?

Mixed Races

Have you ever wondered why God forbade the Israelites from marrying outside of their own people? It is not, as I have heard it said, that God did not want to mix the races. That is a lie from the devil. There is only one race — the human race. God did not want the Israelites' pure, monotheistic beliefs in Him to be contaminated with heathen practices by marrying outside of the faith. Lasciviousness, sexually perverted practices, brought on by carnality, and unbridled lust, are condemned by God. The neighbors of the Israelites, especially the Canaanites, practiced lewdness and lasciviousness, including temple heterosexual and homosexual prostitution and child sacrifice. In short, they worshipped the devil through their adherence to horrific rites and demon worship.

We also must remember the kinds of diseases promiscuity brings. Today, people who contract syphilis and other sexual diseases may be cured with antibiotics. In those days, these diseases meant sure madness and death. The HIV virus was introduced to the United States in the 1980s through homosexual practices, and scientists are still trying to find a cure. Sexual promiscuity would have wiped out all of God's people if they had completely fallen in with the practices of the demon god worshippers.

It is hard to believe that God's chosen people would participate in these practices, but besides not trusting fully in God, the enticement of the base carnality in worshipping false gods brought the ancient Israelites into sin, even to child sacrifice. It is the same in the US today. The sins of promiscuity and adultery may often cause the desire to kill one's own children in the womb. Faithlessness and carnality lead to sickness, death, and abortion.

Dignity and Reproductive Rights

The opposite of the "right to life" has been occurring in our nation. Women are told that they have the right to kill their preborn children. They erroneously call this concept "reproductive rights." That phrase makes no sense. Everyone that can physically create a child has the right to reproduce. This is not China, the country that created the one-child policy. There has never been a restriction on reproducing. Everyone in the United States has the right to bear children. That is a human right.

Murder is not a human right. No one has the moral right to take an innocent person's life, whether it is a child that we created, or not. Because a person is inconvenient or irritating or brings a lot of bills into our mailboxes, does not give us the right to kill him or her. There is an inherent dignity of life. There is no dignity in murder.

Unalienable Right to Life, Reproductive Rights, and Choice

We, in America, celebrate Independence Day on July 4th every year. On that day in 1776, the final text of the Declaration of Independence was given approval by our nation's forefathers. This document is revered because of the stand that was taken to officially break our ties with the tyrannical English Crown and to declare, in detail, who we are as people in this great nation. Its claims on liberty were definitive and profound. The first and second paragraphs read:

> *When in the Course of human events, it becomes necessary for one people to dissolve the political bands which have connected them with another, and to assume among the powers of the earth, the separate and equal station to which the Laws of Nature and of Nature's God entitle them, a decent respect to the opinions of mankind requires that they should declare the causes which impel them to the separation.*

We hold these truths to be self-evident, that all men are created equal, that they are endowed by their Creator with certain unalienable Rights, that among these are Life, Liberty and the pursuit of Happiness.

The first paragraph begins with an explanation of why we separated from England. The second paragraph explains that our Creator-given freedom is "self-evident." Of the three unalienable rights, the right to life is the first mentioned. Without it, the other two — liberty and the pursuit of happiness — are impossible to attain.

The Declaration of Independence implicitly stands on the design of the Creator in claiming these rights. As our republic was formed, our laws were set into place with a deep respect for our unalienable rights and provided for their protection. Yet here in this country, which is founded on the promises of individual rights and freedom, preborn children are so discriminated against that they do not even have the basic right to life! We have become a society of monsters, denying the right to life to our most vulnerable. This is the greatest human rights issue of our time! One of the lies that Satan likes to disseminate, to push abortions, is the bold claim that to kill a preborn baby is a "woman's choice."

Today pro-abortion activists scream about the "rights of women," yet our Declaration of Independence claims a "right to life" for all. Do the rights of women supersede the rights of babies? This is the demonic spirit of Herod in full operation. His master's public guise is that one life is more important than another. Pride and selfishness rule the thought patterns that are directed by our own sinful nature. This has caused us to ride down the slippery slope of tolerance for death.

Nothing in the Constitution of the United States even hints at the right to abortion or requires taxpayers to fund abortions. **The Constitution guarantees the right to life.** Every American, including the preborn, has a God-given unalienable right to life. While the preborn are not specially named here, every single human being is implied. Preborn babies are human beings. Their DNA proves it. The most serious crime that one can be convicted of in the United States is premeditated murder and yet pre-meditating the death of a preborn baby is culturally acceptable! Abortion is premeditated murder.

Right to Privacy vs. Shout Your Abortion

The current legal right to abortion was decided in 1973 upon the "right to privacy" found in the Constitution. The right to privacy is essential in a free republic. The courts will need to re-examine how a right to privacy constitutes the right to take a human life when Roe vs. Wade goes back to the Supreme Court. It will happen! Pro-abortionists will need to prove that the legality of killing a preborn baby somehow equates to a right to privacy.

A few years ago, those who favored abortion often claimed they wanted it to be safe, legal, and rare. We never hear discussions from the pro-abortion group concerning a restriction on the number of abortions any woman should have. There has been a very progressive moral shift. The same people who declared that abortion should be the exception and not the rule now seem to celebrate multiple abortions.

I personally know women who have had more than seven pregnancy terminations. I know of women who have had many more. In recent news, there was a story of a pro-abortion activist who broke the world record for abortions. She was quite proud of her "achievement." It was her twenty-seventh abortion.

A recent popular craze was the call to "Shout your abortion!" We need to do a better job of evangelizing to these lost souls. They need to know the truth of the damage they are doing to their eternal destiny, as well as the destiny of mankind. We usurp the authority of God when we make what are ultimately

His decisions of life and death. Getting in the way of God's plans will always bring us to a bad end because He knows best. He sees all. He knows all.

Now is the time to emerge from the rhetorical fog of those who advocate for the "right to choose" and with a clear vision to see that it is really a mindset to "choose death." It is time to take an uncompromising stand for the right to life and against the abortion and infanticide holocaust. When exercising "choice" about abortion, we are making a choice between the holiness of God and murder. While many women are very private about their abortions, the Constitution of the United States was not originally intended to cover the death of preborn babies.

Euthanasia — Whose Choice?

Assisted suicide of the elderly and infirm is increasing in popularity. In the Netherlands, a little child was murdered by her parents in a hospital bed, and the media called it euthanasia. Do not think that it could never happen here. Anything can happen when the devil runs loose and unabated. The fact that doctors have begun surgically changing the physical anatomy of children to make them look like the opposite gender is proof of this. We are making decisions and forcing our will into situations that only God should handle.

Pro-life supporters absolutely believe in life being led to its fullest, no matter the age or handicap. A few months ago, I heard on the radio a story of a doctor in Holland who was being cleared of charges in a euthanasia case. The patient, who was over seventy-two years old, and suffered from dementia, had asked to be euthanized when she reached a certain level of lifestyle. In the end, she did not want that needle. The doctor asked the family to hold her down as he administered the deadly dose. I was horrified. They reasoned away their immoral actions because that had been the lady's initial choice. It was not her final choice, however, and that woman was murdered. In the end, she valued her life.

When I Chose Life for an Elderly, Sick Man, Against His Wishes

Years ago, it fell on me to take care of an elderly man, whom I will call Ernie Duprey. I did not know was just how sick he was. He coughed a lot, and his phlegm was disgustingly putrid. At eighty-six, however, he was still wonderfully strong and active. He drove, had a business, and took care of himself. Unknown to me at that time was that he had emphysema for many years and before he was fifty years of age, doctors had wanted to put him on an "iron lung." I learned this from his neighbors. He told me his grandfather was a "Maine Indian" that went without a shirt in winter, chopping trees down in the Maine forest. His father was a logger. He came from strong stock. I later learned that Mr. Duprey had lung cancer and that he was already beginning to decline. He made me promise that if he ever got very bad, I would not call the doctor or hospital. It got to the point where he could not walk to the bathroom.

A Broken Promise — the Joy of Life

One day he got dangerously ill. I broke my promise. He refused my pleadings to let me get medical help. I called the doctor and told him the circumstance. That good doctor came right to the house and kneeled by his bedside. He arranged for an ambulance and Mr. Duprey, against his former wishes, agreed to go to the hospital. Medical workers cleaned out his lungs and he came home much refreshed. It was the last week of December 1999. Mr. Duprey and I welcomed in the turn of the century together. He was thrilled to see the year 2,000! He called his family in California and Canada, within my earshot, and bragged to them that I had saved his life! We never discussed the fact that I had gone against his wishes. He was glad to be alive! I learned an important lesson about the strength of the desire for life from that experience. We need to reflect on stories like these when we encounter arguments for euthanasia.

A Matter of Con-science and Science

Conscience is given to all men regardless of their standing with the LORD or their salvation. When we say that our conscience bothers us, it is because we know that what we are doing is wrong. In Greek, the word "con" means "with". The word "science" means "knowledge." When we put those together, we can see that when we are speaking or doing something because of our conscience, it means that we are acting "with knowledge." In Romans 2:14 -15, Paul says that God gave this ability to both the Jews and the Gentiles (anyone who was not a Jew). Up until Paul's time, most of the Gentiles did not know the patriarchal God of Abraham, Isaac, and Joseph.

When we kill babies in the womb, we do so with the knowledge that we are destroying life. Conscience, or "con" - "science," means "with knowledge of the science." Many women struggle before abortions, either because of their Christianity or if they are unsaved, solely because of their consciences. Paul was saying that while The Law of Moses was given to the Jews, the Gentiles also had a moral conscience and knew the difference between right and wrong. Today, we see this with people who are not Christian yet are generous to the poor and needy. We all know that it is wrong to steal and murder. This is the God-given ability for everyone to live within a certain moral framework.

Believers have more than a God-given conscience. Those that are born-again believers, in Jesus Christ, have access to the Holy Spirit of God. Not all Christians understand that. We are indwelt with the Holy Spirit who guides us into all truth. God leads us through His Spirit to walk in love. More than just having a burdened conscience, we have a leading to say what God would have us to say and do what God would have us to do.

To be led by your conscience is a wonderful thing. To be led by the Spirit of Christ is so much better. Because God is love, He leads us into love. Because He is Truth, His Spirit leads us into truth:

> But when He, the Spirit of truth, comes, He will guide you into all truth . . . — JOHN 16:13

All that we must do is ask to be cleansed of sin so that the Holy Spirit will have full reign.

> Wash me thoroughly from my iniquity And cleanse me from sin. — PSALM 51:2

While Christians have no excuse to approve of abortions, even the unsaved know, deep inside their heart of hearts, that abortion is murder because they have been given a conscience. They may choose to ignore their God-given conscience. God gave us all free will.

My Disappointment in the Smithsonian Institute

Some years ago, I visited the Smithsonian Institute in Washington, DC, while on a school trip with my daughter. As we were about to enter the Museum of Natural Sciences, I noticed a disturbing sign that displayed a picture of a cougar. "Come meet your cousins," read the sign. The Bible clearly shows that we are not in rank with animals. Even more upsetting was the voice of a young teacher guiding her students into the building. Content to oblige the message on the sign, she cried out to the children, "Come meet your cousins!" This even goes against common sense.

There is a new movement in many schools, which allows students to create new identities for themselves, whether as an animal or as part of a new "family structure." If children identify with different species from the animal kingdom, they are called "furries." They are also free to "identify with either gender or a mix of new, fictional genders. We should be diligent about learning what is happening in our children's classes and schools. The motives and objectives of every teacher are not always pure, and our children are vulnerable to ungodly deception.

God sets people, whom He has made in His own image, above the beasts of the field and the birds of the air. In Genesis 2:19, we learn that after God created every creature on earth, He brought them to Adam, whose duty it was to name each species. In Genesis 1:28, we learn that God gave man authority over all fish, fowl, and "every living thing that moveth upon the earth" (KJV). All life is valuable, but many believe we are on par with animals.

How are we going to teach our nation's children respect for human life when we pretend that animals are on equal footing with human beings? I love animals very much and respect the fact that they, too, are God's created beings; however, while it is important that we treat animals with love and kindness,[11] we must not treat them as if they are equal to humans. We were given dominion over all God's wild and domesticated creatures.[12] There seems to be a concerted and relentless effort to devalue human life by raising the value of animals, but God values us much more:

> "Indeed, the very hairs of your head are all numbered. Do not fear; you are more valuable than many sparrows. — LUKE 12:7

Stewardship of Creation

Many of us raised during the 1960s and '70s when the need to protect the environment was well-publicized are nature lovers. We all need to be good stewards of the earth.[13] Raised in the woods, I have a deep and abiding love for all that God has created. When recycling came into practice, I was dedicated to separating cardboard from glass and paper long before it was legally mandatory. God tells us that He can be seen in the wondrous beauty of His entire creation. There is no excuse to believe that there is no God!

> For the invisible things of him from the creation of the world are clearly seen, being understood by the things that are made, even his eternal power and Godhead; so that they are without excuse. — ROMANS 1:20

Time spent outdoors in solitude with God can be times of great joy. Everyone should take the time to walk in natural settings, as it can bring great peace. It is a perfect way to relieve stress when the world takes a toll on us. The god of this world wants to steal our peace, but our Creator God blesses us abundantly with the calming beauty of nature:

> He maketh me to lie down in green pastures: he leadeth me beside the still waters. — PSALM 23:2, KJV

Animals cannot call on God because they do not have that kind of spiritual understanding, but they are often more protected by people than defenseless preborn babies. Sometimes, the same people who display animal protection bumper stickers on their cars are the first to say that there are too many people in the world. We human beings are not qualified to make that call. God is Sovereign. That is why we turn to Him in difficult times and in times of oppression.

> . . . Let the LORD be magnified, which has pleasure in the prosperity of His servant. 28) And my tongue shall speak of thy righteousness and of thy praise all the day long. —PSALM 35:27, KJV

Disparity

Who can resist the big loving eyes of a puppy or the cute antics of a kitten? We are awed by the nobility of the lion, and we delight in the wild abandon of birds in flight. We must remember, however, that the most important creature on earth is man because we are made in the image of God.[14] Some people, however, treat animals better than they do people. I would not want to be guilty of trying to convince a little child that animals are more important than human beings and that killing a preborn child is in any way justified. I would not want to face the LORD on Judgment Day.

There are some who advocate for the humane treatment of pets (as we should) but do not think twice about the fact that American abortion clinics continue to murder babies daily. They are suffering spiritual deception and blindness. Helping animals is extremely commendable; rare and exquisite plants are lovely to behold, but what is more precious to hold and view than a beautiful newborn baby? This satanic deception has heavily influenced our culture. Several states with liberal abortion policies are currently considering bans on declawing cats because it is a painful procedure and because it leaves cats defenseless. These states give priority to animals but disregard the defenseless and painful condition of terminating the lives of preborn children!

Adoption

In recent years, a United States senator who sponsored a bill that would protect kittens used in scientific research from being euthanized opposed a bill that would help babies who survive abortion. The Born-Alive Abortion Survivors Protection Act was voted down but hopefully will be resurrected. The "kitten bill" seeks to place the kittens in adoptive homes. It is a travesty that this is more important to certain government representatives than placing human babies in adoptive homes. These children have a constitutional right to life that is often unrecognized.

The average cost of an abortion at about ten weeks gestation has generally been about five hundred dollars, and second-trimester abortions (those obtained between three- and six months of gestation) are about two-thousand dollars. Third-trimester abortions cost eight to ten thousand dollars and even up to twenty thousand dollars — nearly the expense of adoption. The cost of adoption may be ten to fifteen thousand dollars and could even be as much as forty thousand dollars or more, especially when using lawyers. This is prohibitive to many. For those wishing to adopt from foster care, however, the costs may be minimal. I have known many couples who wished to adopt but could not afford the high costs of adopting an infant. There needs to be a total reform in adoption policies.

Reflection: The eggs of bald eagles and sea turtles are well protected by federal law, but preborn babies have little protection. We can call the eagle and turtle eggs "preborn" or "pre-hatched." If you kill one of these, you will have to pay a hefty fine and perhaps be arrested. What do you think of this discrepancy where preborn babies do not have the same protection?

Beatitude 4: "Blessed are those who hunger and thirst for righteousness, for they shall be satisfied" (Matt. 5:6).

Life suggestion: We should give as we are able. The world tells us to hold onto worldly goods. God wants us to share and be generous. We must provide for our families and help other Christians, especially the widows and orphans, but we must also help in the world. That translates to single mothers and children without fathers or anyone who does not have the ability to care for themselves. Ignoring single mothers challenges our walk in Godly righteousness. We must also extend our hearts in Godly mercy to those who need physical and financial help. We should give all we can as we receive God's righteousness by faith. In our giving, we are giving back to Him. If we truly seek God's will, we will realize His full righteousness. We receive God's righteousness by faith in His Son. Proverbs 21:21 says, "He who pursues righteousness and loyalty finds life, righteousness, and honor."

Chapter Five

The Valley of Slaughter

For they have committed adultery, and blood is on their hands. Thus they have committed adultery with their idols and even caused their sons, whom they bore to Me, to pass through the fire to them as food. — Ezekiel 23:37

Burnt Offerings — Burning Babies Alive

The Israelites were fickle! Instead of waiting on the LORD to provide for them, they did not trust Him and sought other ways to accomplish what they wanted. They lacked faith that God's ways are the best ways. We cannot fault them, however, any more than we can fault ourselves. Faith in God's provision can often be a challenge for many of us.

In the opening verse from Ezekiel, above, we see that the babies of God's people belong to God. They were feeding demon gods with the blood of their babies instead of dedicating their precious babies to God! Instead of honoring Yahweh, which is the real name of God, meaning "I AM THAT I AM,"[1] they honored the demons of death and sexual perversion in the cultic Baal religion. When His people turned to foreign idols in rebellion, God referred to it as "adultery." There are many places in the Bible where God accuses His people of worshipping idols.

Yahweh, as written in today's Bible (including the 1611 King James Version), is written as "LORD," with all capitals. The LORD God rebuked his people for placing their babies, as a food offering, in the stone arms of the false god Molech to be burned. In this chapter's opening quote from Ezekiel, this is what is meant by "pass through the fire."[2]

"The valley of slaughter" is the name God gave to the area where the human sacrifices took place, as we read in the following verses. God explains that He never told them to practice infanticide and that it is something about which He never thought:

> . . . they have filled this place with the blood of the innocent 5) and have built the high places of Baal to burn their sons in the fire as burnt offerings to Baal, a thing which I never commanded or spoke of, nor did it ever enter My mind; 6) therefore, behold, days are coming," declares the LORD, "when this place will no longer be called Topheth or the valley of Ben-hinnom, but rather the valley of Slaughter. — JEREMIAH 19:4-6

We learn about the murders of infants in "The Valley of Slaughter" here in Jeremiah 19:6 and in other places in the Bible, such as Jeremiah 7:31. It is the name that the LORD gave to a valley outside of Jerusalem, where many newborn infants were killed and burned as human sacrifices, long before Jesus walked the earth. Jeremiah was told by God to warn His people of impending judgment over this horrific sin, as well as other committed offenses. God's people were not living rightly before Him but were following the gods of their heathen neighbors. They were allowing pagan rituals to infiltrate their religious lives. Just as many do today, God's chosen people followed the world's ways instead of faithfully worshipping the one true God. They began the grisly practice of sacrificing their children in the valley of Hinnom as they began placing their children in the fire for burnt offerings unto Baal, the heathen God, who went by various names, including "Molech":

> 32) Because of all the evil of the children of Israel and of the children of Judah, which they have done to provoke me to anger, they, their kings, their princes, their priests, and their prophets, and the men of Judah, and the inhabitants of Jerusalem. 33) And they have

turned unto me the back, and not the face: though I taught them, rising up early and teaching them, yet they have not hearkened to receive instruction. 34) But they set their abominations in the house, which is called by my name, to defile it. 35) And they built the high places of Baal, which are in the valley of the son of Hinnom, to cause their sons and their daughters to pass through the fire unto Molech; which I commanded them not, neither came it into my mind, that they should do this abomination, to cause Judah to sin. 36) And now therefore thus saith the Lord, the God of Israel, concerning this city, whereof ye say, It shall be delivered into the hand of the king of Babylon by the sword, and by the famine, and by the pestilence; — JEREMIAH 32:32-36, KJV

The Valley — Topheth, Valley of Hinnom, Gehenna, and Hell

All three of the above names describe the same awful location. The old Teacher's Edition Bible Dictionary tells us that Topheth was in the "southeast extremity of the 'valley of the son of Hinnom'" and that it was "defiled by idols and polluted by the sacrifices of Baal and the fires of Molech. Then it became the place of abomination, the very gate or pit of hell."[3] This is where King Solomon, in deference to his foreign wives, originally erected the "high places" for Molech.[4] Later, Kings Ahaz and Manasseh followed through in the same evil idolatry.[5]

These were horrendous scenes. When the infants were placed in the fire, the participants in the ritual would beat drums to "drown the cries of the burning victims that passed through the fire to Molech." Later, this area was called the "Valley of Hinnom." It became the city dump and the fires raged continuously reminding the people of Hell. The "pious kings" who sought to bring the people back to God, began "pouring into it all the filth of the city, until it became the 'abhorrence' of Jerusalem."[6] This is where the inhabitants of the city threw all their waste and dead animals.[7]

In the New Testament, we do not see the name Topheth, but we do see the name "Gehenna" twelve times, indicating the place of future punishment after judgment. The Teacher's Edition Bible Dictionary states that "the later Jews applied the name of this valley . . . to denote the place of eternal torment." Gahanna means "Land of Hinnom."[8]

Who is Baal?

Baal means "master, lord."[9] The description of "lord" for Baal is written in lowercase letters. Our One True God, you will remember, is written, "LORD." Because Satan originated in Heaven, he has underlings in an operative system, which is ranked just as God's heavenly angels are ranked.[10] Satan always conjures up a counterfeit to the goodness and purity of God. He even uses God's ordained order in the heavenlies. The satanic realm operates in an orderly hierarchy like God's angelic realm.[11] The worship of Baal, however, was anything but orderly as we will see later. Even the priests of Baal screamed and cut themselves in a frenzy as their own blood gushed from them.[12]

Most pagan religions, especially in the Old Testament days, were polytheistic, meaning they served many and various gods. Another word for this is "pantheism," which is widely practiced in Eastern and New Age religions today. The ancient Hebrews (later called Jews) were monotheistic and served One God — Yahweh. Their heathen neighbors believed that Baal was the son of El, the primary Canaanite god. You may remember that Canaan is the name of the land where Abraham was called by God to go and establish himself in the "promised land," on which he was to rear generations of promised descendants.[13]

You may know the story of the Hebrews (Israelites) worshipping the golden calf that Aaron made for them while

Moses was away on the mountain with God. Calves were made as representations of Baal. Some things that are a bit confusing are lost in antiquity as Baal was also supposedly the son of the great god Dagon, the god of grain, who was "generally represented as having the body or trunk of a fish, with human head and hands."[14] At that time, a symbol of a fish would have indicated bounty as fish was a diet staple. Either way, he was the son of the chief god in the Canaanite culture. You may see the name Dagon appear in the names of various ancient towns, and you will see the same concerning Baal, with the name even appearing in the composition of the names of people. While there is confusion in historic annals, as to the real names and hierarchy of Baal, Dagon, and Molech, the god of the Ammonites, there is no confusion in our Bible as to the deity of our Holy Trinity and God the Father, God the Son, and God the Holy Ghost.

God of Dung and Abortion

There are also many variations on the name Baal according to different regions, such as "Baalberith," who was worshipped at Shechem.[15] Many of us are familiar with the name "Beelzebul," whom Jesus spoke of in Matthew 10:25. Beelzebul is another derivative of Baal, probably meaning, "god of dung."[16] The Pharisees called Beelzebul, "the ruler of the demons."[17] Beelzebul is also believed to mean "lord of the flies." It is easy to see the connection between the god of dung and the lord of the flies because flies often swarm over dung and anything dead. It is a fitting description of the god of infant sacrifice, who is the enemy of Christ the LORD, who stands for life.

Baal had various cults, and various towns had their own version of Baal, but for our purposes, it is best to understand that he was the head god/demon of nature, including agriculture, thunder, and fertility. The infant sacrifice and sexual deviance of both the Baal and Astarte cults were far from God's call to worship Him "in the beauty of holiness."[18]

Astarte

Baal's female counterpart or consort was the goddess, Astarte.
Throughout the Old Testament, God condemned the worship
of this false goddess. In the Bible, depending on the version
you are reading, you may see her name written, "Asherah" or
"Ashteroth," which is plural and indicates the many idols
made in her image. The King James version uses "Asherim."
Astarte was the goddess of war and fertility, and worshipping
this goddess consisted of flagrant lewdness, "connected with
the most impure rites."[19] Later on, in history, Astarte worship
evolved into the Greek goddess worship of Artemis, the
Roman goddess worship of Diana[20,] and the Roman goddess
Venus.[21] A temple to her was found in old Ephesus, which is in
modern-day Turkey.

> For they also built them high places, and images, and
> groves, on every high hill, and under every green tree.
> 24) And there were also sodomites in the land: and they
> did according to all the abominations of the nations
> which the LORD cast out before the children of Israel.
> — 1 KINGS 14:23,24

King Josiah, the Reformer, Stopped the Passing of Babies Through the Fire

The ancient Israelites were steeped in paganism. They made
vessels for Baal and Asherah that were placed in the temple.
The sun, moon, and constellations were being worshipped.
There were also houses for male cult prostitutes (sodomites) in
the temple. God's chosen people were sinking in sin. Living in
the 7th century BC, King Josiah was a reformer and one of the
few kings who followed the LORD. The Bible tells us that he
was instrumental in ridding Judea of the high places where
incense was offered to pagan deities and the idolatrous priests,
and Josiah ordered the articles related to pagan worship torn
down and burned. He ordered the chariots of the sun to be
burned, and he took away the horses that had been given to

the sun by previous kings. Sun worship was also equivalent to Baal worship. Josiah broke down altars and sacred pillars and the wooden Asherim.[22] It is also recorded that:

> He also defiled Topheth, which is in the valley of the son of Hinnom, that no man might make his son or his daughter pass through the fire for Molech. — 2 KINGS 23:10

Reflection: Living today is a lot like living in King Josiah's time. What false idols can we help take down through prayer? We must pray to reform our ways and save the lives of babies.

What We Saw at the Dead Sea Scrolls Exhibit

When the Dead Sea Scrolls exhibition came to a city near me, I jumped at the chance to go see it! It was a very well-organized event and was educational with many artifacts and displays. What grabbed my attention was something I had not expected to see. In one area, many ancient artifacts, including household idols and amulets, were on display. Amulets were like "good luck charms." You may remember the Bible story of Rachel stealing her father Laban's household gods, or teraphim, and sitting on them in the tent while attempting to hide them.[23] They were small enough to be portable, so nomadic families could transport them easily.

The large number of these false idols that were on display shocked me but gave me a better comprehension of the spiritual adultery God was speaking about in the Old Testament. It also showed the wideness of God's mercy in dealing with such disobedient people. So often, through the prophets, the LORD warned His people of their disobedience of following strange gods because it happened over and again.

Reflection: When we consider the many ways in which we follow various kinds of unbiblical spirituality today, can we be more holy than the ancient Hebrews and Israelites?

What is a Demon?

Demons create much havoc on this earth. When we are not tempted in the flesh, the devil will try to tempt and distract us with his demons. He sends them out to cause discouragement and depression. When we come under attack, we may sometimes want to hole up in a cave and not face the world; but God is greater! The devil, Satan, is a defeated foe, and we need to walk in the victory we have already received from Jesus. The Bible does not fully explain the origins of demons. What I will be sharing is a very brief discussion; a full discussion would require a separate book.

Many believe that demons are fallen angels. While there is no Biblical account of anyone seeing a fallen angel other than in the passage of Genesis Ch. 6 that I discuss in the next paragraph, I do know very believable people who have witnessed manifestations of God's holy messenger angels and warrior host. Throughout the Bible, we can find instances of angels interacting with people, and they take the form of man when they are seen on Earth. On the other hand, I do not know anyone who has ever spoken of seeing a fallen angel. The only time we see them interacting with people is in Genesis Ch. 6, in the pre-flood days, when "the sons of God came in to the daughters of men, and they bore children to them" (v. 4). For brevity's sake, I will not be able to take on a full description of the various viewpoints about this very interesting passage.

Good scholars differ and believe in two views:

1. *The passage of Genesis 6:1-6 refers to the line of Seth, the son of Adam, because Seth was so good. One of the difficulties with this view is that in the Old Testament, "the sons of God" always refers to angels. The second thing I would like to point out is that if the sons of Seth were so good, then God would have put them on the ark and saved them along with Noah and his family.*

2. *This same passage refers to fallen angels producing children with earthly women. It is possible that the "mighty men who were of old, men of renown" (v.4) were such an evil corruption of humanity that God had to send a flood to cleanse the earth of them. These offspring of fallen angels were called Nephilim (v. 4). Fallen angels are those that followed Lucifer out of heaven after a heavenly war.[24] It is possible that the spirits of these crossbred Nephilim had nowhere to go when they died.*

The Bible says that the fallen angels are bound in chains under eternal darkness at this time to be held for judgment.[25] It is possible that the fallen angels are the demons of today, but it is also possible that it is the spirits of their offspring, which were born in their union with women that are the evil demons. In the New Testament, "demons" and "evil spirits" are used interchangeably.

Just as we have eternal life, either spent in Heaven or Hell, angels will always be alive. Jude 1:6 tells us that the fallen angels are kept in chains reserved for "the great day," which is the final judgment of the wicked and unbelievers (KJV). The Nephilim are neither fully fallen angels to be bound in chains nor fully human, to be sent to Hades until the time of the final judgment after they physically die. (Hades, also called Hell, is a temporary holding place for those who have not received Jesus and will not go to Heaven.) There will be a day when Satan and his angels and all evil will all be cast into eternal fire, for then they will no longer have influence in this world.[26]

Even though the Bible is not clear on the origins of demons, the NT shows that they are real. Jesus even equips us to deal with them, under His authority. Interestingly, we see more talk of evil spirits in the NT than in the OT. It seems that the presence of Jesus may have stirred up a lot of demonic activity. We must not be discouraged when we see a lot of demonic activity being stirred up when we are serving the

LORD in righteousness. Christian witness always creates a tempest in the dark, unseen realm. We are safe in the LORD.

I have known people who have seen floating black evil spirits and even small demonic beings. My advice to any Christian who sees anything like that is to cast that spirit out of your presence in the name of Jesus Christ. Announce that you are covered by the blood of Jesus, the King of kings, and the LORD of Lords, and do it in the authority that He gives you as a child of God. If you are not a true believer and do not have faith in the blood of Jesus, you will not have the authority to do this. We know that Jesus encountered demons and when He did, they were always in a human host. Demons do not have their own physical body. Let us look at Matthew Ch. 8 when Jesus visited the country of the Gadarenes:

> . . . two men who were demon-possessed met Him as they were coming out of the tombs. They were so extremely violent that no one could pass by that way. 29) And they cried out, saying, "What business do we have with each other, Son of God? Have You come here to torment us before the time?" 30) Now there was a herd of many swine feeding at a distance from them. 31) The demons began to entreat Him, saying, "If You are going to cast us out, send us into the herd of swine." 32) And He said to them, "Go!" And they came out and went into the swine, and the whole herd rushed down the steep bank into the sea and perished in the waters.
> — MATTHEW 8:28-32

The demon infestation of these pigs caused them to go mad, and they hurled themselves off a cliff. When the Gospels of Mark and Luke give us the same account of this story, they mention only one of the men. Slight differences sometimes occur in the Gospels, but the stories are primarily the same. This may be because they were witnessing from different perspectives. Perhaps one of the men did not stand out as much as did the other. Luke notes that at least one of the men was not fully clothed. Mark tells us that at least one of the men had often been bound in chains and fetters but had abnormal strength enabling him to break loose.

Other details are "cutting" with stones and howling day and night. We see this today as many troubled young people become absorbed with cutting themselves and need deliverance. In news videos, we have been seeing demonic activity in protestors howling in the streets. We know from the Book of Mark that the demons were responsible for giving at least one of the men superhuman strength, which made him uncontrollable. The demon in this man spoke to Jesus and identified his name as "Legion." It could simply refer to a large, unspecified amount, or this is a term that could have meant the number 5,200, which was the number of a Roman legion of soldiers. Legion, therefore, is a military term. This term was also used in reference to the number of angels that God could have sent to help Jesus, numbered at twelve legions, or sixty-thousand angels, in Matthew 26:52. (This word was also referred to when Peter took out his sword and cut off the ear of a servant of the high priest. The "band" was one-tenth of a legion and a military guard.) There are military ranks of demons and a hierarchy just as there are military ranks and a hierarchy of angelic beings.

Notice that the two demon-possessed men were coming out of the tombs. They chose to associate with death. We see this today in an obsession with skulls, certain music, drugs, and abortion. Notice not only their violence but also that they recognize Jesus as the Son of God! They requested that they would be given another place to inhabit if Jesus would cast them out. He accommodated them. There were so many demons in just two men that they were able to fill a whole herd of hogs. If demons can infest a herd of swine, they can also infest a crowd of godless abortion protestors. The hogs went wild and ended up on a short path of self-destruction. Do you see the correlation? Demons seem to be manifesting in abundance in the United States. Demon manifestation has not been as common as it was in countries where the Gospel of Jesus Christ had not yet been fully made known. We are told this by the testimonies of many missionaries that have witnessed demonic activity overseas. It seems as of late, however, as God has been removed from the public square, the number of demonically influenced people in America is increasing.

The Spirits of Molech, Jezebel, and Herod — Satan's Loathsome Trio

Death is important to Satan — especially the deaths of innocent babies. Demons influence events and people. The spirit of Herod is one of many in the demonic hierarchy "upper echelon." I believe that the LORD specifically showed me the spirit of Herod and how he tried to murder the Christ Child because that spirit has influenced the way that the concept of abortion is now sliding into the even scarier realm of approved infanticide in America.

Unlike God, who can be everywhere at the same time, angels, Satan, and demons can only be in one place at one time. There are many in Satan's army, working under him in a vicious network to do harm. The Molech, Jezebel, and Herod spirits, are all high-ranking demonic beings. The idols of Molech had demons of child sacrifice attached to them. The spirits of Jezebel and Herod have names that associate themselves with the actual person most known for certain demonic activity.

Queen Jezebel, mentioned in Ch. 2, was responsible for bringing both Baal and Asherah worship to Israel. The prophet Elijah said that there were eight hundred and fifty prophets of these gods that Jezebel supported.[27] She taught her husband, King Ahab of Israel, to build places for child sacrifice in Israel. Her background was full of murder because her father was a Baal worshipper.

In 2 Chronicles, we see how the occult is mixed with child sacrifice in King Manasseh's worship of Baals and Asherim:

> Manasseh was twelve years old when he became king, and he reigned fifty-five years in Jerusalem. 2) He did evil in the sight of the LORD according to the abominations of the nations whom the LORD dispossessed before the sons of Israel. 3) For he rebuilt the high places which Hezekiah his father had broken down; he also erected altars for the Baals and made Asherim, and worshiped all the host of heaven and served them. 4) He built altars in the house of the LORD of which the LORD had said, "My name shall be in Jerusalem forever." 5) For he built altars for all the host of heaven in the two courts of the house of the LORD. 6) He made his sons pass through the fire in the valley of Ben-hinnom; and he practiced witchcraft, used divination, practiced sorcery and dealt with mediums and spiritists. He did much evil in the sight of the LORD, provoking Him to anger. — 2 CHRONICLES 33:1-7

Joint Influence — The Spirits of Herod and Jezebel on Queen Athaliah

Evil spirits can continue to attach themselves to generations of the same family. In Exodus 20:1-5, part of the Ten Commandments, God condemns those who worship and serve false gods. He speaks of the sin that is passed on to the third and fourth generations because of idol worship. Idol worship is demon worship. Just as the demons of child sacrifice were spiritually attached to ancient statues of Molech, spirits of murder and other vices may attach themselves to generations of the same family. All carry the same spirit of death and destruction because that is the devil's goal. The wonderful thing is that when we are aware of it, we can make the choice to be delivered of any bondage. I have witnessed individuals breaking the spirit of abortion in their families!

Queen Athaliah of Judah, the daughter of Queen Jezebel and King Ahab, sacrificed infants to Baal by placing them in the arms of the demon god, Molech, as well. She was married to Jehoram, King of Judah (the Southern Kingdom, where Jerusalem sits). The demonic spirit operating in her mother also operated in her and she influenced her husband, King Jehoram, to worship Baal.[28] Her mother was Queen of the Northern Kingdom of Israel. Queen Athaliah is infamous for her demonic killing of all the children who were royal heirs to the historic throne of David, in her evil desire to control the land of Judah.[29] She killed her own grandchildren!

I believe that Athaliah was also influenced by the same spirit that later influenced Herod and a Jezebel spirit because she killed her own descendants out of lust for the power of the throne. These spirits are all part of Satan's family. Remember that it was Satan's lust for the Throne of God that caused his fall! Queen Athaliah obviously had demons driving her to do her malicious deeds. Grandmothers have a natural joy in caring for their baby's babies! One little baby escaped his evil grandmother's bloodthirstiness and was hidden from her for six years by his aunt, Jehosheba, the wife of the high priest. Young Joash became king at the age of seven after Queen Athaliah was killed.[30]

The spirits that worked through Queen Jezebel, Queen Athaliah, and King Herod are spirits of witchcraft and control. Even in 21st-century America, these ancient evil spirits are all on the prowl as they work for their master, Satan. They work through high-level politicians in America now, and not kings and queens because we are a republic and not a monarchy. While we associate a female with the spirit of Jezebel, there are no boundaries on the sexual identity of demons and so they can also work through males. The spirit of Herod may work in females. Demons can operate singularly or in multiples within a single human. Remember that Mary Magdalene was delivered from seven spirits.

Demons, which are evil spirits, need a body to inhabit, unlike created angels. That is why I hesitate to believe, as some do, that demons are fallen angels. Angels have their own bodies as we see again and again in scripture. I do know a few people that have seen black wispy spirits but that cannot be backed up by scripture. As I understand it Biblically, however, demons always seek a body to inhabit. Because the Bible is not clear on the full nature of demons, I do not think many of us know the entire picture of the demonic realm. We can only speculate.

Spirit of Molech, the Sin of Witchcraft, and Abominations

> And thou shalt not let any of thy seed pass through the fire to Molech, neither shalt thou profane the name of thy God: I am the LORD. — LEVITICUS 18:21

The spirit of abortion is also called by many, "the spirit of Molech." This is because of the method of worship, as described previously. Molech, in ancient times, was variously pictured as an owl and a man with the head of a bull. This was an idol of provision, fertility, and sexuality. For now, we will be concerned with his representation as a bull, as the Old Testament Hebrews and Israelites knew him best. The Teacher's Edition Bible Dictionary calls Molech a "fire god" and gives this description of this ancient idol:

> Fire-gods appear to have been common to all the Canaanite, Syrian, and Arab tribes, who worshipped the destructive element under an outward symbol, with the most inhuman rites. According to Jewish tradition, the image of Molech was of brass, hollow within, and was situated without Jerusalem. 'His face was that of a calf, and his hands stretched forth like a man who opens his hands to receive (something) of his neighbor. And they kindled it with fire, and the priests took the babe and put it into the hands of Molech, and the babe gave up the ghost.' Many instances of human sacrifices are

found in ancient writings, which may be compared with the description in the Old Testament of the way Molech was worshipped.[31]

Possibly the strongest admonition we find in the Bible against infant sacrifice to Molech is in Chapter 20 of Leviticus and Chapter 18 of Deuteronomy. It is clearly associated with witchcraft and demons (familiar spirits). Remember that "seed" refers to one's babies or children.

> Again, thou shalt say to the children of Israel, Whosoever he be of the children of Israel, or of the strangers that sojourn in Israel, **that giveth any of his seed unto Molech; he shall surely be put to death**: the people of the land shall stone him with stones. 3) And I will set my face against that man, and will cut him off from among his people; because he hath given of his seed unto Molech, to defile my sanctuary, and to profane my holy name. 4) And if the people of the land do any ways hide their eyes from the man, when he giveth of his seed unto Molech, and kill him not: 5) Then I will set my face against that man, and against his family, and will cut him off, and all that go a whoring after him, to commit whoredom with Molech, from among their people.
>
> 6) **And the soul that turneth after such as have familiar spirits, and after wizards**, to go a whoring after them, I will even set my face against that soul, and will cut him off from among his people. 7) Sanctify yourselves therefore, and be ye holy: for I am the LORD your God. — LEVITICUS 20:2-7

Deuteronomy 18 also includes a similar warning:

> There shall not be found among you *any one* that maketh his son or his daughter to pass through the fire, *or* that useth divination, *or* an observer of times, or an enchanter or a witch, 11) or a charmer, or a consulter,

with familiar spirits, or a wizard, or a necromancer. 12) For all that do these things *are* an abomination unto the LORD. . .” — DEUTERONOMY 19:10-12a

Obviously, **God considers killing your own child an abomination.** There is no word in the Bible that carries a stronger condemnation. The punishment for murder is death.

We hear no more about child sacrifice after the Israelites were taken away into Babylonian captivity in 586 BC and then came back to Judea, 70 years later with the new name of "Jews." It appears that the child sacrifice had finally stopped because there was no Molech worship in Babylon, although that land had a plethora of false gods. The problem is that the spirits attached to the Molech idols continue to exist. The demon god Molech, under Baal, worked through Herod the Great, his son Herod and all others who work to kill children around the world. This spirit permeates the abortion industry and the United States politicians who further his bloody work.

Historic Worldwide Child Sacrifice

It seems that fire gods were popular all over the ancient world, probably having their start in ancient Babylon before the spread of humanity around the globe, which occurred after the Tower of Babel. You are probably familiar with the stories of throwing young girls into the mouth of a volcano, which was a real practice made known to many modern people through movies and television. You may remember that the Aztecs also practiced child sacrifice. There is nothing new under the sun. The ancients who had left the counsel of the One and True God, and migrated around the world, became fixated on appeasing their false gods in times of drought and need for provision.

I can remember reading about Pozo Moro, in southern Spain, where there is a relief on an ancient Phoenician funerary tower. The Phoenicians were the neighbors of the ancient Israelites and were known for their shipbuilding and navigational skills and had traveled to that part of the world. The Phoenicians were descended from the original Canaanites and shared worship of many of the same gods.

The funerary tower relief seems to picture what some call a two-headed monster holding a child in a bowl in his right hand and a piglet in his left. This is a clear picture of child sacrifice. In the ancient world, when food sacrifices were brought to the gods, even in the Bible, those who gave the sacrifice participated by eating the sacrifice. It is a difficult subject to think that this picture may show ancient cannibalism. I have not been able to find any verification one way or the other, as regards this artifact, but it has been speculated. If it is true, then there would have been cannibalism as the ancient priests ate the burnt offerings.

Sicily is a large island at the tip of the toe of the boot of Italy. Years ago, God led me to investigate the practice of child sacrifice on that ancient island. I found more than I wanted to know. This was another place where the Phoenician neighbors of Israel had traveled. The Carthaginians who settled in some parts of Western Sicily sacrificed their infant babies to "the gods." There are actual stones that are inscribed with "dedications" to the gods by the infant's parents. Carthaginians were Phoenicians who had traveled to Sicily from their settlement of Carthage, just as they had traveled to Southern Spain. Carthage was a city-state in North Africa in the years before Jesus lived and was even larger than Rome and Athens in its time. Thousands of urns have been found filled with the bones of infants.

Controlling Spirits

Insecurity, rejection, pride, arrogance, manipulation, and control are characteristics of someone controlled by the spirit of Jezebel. Many women and men involved in promoting abortion are very influenced by this spirit, as mentioned previously. The controlling spirit is a spirit of witchcraft. That is why those of us, who are sensitive and spiritually discerning, sometimes see the demonic at work in certain people's words and the expressions on their faces.

About King Ahaz of Judah, husband of Queen Jezebel, we read,

> But he walked in the way of the kings of Israel, and even made his son pass through the fire, according to the abominations of the nations whom the LORD had driven out from before the sons of Israel. — 2 KINGS 16:3

In my experience and in the testimony of others, we see that this spirit of Jezebel can influence a man as well as a woman, although many say it is seen more in women. King Herod was also under the influence of the spirit of Jezebel, as he had the same character flaws. His own penchant for control, through spilling the blood of others, shows us the demonic influence that affected his life. People feared him because his attempts at manipulation included murder, just as Jezebel tried to kill the prophet Elijah, and just as she had killed Nathan, the owner of the vineyard that she desired for her husband. The spirit of Jezebel is a controlling spirit of witchcraft. Just as Herod the Great killed his children to exert control over his kingdom, some women abort their young to maintain control over their immediate kingdom that surrounds them or to keep or gain a societal position. This includes concerns over career and money. The spirit of witchcraft even inhabits high offices in our land, which is why abortion is constantly on their mind. "Abortion rights" is included in every single major bill that one political party tries to pass.

Be a Jehu

In addition to prayer, we need to be proactive in defeating these spirits. Jehu is the prophet whom God sent to destroy Queen Jezebel to keep her from killing many others. Jehu was known for riding fast and "furiously." He did not fool around.

He did not tolerate Jezebel or fall to her whims when she sat in the window painted alluringly to entice him.[32] Remember, the devil's agents are always masking their true intentions and the devil can come as an angel of light.[33] Jehu did not tolerate or converse with Jezebel. In the Book of Revelation, Jesus found fault with the Thyatira church because they tolerated the woman named Jezebel who called herself a prophetess.[34] This woman operated under the same spirit of false religion, control, and sexual immorality, as did her Old Testament predecessor. Herod also operated in all those demonic arenas. While by name he was a Jew, he was not a Jew by birth or at heart.

God judges the heart, and He is the only One that knows our hearts.[35] Jehu was anointed by God, to deal with the severe issues surrounding the murderous Jezebel. If there is a Jezebel in our church or even in our circle of Christian friends, we must not tolerate the spirit that works in that person. In the same way, we must not tolerate any spirit that defies Christ. While the culture around us tells us to be tolerant of nearly everything, Jesus condemned that kind of compromise. We cannot walk arm in arm with evil but must stand up, call it by name and deal with it, in the spirit of love. If someone carrying a spirit like that which influenced Herod, is told the truth, they may repent. We must love the person, but we must not appease the spirit.

The Spirit of Herod in Government

There is a spirit of Herod in our government today. It is a spirit that loves the grandiosity of Washington DC and other impressive seats of government. It may even celebrate beautiful churches and cathedrals and call itself religious, but it is evil. Those operating in this spirit crave power and they will stop at nothing to gain it. They serve the most hardened hearts by glorying in the blood of preborn babies and newborn infants. It is a bloodthirsty, antichrist spirit. This spirit does not ever seek the LORD to meet the needs of the people but serves a different master. Someone operating in this spirit may call himself a Christian, but as Herod called himself a Jew, it is in name only.

The Jezebel spirit working alongside the spirit of Herod will seek to imprison and kill the prophets who speak Truth. You may remember when Herod's son, Herod the Tetrarch, imprisoned John the Baptist at the bequest of his wife, Herodias, for speaking the truth about their immorality. Not only was she his half-brother's wife, but she was also his niece! This woman worked in the spirit of Jezebel. This spirit always likes to stay near a powerful person in order to control that one. In chapter two, we saw how Herodias' daughter, Herod's stepdaughter Salome, danced enticingly before Herod and his guests. It manipulated him to cause him to offer her half of the kingdom, which was an idiom expressing his desire to give to her generously.[36] We see an incestuous and possibly pedophilic spirit here. Many authorities express that the name Salome in the Bible means "girl," meaning still a child. Salome later married her grand-uncle, Philip.[37] This is an example of how demonic spirits often work together in a massive onslaught against humanity and all that is of God. In this intriguing saga, we next see how surprisingly, yet smoothly, the spirit of murder introduces himself onto the scene.

When Herod offered her a gift of her choice, Salome, as a child would do, consulted with her treacherous mother, Herodias. Herodias advised her daughter to ask for the head of the prophet, John the Baptist, on a platter.[38] Herodias was operating in the same spirit as Queen Jezebel, who sought the life of the prophet Elijah. Remember that John the Baptist came as Elijah, the very prophet that Queen Jezebel declared to kill. These spirits work incessantly, through all time, to destroy the plans of God, the prophets of God, and all that is good.

If we do not go on the spiritual offense in prayer and rebuke these spirits, the day is coming when God's true prophets will not be physically safe in America. The truth is already being censored, and falsehoods born by conniving minds rule the media. The spirits of Herod and Jezebel are working nonstop to destroy the Godliness of our nation. We, however, need to be proactive in our faith, courage, and authority given to us in the name of Jesus. We must stand up to the abusive and murderous spirits. God is in control. Satan's minions, even those in the upper ranks, can only do as much as they are allowed. In Christ, we have the authority over evil.

> And these signs shall follow them that believe; In my name shall they cast out devils; they shall speak with new tongues; They shall take up serpents; and if they drink any deadly thing, it shall not hurt them; they shall lay hands on the sick, and they shall recover. — MARK 16:17,18, KJV

The Powerlessness of False Idols

Do you remember the story of the Philistine's theft of the Ark of the Covenant? The Israelites had not been respecting and honoring the ark in the way they should. In fact, they had been using it as a kind of charm for good luck. The ark was supposed to be reverenced for the holiness of God, so God allowed it to leave His people. God displayed His power over the demons of darkness in an unforgettable way to the inhabitants of Ashdod, where the stolen ark was brought:

> Now the Philistines took the ark of God and brought it from Ebenezer to Ashdod. 2) Then the Philistines took the ark of God and brought it to the house of Dagon and set it by Dagon. 3) When the Ashdodites arose early the next morning, behold, Dagon had fallen on his face to the ground before the ark of the LORD. So they took Dagon and set him in his place again. 4) But when they arose early the next morning, behold, Dagon had fallen on his face to the ground before the ark of the LORD. And the head of Dagon and both the palms of his hands

were cut off on the threshold; only the trunk of Dagon was left to him. 5) Therefore neither the priests of Dagon nor all who enter Dagon's house tread on the threshold of Dagon in Ashdod to this day. — 1 SAMUEL 5:1-5

The Philistines had placed the ark before their false idol, Dagon, but in the morning, in a marvelous demonstration of God's power, their "god" was found flat on his face before the presence of the LORD in the ark. They set it in an upright position again, but the next morning found their god once again flat before the presence of God. This time, however, the head and hands were removed! All false idols are powerless before God. The abortion demons, likewise, will not have the final say. As Christians, we need to invite the presence of God and His Glory back into our nation. Amazingly, some pastors, in some churches, believe they are doing God's work by affirming abortion and even going so far as to "bless" abortion clinics. They are disregarding the Biblical position on the sanctity of life and are declaring war on God.

Abortion was once the scandalous secret of civilized society, but it has now exploded, often unashamedly, into the public in such predominant places as print advertisements for clinics and centers, and even proudly displayed on tee shirts. The embarrassment over the concept of abortion is lessening as these shirts proudly proclaim bold sentiments and exclamations, such as, "I Had an Abortion!" A woman that would wear such a tee shirt is one that is filled with overwhelming emotion. If she has any shame about her abortion, she is doing her best to cover it up and ignore it. She is exposing and expressing deep, angry thoughts. It is very sad to realize the depth of such psychological torment.

In the United States, until 1973, the womb was a legally protected environment. A Supreme Court Justice ruling, which was partly the result of a fraudulent court case, changed all that. With Roe vs. Wade, the inherent safety of the womb became a thing of yesteryear. At the pronouncement of that ruling, mothers and abortionists obtained full legal rights to exterminate the life of any baby, if the mother and the abortionist agreed to kill that child. The Valley of Slaughter opened wide. We need to be led by the Spirit of God to climb back up out of the pit:

> Now concerning spiritual things, brothers, I do not want you to be ignorant. You know that when you were heathen, you were led away to those mute idols, however you might be led. Therefore I make known to you that no man speaking by God's Spirit says, "Jesus is accursed." No one can say, "Jesus is Lord," but by the Holy Spirit. — 1 CORINTHIANS 12:1,2

Today's Occult and Baal Worship

The 1960s and ''70s saw a cultural revolution regarding occult practices in America. During the last half of the 19th century, occult activity was rampant, especially in places like Southern California, New York City, New Orleans, Florida, and the Carolinas, but even existed in the farmlands across the United States. Along with a sense of freedom in the sexual arena, people started freely exploring the mysteries of the occult. Many became reliant on astrologers, psychics, and mediums to help guide them through their daily lives, especially to help with finances and relationships.

Many believed the devil's promises. In the Bible, the sins of witchcraft, promiscuous sex, and drug use are linked together as sins of rebellion. Abortion is tied significantly to all these activities, just as in Biblical times. This rebelliousness began a strong return to Baal worship, allowing the spirit of Herod to work insidiously to the point where we now have advocated for not only abortion but also infanticide. The mind-numbing brazenness of the politicians pushing this is one way to tell that there are demons behind their words. The move toward infanticide is heartless and irrational. They do not recognize the Baal worship. They are spiritually clueless.

Witchcraft and Suicide

When God had me begin a music and teaching ministry in a non-denominational church, I spoke with the pastor, relating to him my dismay about the number of suicides I had become aware of in that section of our state. The small church in which I had previously served as the senior pastor had suffered through three suicides in the few years before I arrived. One suicide was that of a granddaughter of a former pastor. It was heartbreaking to find out that she was only in her early teens and had hung herself. The pastor with whom I spoke told me that he was not surprised because during the 1970s, southern New Jersey, where I was raised, was a major center of occult activity in the United States. That shocked me! On reflection, though, I knew he was right. As a child, I had witnessed séances and occult games, such as the Ouija board, played casually and loosely at the homes of friends and even at 4-H camp. My mother had a friend whose friend was a self-proclaimed witch! We found out later that both of those women were lesbians. That was not discussed, or even something that I knew about back then. I know women who have demonic issues that once played games like "Bloody Mary," a game played with a mirror when they were young.

In my adult years, an elderly woman I knew who was involved in occult practices and spells told me that when she was a child, her mother would sometimes send her to the drugstore for a certain drug that would induce abortion. She never told me the name of the drug, but she did inform me that her mother had aborted twelve babies in all. It is hard to imagine the impact of this cruel task on this elderly woman's young life. How could she have learned to respect life in the home in which she was raised? This woman led a very sad life. She lived with a spirit of confusion. She told me that she prayed to God, yet she continued to speak about casting spells and practicing witchcraft even up to the last years of her life. She had children and grandchildren but was estranged from them.

Reflection: With the historic amount of occult activity in New Jersey, is it a coincidence that abortion is legally allowed in that state through the total nine months of pregnancy and is often paid for with the taxes of New Jersey citizens through Medicaid?

America's Chemical Burning Abortion — Passing Through the Fire

Just as in ancient Israel, where babies were horrifically burned as an idolatrous practice, there is an abortion procedure that involves chemically burning the young baby in the womb, which is called instillation abortion or saline infusion abortion. In this kind of abortion, which is considered surgical, the baby is poisoned, and his outer layer of skin is burned off before he is expelled from his mother. This kind of abortion is no longer popular but was in common usage until recent years. Both spiritually and physically, the burning nature of the deaths of these children can be compared to burning children to Molech. Survivors of the cruel chemical abortion burns have grown up to share their testimonies today. They do a great service in telling their stories because they expose the horror of abortion to us all. A quick search on the internet will enable you to listen to the testimonies of their very difficult beginnings in life.

In my volunteer training for a pro-life pregnancy center, I learned about various types of abortions. Spiritually, they are all like passing a baby "through the fire." We sacrifice our unwanted babies for many reasons, but in the end, we hand them over to a false idol instead of the true God, who will take care of all our needs when we trust in Him.

Because abortion method descriptions are available from a variety of sources and because procedures sometimes differ from case to case, I will not give explicit details. What follows is a generalization. If you are interested in more precise descriptions, I advise you to do your own research, which is not difficult.

Kinds of Abortions Today, Including Birth Control and Abortion Pills

Birth-control pills can work as abortifacients. The older variety of "the Pill," which was considered more dangerous physically to the health of the mother than the newer birth-control pills, were less likely to act as an abortifacient than the newer, safer pills. Birth control pills do not fully stop contraception but instead, greatly inhibit it. The newer "mini-pills," however, still allow a woman to ovulate. When a baby is conceived, this kind of pill is designed to keep the fertilized egg from implantation. Most women using this kind of birth control do not know that there is a likelihood they may have been pregnant.

An abortion pill or a medical abortion can only be used during the first trimester. In the United States, this is typically a combination of mifepristone (RU-486) and then misoprostol is given to a woman who is about seven to nine weeks pregnant, or up to about ten weeks after her last menstrual cycle. The baby is then delivered dead. This is very painful to think about because babies at seven weeks are already stretching and moving and heartbeats can be detected. Their little arms and legs are already starting to form, although they are very tiny. It is also painful to think about the client when she is all alone, expelling, which is giving a painful birth, to a dead, not fully developed baby. There is a push by the abortion industry to allow this abortion method to be widespread by telemedicine and mail-order. This means many more abortions would occur in seclusion with no medical supervision. **These young women are told to go into a bathroom and sit on the toilet to expel the baby. They are told not to look but, of course, they look! What they commonly see are tiny arms and legs and heads**

of their dead babies floating in toilets. Blood is often described as being "everywhere" during these abortions. I cannot imagine being more alone than that. More than half of abortions performed today are dangerous medical abortions!

A common type of surgical abortion from five to thirteen weeks, or a little more, after the first day of the last period, is suction and evacuation abortion or vacuum aspiration. This is otherwise known as D&C or Dilation and Curettage. The vacuum uses extreme force. It involves dilating the cervix and then dismembering the child in the womb by tearing the baby apart piece by piece by force as the abortionist suctions the baby's legs and head and every other body part out. An abortion worker organizes the baby's body on a tray to be reassembled. They must make sure that they do not leave any parts of the baby or the placenta behind because a deadly infection may occur. The lining of the uterus is then scraped with a device called a "curette" to make sure that the abortion is complete.

Manual Vacuum Aspiration or MVA is used as early as three to twelve weeks after the last period and is considered not as invasive as other abortions. A syringe is used instead of a vacuum. There is still a small risk to the mother in this abortion procedure.

D&E or Dilation and Evacuation is used after thirteen weeks have passed since the last period, and up to twenty-four weeks, during the second trimester of pregnancy. This procedure uses an even more powerful suction, or vacuum, to evacuate the amniotic fluid. Then the abortionist uses a sharp-toothed clamp to grab and tear the baby's limbs, organs, and other parts and crushes the baby's skull. The uterus is then scraped, and the placenta is delivered. At thirteen weeks the baby already has visible fingerprints and is about three inches long. By the end of the fifth month or about twenty-one weeks, the baby is already eight to ten inches long and has had the capacity to feel pain for at least a week. This baby can live outside the womb with proper medical care. It is hard to believe that some would have no trouble killing this baby by dismembering him or her while still alive and able to feel the pain. This baby may still be aborted by this method for the next three weeks as he grows bigger and stronger daily.

Partial-birth abortion is like the previous procedure but is called a D&X. This procedure first involves partially delivering a baby, body first, until only the head is left in the birth canal. The baby is still alive at this point but even though he is moving, he is still not considered to be born because he has not taken his first official breath of air outside the womb. Then the abortionist uses scissors to cut the baby's skull at the back of his head to create a hole in the baby's brain. A suction machine is applied next, and the brains are drained out.

The Evil Spirit of Herod, Late-term Abortion, and After-Birth Abortion

Consider a country where everyone lives in the love and peace and freedom of God. This ideal cannot be realized in a country where killing innocent human life is permitted. We have many representatives in government that proclaim abortion to be a "right." The words they use concerning abortion are misleading and are politically correct, but not ethically, morally, or factually correct. Especially now that many are espousing the death of an unwanted baby even up to the moment of birth and after, we must question their motives. While many of those that promote this claim say that killing a baby at a late date would only be for the benefit of the "health" or the "life" of the mother, we must investigate those words carefully.

Promoting the death of newly born, unwanted babies was once rare, but we live in an era of slippery slopes. Just as the institution of same-sex marriage began a ridiculous slide into calls for polygamy and other culturally dangerous practices, legalizing abortion up to twenty weeks gestation grew into performing late-term abortions at the rate of at least 8,296 a year and I have read much greater figures. The Center for Disease Control does not receive figures for every state, but it reports that 1.3 percent of abortions occur after twenty weeks of gestation. In the year 2015, according to the Center for Disease Control, there were 638,169 reported abortions, with all states not reporting, so there were more.[39] There are a minimum of 8,296 late-term abortions in the United States per year. I have seen a figure of around twelve thousand and have heard that there are tens of thousands. The actual figure would be much higher if all states reported to the CDC. They are not legally required to do so.[40] We also know from personal testimonies that illegal late-term abortions occur in some places.

Considering the Life of the Mother

First, we must consider that **there is never a need to abort a baby to save the life of the mother.** If the mother is in danger, she should be cared for, and the child should be delivered early. Ideally, every attempt should then be made to benefit both the life of the mother and the baby. My fourth child was a breech baby — he did not turn downwards in order to be born, as would be normal. The doctor attempted to take him early so that neither of us would die. In that case, it was an unsuccessful maneuver, and we later went through an emergency C-section, but the attempt was made early to lessen the danger. There was no need to kill him in the womb to save my life. That is a simple example. Even when the health concerns are more complicated, most doctors say that there is no need for an abortion to be made up to the day a baby is due, because a baby can simply be delivered with every effort made to give life-supporting measures for the health of the baby. There is never a need to kill the baby.

Second, the word "health" can be, and often has been expanded to include psychological, mental, emotional, and even financial (if that affects one's mental well-being). Essentially, those that promote abortion up to birth are clearing the way for any baby to be aborted at any time, even when that baby is fully formed and able to live entirely on its own. This is pure evil. It is witchcraft and it is satanic. Infiltration of demons into the elected officials of the highest offices of the land has caused us to become a bloodthirsty nation wanting to see preborn and even just-born babies die in a new call for "after-birth abortion." **The United States is only one of a handful of countries that permits late-term abortion including North Korea and China. We must pray for the spiritual eyes of the nation to continue to be open to the things of God and the importance and sanctity of life.**

The Slippery Slope of Abortion and Acceptance of Infanticide

Late-term abortions are accomplished by injecting poison (Digoxin) into the baby's heart through the mother's uterus. The mother is then told to go home where the baby is usually delivered dead in about three days, often as the mother sits on the toilet. All abortion procedures are gory and no matter how it is done, the result is still usually a dead baby.

God calls infanticide "slaughter."[41] The Bible never mentions abortion because it is not something that the Hebrew people ever thought to do. When they were living rightly with God, children were considered a blessing to these people. When their thoughts became contaminated by the false idol worship of their worldly neighbors, they then sunk into depravity.

Our culture once greatly honored motherhood and babies. Historically, we have always said that a pregnant woman was "with child." Both the preborn child and the pregnant woman were culturally afforded dignity and respect. Now some, in a truly barbaric fashion, are deceptively calling the preborn child a "parasite." The dignity of being "in the family way," as we used to say, has gone the way of the horse and buggy. Just as King Herod had no regrets in killing small children, many of our American politicians are advocating for babies to be killed up to the moment of delivery and even after, if the mother does not want that child after a botched abortion. A botched abortion is the delivery of a live child. Especially after about 22 weeks of gestation, the born-alive baby of abortion has a great chance of survival. Respect for life has diminished in some circles; there are people that disregard the life of a baby "accidentally born" in a botched abortion. In the news, recently, a little girl was featured who was born in 2014 at 21 weeks. Today, she is a beautiful preschooler! A friend shared with me pictures of his nephew, born last year at 28 weeks. I saw the progression of his development through photographs. He is now a very healthy and beautiful baby boy!

All Abortions in the Third Trimester are Infanticide

I have read many testimonies of women who aborted their viable babies and later regretted it. Many regretted it as it occurred. There are no statistics available for the number but the stories we do know are full of anguish and pain. Many post-abortion mothers have confessed to seeing their dead babies at some point during the abortion procedure, although every effort is usually made to prevent that from happening. When mothers see their dead babies, the abortionists cannot lie anymore about what they are doing — committing heinous murder. Many of these babies could have lived on their own or with minimal help.

There is plenty of evidence that there are many babies accidentally born alive during abortions because of cases such as the case involving abortionist Kermit Gosnell and several of his workers in Philadelphia, a few years ago. He was found guilty of murder. At least one woman and seven infants born alive during abortions were killed in his care. He was eventually convicted of the deaths of one mother and three babies.

Many abortion survivors have missing limbs or other physical problems caused by abortion attempts. At the Conclusion of this book is a letter written by a friend of mine who is an abortion survivor. Her mother attempted to abort her three times, but the abortionist was unable to complete the job. If you watched the news during the Gosnell case and others, you would know that born-alive babies were murdered after delivery. There are other cases.

After-birth Abortion

The "after-birth abortion" proponents are hard to understand. Words cannot truly express the horror of the proposal that this practice could be deemed acceptable to society at large. Abstracts for papers on this very startling concept are available on the internet. I have also seen the same concept described in intellectual, elitist publications. The general idea of this is based on an acceptance of abortion!

People that defend the after-birth abortion position believe that both preborn babies and newborn infants are not actual people and do not have the same moral status. They believe that the killing of these children, even completely healthy infants, is defensible based on the concept that they are not morally relevant. Essentially, they are arguing that if the baby is unwanted by the parents, and if adoption is not something that they want to consider, that little baby should be destroyed, even after birth.

Financial Concerns

In talking to people, I learned that financial hardship is the reason that many parents give as the reason to end their baby's life. Young women and men do not always understand that this is idol worship. Just as in the ancient days of the Canaanites, when worshippers relied on Molech and Baal for financial provision, those who seek abortion do the same. Focusing on the dollar, they are worshipping an idol of financial greed and not following God. America is advancing down the slippery slope to its own destruction by killing our young in "the valley of slaughter." We sacrifice the babies on the altar of Baal and their little bodies are taken away to be sold or burned to ashes in incinerators.

It takes money to raise a child, but along with honest work, it takes faith in God's providence to provide for that child. Money should not be the determining factor in whether a person lives or dies. The determination should be based on the value and sanctity of life. **We need to let go of fear and hang on to God.** Throughout the Bible, He tells us, "Do not fear." It is mentioned three-hundred and sixty-five times — one admonishment for each day of the year! There is a reason for that! It is very easy to fall into fear when we are uncertain of the future. The devil wants you to feel that God has abandoned you. God says He will never leave you nor forsake you.[42] When we are afraid, we need to remember to turn fully to Him.

> Consider the lilies how they grow: they toil not, they spin not; and yet I say unto you, that Solomon in all his glory was not arrayed like one of these. — LUKE 12:27

In the verse above, Jesus gives us comforting assurance of God's provision for His children. We need to lean into Him and trust Him with our very lives. God is magnificent and worthy of all our praise and worship. The Bible shows us that we need to pray and sing songs to Him both before and after the battle has been won in the natural realm. In the supernatural, the battle of abortion has already been won. It was won on a hill called Calvary when Jesus took the punishment for our sins two thousand years ago. "By his stripes, we were healed."[43]

The Best Way to Leave the Valley of Slaughter

"The Valley of Slaughter" exists in America today with modern-day Americans being no less guilty than those who sacrificed their babies to demon gods long ago in ancient Israel and surrounding nations. Babies are sacrificed to idols of greed, convenience, and selfishness — all of which represent modern-day Baal. Their blood is on all our hands. We are responsible participants if we do not declare this ungodliness to the masses. How can any of us be silent in the face of such horror, especially when, with our tax money, we are paying to have these babies killed?

Beware, no matter what the political rhetoric may be, there are many politicians who are always trying to slip laws in through the side door, which will cost taxpayers to abort babies, even though most taxpayers do not approve. There are politicians in Washington, DC who are trying to create plans, which will stop taxpayer funding of abortion altogether, but they need our prayers and support. Remember that when Roe vs. Wade gets overturned, the authority to permit taxpayer funding of abortion will move down to the state level. Most states are already working on providing a legal structure that will either allow or not allow any abortions. Some are proposing to allow abortions only up to the hearing of a heartbeat, or up to the time it is scientifically proven that a baby will feel pain, or up to the moment of delivery.

While I believe that abortion should be outlawed, I believe the most effective way to curb the killing of the preborn is through teaching what the Bible says about life and helping young women to follow God. The best tangible way to stop abortions is to help a young woman get an ultrasound of her baby. Pregnancy care workers testify that an ultrasound is the most effective way to convince a woman that she is truly carrying a living child in her womb.

Reflection: How many abortion clinics try to encourage and counsel a young woman in her finances so that she can support her baby?

Beatitude 5: "Blessed are the merciful, for they shall obtain mercy" (Matt. 5:7).

Life suggestion: Plant a garden of hope. As we extend mercy to the children that have no voice, we must also extend God's mercy to those who have fallen into sin with abortion. Sowing seeds of forgiveness and mercy will yield a harvest of love and blessings. Do not worry about whether someone deserves to be forgiven. That is not your problem because God will vindicate you when necessary. It is out of your hands and not your responsibility.

The strong and important doctrine of forgiveness is paramount in all our interactions with others. We must continually rely on Christ and His death on the cross for the forgiveness of all our sins, so that we can, in turn, exercise mercy on others. As we did nothing to receive this forgiveness except to give our hearts to Christ, we must expect nothing. Even our faith is a gift from God.[44] Jesus did this for us before we received Him. In Matthew 6:14-15, Jesus tells us, "For if you forgive others for their transgressions, your heavenly Father will also forgive you. But if you do not forgive others, then your Father will not forgive your transgressions."

Chapter Six

Spiritual Battle for the Heart and Soul of America

"I am the vine, you are the branches; he who abides in Me and I in him, he bears much fruit, for apart from Me you can do nothing." — John 15:5

The Battle is Real

In an amazing testimony, a longtime friend of mine, who was a producer of my former radio show, related to me that she had awoken in the middle of the night to a vision of a demonic battle going on in the spiritual realm. Even more amazing was that her husband, also a professional person, awoke to the same vision. He asked her, "Do you see that?" God's faithful warring host was battling with demonic beings over the tops of tall buildings, cathedrals, and churches. They watched as gargoyle-like statues morphed into demonic beings. Together they watched the fascinating cosmic battle between good and evil. God allowed them to see into what I believe is the second heaven where the battle rages out of earthly vision. When people whimsically say, "the battle is real," I do not think most of us know just how real it is!

Spiritual Warfare for the Soul of Women

When a young, unmarried woman finds herself pregnant with a child, she has already been in spiritual warfare for her very soul, because of many factors. After she finds that she has conceived, new warfare begins in her mind. Where will she live? How will she afford diapers and formula (although I personally believe breastfeeding is best)? How will she work? All these legitimate thoughts and worries fast forward through her mind like an express train and she is genuinely frightened.

That is very understandable. She then thinks that if she makes the problem go away, no one will know about it. Her parents will be spared the shame and her neighbors, schoolmates or co-workers will be none the wiser. Life will go on just as before. It seems simple. Abortion seems to be the only answer. The problem with all of that is that even if no one else knows, God knows.

Perhaps, though, she may double back and consider the fact that an abortion can be extremely painful and expensive. There is also the fear of the unknown. It can be scary. If she has never had an abortion before, then she probably does not know anything about the procedure, or the cost. She may live in a rural area and may have difficulty finding transportation to a clinic. Where will she find the money? Another scenario is that she would never consider ending the life of her child, but her boyfriend is frightened at the prospect of possible marriage or child support payments for a baby that he never wanted in the first place.

Sadly, our secular culture now separates sex from parenthood. God first ordained sex as a benefit of marriage, but it has been now designated for the young, fancy-free, and single, in today's media and culture. Sex was designed as a wonderful way for married couples to procreate and populate the earth.[1] There is a temptation in our fallen nature, however, that walks us out of this blessing when we voluntarily walk outside of God's will for marriage and into promiscuity. Then, sometimes, when children are conceived, we do not know what to do with them! It seems ridiculous that we do not consider pregnancy as the blessing it was meant to be! The abortionist says that he has the easy answer to the question of what to do with an unplanned baby. Too many times the parents take that option.

Coerced Abortions — Real Stories

Many times, the parents of a pregnant young woman may pressure her to end the child's life. I have a friend whose father and stepmother, without her consent, brought her to an abortion clinic many years ago, when she was 15 years old. She was five months pregnant before the abortion and the experience haunts her today. "That was a baby!" she told me. I was astounded when she told me that both parents were very involved in their churches. Her father was a church elder, and her mother was a Sunday School teacher.

There are, from time to time, news releases about women who are killed by their partners because they refuse abortions. We do not know the number who are not killed but do abort their babies because they are intimidated, bullied, terrorized, or gently coerced. I know a young lady who was pregnant and in a very bad situation. While she was very much in love with her boyfriend, he refused to marry her and was very angry about the pregnancy. He screamed and cursed at her many times, demanding that she get an abortion. He accused her of being a "gold-digger" and of wanting to have a baby to receive child support. She was strong in her belief that abortion was wrong.

While on the telephone with him one night, he began screaming at her and calling her vulgar names and she, through her tears, struggled to verbally defend herself. She believes the stress of the situation caused her to begin to miscarry her child, who she knew to be a girl, because she started spotting blood and went into painful contractions while he was raging, humiliating her, and cursing at her. She begged him to stop, crying, "I'm losing her!" but he continued.

She hung up on him and called her doctor. She was able to reach him as he was driving because it was an emergency. She was heavy-hearted when she heard him say that he could not do anything at that stage, but he did advise her to lie down with her feet up, which she did. She tried to relax and calm herself as the contractions came and went and came back again. Eventually, they stopped, and her baby was safe. The same scenario played out one more time, a few weeks later, as he screamed at her over the telephone again but this time she knew to hang up and lie down again with her feet up to protect her child.

It was an unplanned pregnancy and even though she did not want to be pregnant, she was not about to let that baby die if she could help it. Her motherly instincts kicked in, even though she rationally believed that this pregnancy was very devastating to her life because of her situation and many other reasons including a desperate financial state. There was a problem with her fluid level after that and her doctor ordered her on complete bed rest. Her boyfriend humiliated her over that as well. As soon as she told him, he called her "lazy" and insisted she go into the kitchen and make him soup and do things for him, even though they did not live together. During the pregnancy, he began pulling her hair and breaking her belongings, such as her telephone, camera, vacuum cleaner, and an inherited antique table with strong sentimental value. After her baby was born, he began punching her in the head as she held her infant daughter, unable to raise her hands to shield herself because she was protecting her baby. He spit on her and bit her arms, kidnapped her and her baby, took them on wildly dangerous car rides, and beat her up many times. She praises God today that she gave birth to a very healthy baby at the expected delivery date. It took her some time but eventually, she found the strength to leave that very abusive relationship. She believes her boyfriend was under demonic influence and once saw intense evil coming from his eyes as a demonic presence. At that moment he was not raging but it was a prelude to things to come. She attributes the strength she gained to the LORD who she learned to rely on as her Deliverer.

The LORD is my rock and my fortress and my deliverer, My God, My rock, in whom I take refuge; My shield and the horn of my salvation, my stronghold. — PSALM 18:2

Choosing Her Baby's Life over a Military Career

Another young lady I know had just turned 18, was in the delayed entry program for the U.S. Army, and was temporarily staying with her Army recruiter when she discovered that she was pregnant. She dearly desired to be in the military believing it would create a better life for herself. She came from a military family and loved her country, so she wanted to serve. Her father told her that he would pay to abort her child because he felt she had ruined her life. Her army recruiter also wanted her to abort. She had scored extremely high on the job placement exam and was the top recruit. These are her own words:

> I stood firm, said no, that there was a life and I'm not taking it away. I remember it was right after Christmas I found out and I drove to a rest area, and I went to the bathroom there and I looked down at my belly and I promised my baby, "I will do everything in my power to protect and love and take care of it."

She went to the doctor to get a release from the army because of her pregnancy and her doctor offered her an abortion, telling her that they could take care of it for her by giving her a chemical abortion pill. She was already sworn in and ready to leave for basic training, but she declined his offer. She asked him to fax her doctor's note to the Army for release.

Still, she felt fear that, although Army policy is to release a pregnant woman, someone might slip her an abortion pill into a drink. There was a man, she was told, already on his way to pick her up for basic training. She did not understand why someone was still coming for her since she was getting a pregnancy release. Fearing for her baby's life, she fled in the middle of the night, while her recruiter was sleeping. Her dream of a military career was over, but she used every bit of that energy in raising her child, who was later diagnosed with autism. She loves being a mother and absolutely believes that her child was born with a purpose. He is almost in high school and is already being recognized for his artistic abilities. He has even earned quite a bit of money from his art, which will be applied to his dream of art school. I believe her resolution to protect her child, while all around her were encouraging her to abort, shows her strength of character and will bring her many blessings in life and in the hereafter.

Abuse Often Begins During Pregnancy

Many testimonies I have heard involve abusive situations where a boyfriend, who at first seemed very attentive and loving, became angry and abusive at the news of an unplanned pregnancy. If a young man has trouble with anger, it often first becomes evident during pregnancy because he feels out of control. We all need to be alert to these situations because this is when a woman or girl is extremely vulnerable. Many women become victims of physical abuse, especially when they are living with their partners. This results in many women making appointments with abortion clinics under duress. They may fear their boyfriend, either because of physical and verbal intimidation or because they fear losing his "love." At the clinic, they may be given a form on which they have to proclaim they are there of their own free will. **In cases of coercion, the little box they must check off is virtually useless in trying to screen abuse victims. The abused young woman will often lie because she fears what will happen if the abortion does not occur.**

Victims of physical abuse are often too intimidated to report their partners to law enforcement. They are living in confusion and often do not understand that without Jesus, their boyfriend or husband will never be capable of offering the kind of love she needs. Just like any sick person, an abuser needs healing of his (or her) problems. For him to love his wife as Christ loves the church — enough to die for her, if need be, as is Biblically mandated,[2] he first must be willing to accept Jesus Christ as his LORD and Savior. He will never change because of her. In my experience, I have found that he usually does not even consider himself an abuser.

Often, the women are addicted to the relationship, much as one is addicted to a drug. They do not even understand why they cannot break free. They want to get out but are so needy for love that they continue to try and please the abuser. Many policemen and judges have trouble understanding why a woman continues to drop restraining orders against the men they love. These ladies and girls feel that they literally have no one to turn to for real help. Women in a domestic abuse situation need to learn that the love of God will help them grow into being the kind of wives and mothers that will bless their families. Once a young lady gives her heart to Christ and grows into a strong relationship with the LORD, her heart will change, and she will stop allowing herself to be abused. God's love will help her stop accepting what is unacceptable. We need to reach out to these young women in loving guidance. They need deliverance.

Those who proclaim abortion as a woman's right, often ignore the fact that many abortions are performed on domestic violence victims who are not in an emotionally or spiritually healthy situation. Abortion will affect the rest of her life and she will never know her baby. The decision to abort cannot really be called the freedom of choice when she is often not given time and space to pray, seek God's will, and heal from the abuse. Abortion clinics are not domestic abuse or mental health counseling centers. They are there for one purpose — to make money. They are not trained in, nor do they seem to be interested in, training their employees to offer help to clients who need help with domestic violence issues.

Rape and Incest Victims and Hiding the Evidence

Rapists, child molesters, and child abusers love abortions and need abortions to be legal. The crime is hidden when the baby dies. There are many recorded reports of older men bringing young girls to abortion clinics without the clinic reporting the incidents to authorities. The baby is the evidence of the crime and so is disposed of, which leaves the abuser free to continue his evil. Whether rape or promiscuity causes the pregnancy, abortion solves the problem of consequences for one's actions.

Many good people believe that rape and incest are good reasons for an exception in a ban on abortion because, after all, it was not the woman's fault or intention to be pregnant. The Bible offers hope for even those who have been emotionally and physically brutalized by incest and rape. To be clear, every incest victim is also a rape victim and so the conflict and hurt are magnified. An incest victim often feels as if he or she has no one to trust because the one who has been given the responsibility of love and care has been acting as an agent of Satan.

We must isolate the mother from the baby in our minds, to understand why abortion does not solve anything. The baby is innocent. The baby has done nothing wrong that would merit death. We must trust God. What if the baby has no father? The Bible tells us that God will protect and defend the fatherless.[3]

Victims of rape and incest need special care and counseling. It seems to lead to spiritual confusion nearly always, which leads to promiscuity. Promiscuity leads to abortion. We need to reach these young ladies with the special message of love and spiritual healing through our Savior. Most women and girls who become pregnant because of rape keep their babies, raising them with love despite their traumatic beginnings. Many rape victims give testimony that they found healing through their children. If a young lady does not feel emotionally able to raise a baby, there are many couples that would love to adopt because they yearn for a newborn to love and cherish.

The mother of one of my dearest childhood friends was a "rape baby" from Cincinnati. If she had not been born, I would never have had the pleasure of knowing her and her family. She played the organ in the Catholic Church and was very kind to me and everyone she met. The thought of her being aborted is inconceivable. I am thankful for her life, and the happy times I spent with her, and am blessed to have known her.

Reflection: *Do you know anyone who was born because of rape?*

Reflection: *A question we should contemplate is this: Will an abortion make the rape go away?*

Replacement of God

The United States of America has become a stronghold of many kinds of corruption, but abortion is our greatest national sin. As soon as the Bible was taken from the public square, rebellion and narcissism took their place. It was not long before the general abhorrence of abortion began to slide away and the deceptive phrase "my body my choice" took its place.

It seems that the concept of integrity has lost its hold on the American mind. This is especially true of Biblical integrity. We have replaced the standard, on which Americans have historically relied — the Bible — with moral relativism, which relies on individual standards. In a world where critical thinking seems to have largely gone by the wayside, people are proclaiming that there are many truths, and that people must follow "their truth." Christians know that there is only One Truth. We took God out of the schools, however, and replaced Him with secular humanism. The church has lost its voice.

When integrity is considered important, the understanding that the little body in the womb is also a person with rights is accepted without question. When we, in this country, lost a grasp on integrity because of a loss of respect of Biblical moorings, our respect for human life began to drift out to sea leaving a tide of dead preborn babies in its wake. Getting back to the Bible is the only way to win back the heart and soul of America.

America's Encounter with the Spirit of Herod — Roe vs. Wade

In the United States, until the Roe vs. Wade decision to legalize abortion on the federal level five decades ago, the womb was a legally protected environment except in states where abortion had already been legalized. The Supreme Court Justice ruling, which was partly the result of a fraudulent court case, compromised the inherent safety of the womb. At the pronouncement of that ruling, mothers and abortionists obtained full legal rights to exterminate the life of any baby if the mother and the abortionist came into full agreement to kill that child up to 24 weeks gestation. Nevertheless, as stated earlier, many abortions take place through nine months' gestation.

The devil wants to take all our babies and God wants them to live. It is a simple matter to distinguish between life and death, but the issue of abortion became an incredibly convoluted, complicated, evil mess. It will take the power of God to get us out of this pit of destruction. As I write this, we are watching some of Satan's strongholds fall as many states are starting to limit abortion but much more needs to be done. The only way to reach the hearts that are still hardened to abortion is through lovingly reaching out with the Word of God. God's word does not return void.[4] It always effectively serves a purpose. It is sharper than a two-edged sword and gets to the "heart" of the matter.[5]

Roe vs. Wade is a national disgrace. In a misguided attempt to play the role of God, judges declared that legal personhood does not begin until a baby is born. This law was created from the judicial bench, which is contrary to the design of our republic. Laws must be voted on in the House of Representatives and enforced at the judicial level. That abortion is called a "right" is one of the most twisted and heinous lies ever told to the American people. In 1973 the Supreme Court of the United States declared that somehow the right to privacy, a constitutional right, includes the right to abort your own baby. This was not the plan of our founding fathers. This law will be overturned soon.

Roe vs. Wade seems to presume that a preborn baby does not carry the same DNA as he carries just one second after birth. At conception, a baby has its DNA established along with the same characteristics that define his or her physicality. A baby is nothing less than a human being. It is a logical conclusion to determine that abortion is the killing of preborn babies. Even so, Satan has inspired many to succumb to the idea that a baby in the womb is just a "blob of tissue." The progressive, feminist point of view, for a long time, has been that a preborn baby is just a "clump of cells." That is either a wishful, delusional fantasy or a lie.

Lately, the pro-abortion movement has been moving away from that position precisely because it is so unscientific, but the direction they are heading in now is even more dangerous. This spirit that is manifesting through the pro-choice movement seeks to kill the babies when they are fully developed and there is no doubt in my mind that this is the spirit of Herod. Herod had no problem killing young children. This spirit has insidiously crept into our culture and has begun to infiltrate American thinking. It has not yet become the mainstream body of thought and we must work to keep it from becoming so!

A Famous Pawn

Norma McCorvey (the "Jane Roe" of Roe vs. Wade) eventually became a born-again Christian and wrote a book about her journey. Many years ago, I heard her talking about working in the abortion industry in videos. In fact, I read a lot about her and followed her website when she was living. She explained how she was trained to dehumanize the tiny person who was being killed. The idea was to lead clients to believe that what was being removed was just a blob of tissue, not a human being. There are many of these same kinds of reports available to be read online, including Ms. McCorvey's testimonies. She sincerely regretted having been used as a pawn in the infamous trial, which created an open door for legal abortion in our nation. The devil is a liar and a deceiver, and abortion was legalized under the cover of lies. Norma McCorvey claimed she was raped but she later admitted that was a lie she told to advance the case before the Supreme Court.

Other Lies and Coat-Hanger Abortions

One of the lies perpetuated by pro-abortion activists is that legal abortions stop thousands of deaths from back-alley coat-hanger induced abortions. The National Center for Disease Control has been collecting abortion data since 1979. The total number of deaths from abortions was 63 in 1972, the year preceding the passage of Roe vs. Wade. 24 deaths were attributed to legally induced abortions and 39 were from illegal abortions.[6]

During the Supreme Court battle to legalize abortion, Dr. Bernard Nathanson, founder of the National Abortion Rights Action League, gave the Supreme Court a false, very high, number concerning the number of women who died from illegal abortions. I personally heard Chuck Colson speak on the radio, about fifteen years ago, about Dr. Nathanson's confession to him. I distinctly remember him saying that he picked the number of so-called coat-hanger abortions "out of the air." He said that he lied to get Roe vs. Wade passed. It was good for his business! Thankfully, Dr. Nathanson became a Christian and worked the rest of his life to end abortion, as did Norma McCorvey. You may search for both of their videos on the internet, and you will be amazed at what you find. I will not name his video because of possible copyright issues. Other former abortionists have also produced excellent videos on this topic.

It is not commonly known that there was a companion case that was heard in Georgia along with Roe vs. Wade. It was called Doe vs. Bolton. "Mary Doe" later stated that she never wanted an abortion and that she was lied to by her lawyer. She claimed that nothing was explained to her.

In 1997, the executive director of the National Coalition of Abortion Providers admitted that he lied about the number of partial-birth abortions performed because he feared that it would hurt the abortion industry. A proposed law that would have outlawed partial-birth abortion failed to pass as a result. There are women and girls who desperately and dangerously try to end the lives of their babies. Access to counsel at a crisis pregnancy center will help them but they obviously also need mental health counseling.

There are many other stories that I have heard and there is no room in this book to talk about them all, such as the woman who told me she was pressured by the Department of Social Services to get an abortion but declined. The battle for the soul and heart of the Nation centers around the disregard of the God of the Universe — the Creator of all life. The mysterious and wondrous love of God is evident in the beauty of His creation. Even if we do not completely understand the miracles behind the science, we must still strive to stay in God's perfect will and respect life. We cannot fully comprehend many things, on this side of eternity. **Is it not better to leave these things in the hands of God, who is Truth, and who has understanding?**

Dictionary Definition — Aborticide, not Abortion

The 1913 edition of Webster's Dictionary defines abortion as "The act of giving premature birth; particularly, the expulsion of the human fetus prematurely, or before it is capable of sustaining life; miscarriage." This 1913 edition of Webster's defines "aborticide" as "The act of destroying a fetus in the womb; feticide." This dictionary also includes a note, which says, "It is sometimes used for the offense of procuring a premature delivery."[7] The current Webster's New World College Dictionary, 4th Edition online, defines aborticide as "destruction of the embryo or fetus in the womb." The term "aborticide" has at least two characteristics that should make it a preferred term, over the term "abortion," because it is more accurate and precise:

1. It does not mean "miscarriage," as does "abortion." An aborticide is elective - it is something someone chooses to do.

2. It ends in "-cide," a suffix that means "to kill."

In earlier times abortion was not thought of as deliberate and so the word "birth" was used. Now that abortion has become so popular, we recognize that it is done deliberately and so now Webster's Dictionary uses the word "destruction."[8]

A sum-up of a recent politician's speech is telling of the real thoughts of many in our generation. He said that is better to kill unwanted babies in the womb or else we will end up killing them after they are born. He seemed to mean that killing them would be a result of having them born into a world where they were not wanted. I know of many parents who have been unable to have children and want to adopt the "unwanted" and so his argument falls to the ground.

More of Satan's Deceptions

This book is a cry to America to listen and obey the Word of God. **"Thou shalt not kill" should be very easy to**

understand.[9] The deceptive spirit of Herod, however, seeks to cover up the true motive and reality of murder. King Herod revealed his deceptive nature when he told the wise men from the East that he wished to know the location of the child so that he might worship him. This evil spirit lies and deceives as does his leader, Satan. When Satan deceived Eve, he told her that she would not die if she ate the forbidden fruit. She listened and believed him when he told her that she would benefit if she went against God's command![10] Although God forbids the murder of innocent life, the spirit of Herod and his network of demons work to deceive women into believing that killing their preborn babies will somehow benefit them. The lie created in Satan's realm whispered into a vulnerable woman's ear, is that the life she carries within her womb is unimportant and dispensable. Satan creates doubt.

Think about the havoc that lies, miscommunications, and misunderstandings play in our individual lives. When these things happen on a national scale, the results are often cataclysmic. Lies can cause bombs to go off in our personal lives. Unfortunately, mainstream media and many politicians and entertainers lie to pridefully push their personal agendas. We often hear that Satan's sin was pride. Pride is a lie. It is the lie that our personal importance is of any lasting merit. Jesus told us that in His Kingdom, the first shall be last and the last shall be first.[11]

Not only is Satan the father of lies, but he is also the prince of the power of the air.[12] Although God is ultimately in control, during the current dispensation of time, he still has the authority to act within God's limits. That is hard to understand but we must remember that individuals give him authority in their lives when they indulge in sinful practices. There are many doors that allow the entrance of demons. Before we start poking fingers at others who are suffering, however, we must also remember Job. He was an upstanding man of God, but

God still allowed Satan to test him. If you ever feel like you are going through a "Job season," you are not alone. Just remember that when Job came out of the hard times he got twice blessed.[13]

The Truth of Parenthood

Satan loves to twist the truth. I once heard it said that a certain number of women having abortions are mothers. They were implying that if a woman with no previous children has an abortion, then she is not a mother. It seems obvious to me, however, that 100% of women obtaining abortions are mothers. The life within them causes them to be a parent. Likewise, 100% of the males whose babies are aborted are fathers. It can be said that a certain number of women obtaining abortions also have other children. Once they have had an abortion, they are the mothers of dead babies. **Once the father's baby is aborted, he is still the father of a dead baby.**

If a woman or man does not consider him or herself a parent, when they are expecting a child, then it may be because that mindset serves as anesthesia to the heart and mind. If one chooses to look at a preborn infant as a "thing" to be gotten rid of, it could possibly relieve the parent of any guilt or shame. The problem with this is that in their hearts unless they are truly lacking in intelligence and empathy, they really do know the truth of the matter. They are just lying to themselves by mislabeling reality.

Recently, I heard in the news that ultrasounds of babies do not actually pick up heartbeats. How far can they go with lies and being anti-science? I had ultrasounds and saw all four of my beautiful children. I am here to tell you that I also heard their heartbeats! Since I was heavily monitored with my last baby, I heard his heartbeat very early on! It was wonderful!

Reflection: What place do you think logic has in the pro-life movement? Can we win others to an understanding of the reality of life through logic, scripture, or a mixture of both?

"Parenthood Clinic" Deception

A young lady I knew called a local clinic that was advertised in the yellow pages of the telephone directory. This occurred during pre-internet days. The ad offered help for unplanned pregnancies. It was one of many in a very well-known nationwide chain. When she called, she was surprised to find that the woman who answered the phone offered her an abortion. While the young lady was looking for help for an unplanned pregnancy, because she was uninsured, the woman on the other end of the line told her that she could only help her if she wanted an abortion! This business advertised that it offered pregnancy help for unplanned pregnancies, but that was deceptive. The young lady felt that it was very disturbing that they only offered an abortion to her. When she declined their services, the representative's reply was to tell her to call them back if she changed her mind!

Another woman, who had worked for an abortion clinic, recalled reading from scripts to any potential client who called in. They had scripted answers for every possible question that could be asked, and all answers were geared toward guiding the young woman into the clinic for an abortion. The more women they got to come in, she said, the more money they all made. There was a quota on the number of abortions they had to perform to make their budget.

God is Sovereign

Man has stepped into what is the rightful place of God. By usurping His position, legalizing abortion was the greatest affront to God that this country ever committed. America was founded on Christian principles with the Bible as our standard on morality. God has never condoned the murder of innocents. In His sovereignty, God commanded, "Thou shalt not kill."

This should be easy to understand. Yet, here we are, almost fifty years after the passage of Roe vs. Wade, and many still vehemently deny the sanctity of life. The spiritual deception is on a very large scale, and we ignorantly behave as if we are immune to the judgment of God.

Some people act as if they do have a complete understanding. Their confidence may seem baffling. Because they are Hollywood actors or musicians, they believe they have the answers to everything, yet, they say the craziest and most contradicting things! For instance, one very famous television personality seems to agree with her contemporaries that abortion is "a right." That same woman said recently that she thinks a baby in the womb can "feel" if they are male or female. Why does she think it is acceptable to kill a human being that is so self-aware, even while still in the womb? How can she defend her stance without condoning murder? She is very wise in her own mind. 1 Corinthians 3:19a tells us, "For the wisdom of this world is foolishness with God."

A Rose is a Rose — the Deception in Playing with Words

Years ago, we used protective language concerning pregnancy. We used the terms which gave honor to the pregnancy and the woman such as "expecting," "with child," "in a delicate condition," and "in a family way" because the word "pregnant" was considered impolite to use in mixed company. My high school friends used the slang term "p. g." Another term I heard was, "she's wearing her apron high." When parents were not yet ready to explain the facts of life to children concerning how babies were born, they used phrases like, "found under the cabbage leaf" or suggested that "the stork" brought the babies. My own mother claimed it was the angels that brought the little ones!

The current games being played with words in our present culture are both dangerously deceptive and ridiculous.

Abortion is now called "healthcare." This is part of the abortionist's branding and deliberate propaganda by abortion supporters. That term totally skirts around the issue that abortion is the intentional death of the preborn. Since when did health care involve killing? Words are used as trickery to get across points of view rather than to describe reality and real science. I am reminded of William Shakespeare who in Romeo and Juliet wrote that "a rose by any other name would smell as sweet." We can say that the murder of a baby, by any other name, is still the murder of a baby. **Abortion is not healthcare.**

I'm Having a Fetus! The Truth of the Choice Between Life and Death

I recently received an invitation in the mail for a baby shower. I have never heard of a fetus shower, but the word "fetus" is the word of choice with abortion centers. It is a word that is used as a sort of sanitizer or bleaching agent. We use bleach when we do not want to see any of the dirt. The word "abortion" sounds so much cleaner and medically perfect than the word, "kill." Another attempt at bleaching the concept of abortion is in the use of the phrase, "freedom of choice" or "freedom to choose." The freedom to choose what? The choice is between life and death.

"Gestation" refers to the amount of time it takes a baby to develop in the womb, which is typically nine months. At what point of gestation, in our present culture, should we call a baby a baby? When a young woman announces to others that she is pregnant, what does she say? "I'm having a fetus"? The twelve-week gestational age is the cut-off point for abortion in some states. Do we then start calling the child a baby? Perhaps we should continue to call the baby a "fetus" in order not to hurt the feelings of those who cannot come to grips that the baby has been a baby all along. We could be politically correct so as not to offend. A mother could say that she is pregnant and then not call her little one a "baby" until after it is born at nine months. These are all silly suggestions but there are some that believe abortion should be accessible all the way up to nine months gestational age and even, incredibly, beyond. When a young lady is happily pregnant, however, she very naturally says, "I am going to have a baby!" and she would be declaring the truth.

Mind Control

How many women, who have suffered a miscarriage, have used the words "aborted" or "fetus?" The grieving mothers and fathers most commonly say that they have "lost a baby." Once, I heard the word "fetus" used by a father who desired to have his wife abort a baby. Emotionally detached from their offspring, both mother and father willingly aborted that little one. Perhaps they were too embarrassed to call their child a baby because that would have declared the child's humanity. It is emotionally easier to abort a "fetus" rather than a "baby." How much better would it have been if they would have at least attempted to adopt their baby into a loving home? Instead, that precious baby was thrown into a garbage can full of a heap of medical waste to be taken to a landfill, sold for research, or burned in an incinerator as fuel — all of which have happened and are possibilities for any aborted baby.

Just as abortionists use the word, "fetus" as an intentional, emotional disconnect, they do the same with the words, "abortion" and "pregnancy." When clinic workers speak about aborting the baby, they refer to it as "pregnancy" as in "aborting the pregnancy." We do not usually call this practice of killing preborn babies, "massacre," or "slaughter," although either of those names fits the circumstance. We have sterilized the "procedure" for our sensitive, modern ears and so we call it by the word, which evokes the least emotion — "abortion."

Of course, if a woman uses the word "fetus" at all before birth she would always be correct. It is simply the Latin word for "unborn young" or "unborn baby." The Miriam-Webster online dictionary states that the definition of "fetus" is "specifically: a developing human from usually two months after conception to birth."[14] In Webster's 1913 dictionary, the word may have only been used for the animal world. The definition reads, "The young or embryo of an animal in the womb, or in the egg; often restricted to the later stages in the development of viviparous and oviparous animals."[15] My, how things have changed.

By using the word "fetus," abortion centers and pro-abortion warriors attempt to detach the mother and father emotionally from the baby. Manipulating the words serves their greed. Recently, a radio station that is heard all over America, was revealed to have typed up a memo concerning what words could and should not be used on the air concerning abortion and pregnancy. An unborn baby was a "no." "Fetus" was a "yes."

The bottom line of the abortion business in this country is an economic one. They use government money, corporate, and individual donations to fund abortions. They are hypersensitive to criticisms of their real aims and actions. They are using any tool they can find to aggressively campaign against preborn babies' lives. Their agenda is slick, seemingly caring about women but they are trying to control our minds as to how to conceptualize abortion. Is it a death or is it a "choice"? Abortion is the killing of life. Abortion centers need to be truthful in calling abortion what it is — terminating, extinguishing, ending, killing a life. **They need to call a "fetus" what it is — Latin for "unborn baby."**

Abortion Doula

Have you ever heard of an abortion doula? A doula is one who generally gives emotional support to a woman during pregnancy and delivery but is not medically trained, as opposed to a midwife. While preparing for a pro-life rally I received a threatening call from an anonymous, self-identified "abortion doula." Screaming with the most vulgar language, she let me know that I was not welcome in her town. I highly suspected, in my spirit, that this person was also into a type of witchcraft that is prevalent in my area. The weekend of the rally my tire was slashed. When she could not get, by threats and intimidation, my compliance with her wants, she took the matter physically into her hands. The person that operates in this type of spirit operates in fear and intimidation because they are too cowardly to speak like adults. They know they cannot win the argument. A preborn baby is still a human baby, and they know it.

Many Witches Desire Abortion

Witchcraft, New Age philosophy, prescription, and illegal drug use are being substituted for a relationship with the God of the Universe. In our government, there are also people that are open to demonic influence because they are under a strong delusion. We are living in the days when people call good evil and evil good.[16] The devil works day and night to undermine the God of the Universe. The demons follow instructions to manifest through people that carry out Satan's will against the Kingdom of God. Witchcraft and New Age activity, which are so common today, invite demons to enter through portals that people willingly, or naively, open to them.

Earlier in this book, I explained how witchcraft is closely aligned with abortion. In this example, we can see how they are interconnected in the following verse about King Manasseh. Remember that to "pass through the fire" means burning an infant alive:

> And he made his son pass through the fire, and observed times, and used enchantments, and dealt with familiar spirits and wizards: he wrought much wickedness in the sight of the LORD, to provoke him to anger. — 2 KINGS 21:6

"Observed times" refers to the sin of astrology. Enchantments, wizards, and familiar spirits are all abominable to God because they are pagan worship and take our focus off His love and guidance.

What are the main topics of the complaints of "witches" that we read about in the news? They are abortion and politics. Self-proclaimed witches have been videoed casting spells on pro-life politicians. We never hear about witches casting spells on the politicians who support abortion. One politician has been recorded encouraging people to verbally assault and physically surround our pro-life politicians. This has been played on many news broadcasts. If the spellcasting did not undermine the plight of true victims of physical assault — the babies — it would all seem like a bunch of silliness, but the violent intent is real.

If the encouragement of violence against our politicians does not alarm us about the potential of a disastrous civil war in our country, then we are blind. Never in my life have I seen politicians encouraging violence against other politicians until now. The demonic influence is obvious. Many pro-life politicians and protestors have been physically attacked by pro-abortion activists. The devil is trying to thwart God's plan for America at every step. The only way to extricate the demons from the mobs is to cast them out in the authority given to us by Jesus. We cannot entirely blame this new generation because they have not been taught the Bible. We all need a moral framework — something that we can rely on and stand for when choices need to be made. If God is not the center of our lives, something else will move in and take God's place.

Sorcery — Pharmakeia

The sin of sorcery in Revelation 9:21 and 18:23 is the sin of witchcraft and drugs. This can be understood by searching out the original Greek word, "pharmakeia," in a word study.

"Pharmakeia" is the Greek word that the Bible uses for mind-altering drug use and witchcraft. It is where we get the word "sorcery." Being under the influence of the spirit of "pharmakeia" causes deception and estrangement from God. It allows demons to get a foothold in one's life. Not only does drug use open one up to spiritual attacks by the devil, but drugs have historically been used to abort babies, just as the abortifacients (abortion pills) are used today.

Drugs, witchcraft, and abortion all work hand in hand. I have heard testimonies of former witches and warlocks on television and videos, who were present at ritual abortions even inside abortion clinics. You may have learned in school that the Ancient Greeks used drugs in their pagan temple rituals. Galatians 5:19-21 uses the word "sorcery," as Paul speaks of the "deeds of the flesh." In Greek, the root of the word sorcery is also "pharmakeia."

Prescription drugs may be necessary, but the overuse of both illegal and prescription painkillers may be responsible for a lot of the angry outbursts from the pro-abort crowd, although they would probably deny it. Access to mental health care needs to be increased in America. I have heard stories of people on painkillers that did things they never would have done before taking them. Remember the devil seeks whom he may devour.[17] Any kind of mind-altering substance, if abused, can be a demonic gateway. The use of many mind-altering drugs has helped increase the demonic influence on people in America today.

Another problem is that we are raising kids to be addicted to cell phones, computers, and electronic games. Living in a fantasy world of deception, many children do not know how to interact relationally with other human beings. It is no wonder that life inside the womb, let alone outside the womb, is not precious to many of them.

"Women's Lib"

Those of us, who grew up in the 1970s, were exposed to a cultural revolution. When I was a little girl, my mother was one of the few who held a job outside the home. This was hard on me in many ways, including when many other mothers attended daytime school functions that my mother could not attend. The American landscape was changing at that time with feminists promoting a women's liberation movement. It was during this time that we female junior-high students argued for the right to wear slacks to school.

As a 7th-grade classroom representative, it was required that I meet with a group of other representatives with the principal. I do not know how many of my classmates cared about a feminist agenda at that point. We were wearing our dad's neckties to school as a fashion accessory to go along with our 70s fashion vests. Most of us were not making a political statement but were more concerned with wearing cute clothes that were coming out at that time, such as bell-bottomed jeans and nice two-piece slacks outfits. Around that time, I do remember bra-burning was becoming a radicalized exhibit of the feminist agenda but that was something we might have seen on television news or in the papers and not in real life. We were in a rural, somewhat conservative district.

Feminism was not taught in school, and I suspect that few of my classmates read the daily papers. I do not think that any of us thought we were not free, as the "women libbers" claimed! I am sure there were things that needed to be addressed such as adequate salaries or being passed over for promotion in favor of a man but, in our little world, women seemed to be in charge. My homeroom teacher was a lovely lady of African American descent. The truth was that when I met with the school principal, along with the other classroom representatives, my entire reason for wanting the freedom to wear pants to school was that I suffered terribly from the cold at school! Waiting in lines before school began, going to the cafeteria, and being outside for recess during the winter months, was almost unbearable for my little 72-pound body. Of course, the fact that the fashion at that time was to wear tiny little miniskirts did not help! By that time, the old-fashioned wool leggings we wore under our dresses in earlier years were embarrassing and "not cool."

The big day came when we nervously gathered around the desk of Mr. Davies. He was a throwback to the days of the old-time school administrators. Large and stern with a decided no-nonsense attitude, his presence in the halls was a little intimidating, even for the "good kids." The children respected him, and I think that many feared him a bit, based on the comments that I heard. He was an older man and had, in fact, been my mother's teacher. In our meeting, he gave each of us young ladies an opportunity to speak. He asked us why we wanted to wear pants to school. I presented my case of always being cold. He probably thought, "It's no wonder! Look how short your dress is!" We won our case. At the time, we were surprised that he gave us what we asked for! Looking back, I suspect that he knew the trend was for every school to acquiesce to the cultural demands of allowing girls to wear slacks. I truly believe, however, that this old-fashioned, mannerly, gentleman was secretly thankful for the opportunity to see the young girls cover up!

Little did we know, at that young and innocent age, that sexual promiscuity was rising to previously unknown heights in the United States. The introduction of the birth control pill occurred only ten years before. The success of the Roe vs. Wade court case, which opened more access to abortions across the nation, facilitated a more sexually promiscuous culture than had ever been realized in America. What was not publicly known at that time, was that along with serious physical side effects for women, "the pill" could cause an abortion. There is always a chance that an egg may be fertilized, despite having taken a contraceptive pill, and that fertilized egg, now containing all the necessary DNA of a person, will be killed. I believe there are many babies in Heaven today waiting for mommas who never even knew they were pregnant.

Control of the Home

Men have been de-masculinized by the feminist movement. Government money has replaced man as the breadwinner. We hear more about men committing suicide these days. We hear more about men being depressed than we heard years ago. The problem is even showing up on college campuses where young women are now much more likely to graduate than young men.

God gave us order for the home. Men are one hundred percent necessary to the family structure. The Biblical family consists of a man and a woman — a husband and a wife — with the man in the leadership role. This role is loving, leading, and forgiving, just like our Heavenly Father in many respects. He is not to lead by force but by love, a love so great that he would lay down his life for his wife as Christ laid down His life for His Bride, the church.[18] Husband and wife are allies of each other. Children raised in that kind of environment are usually kind, loving, and respectful as they are raised in an atmosphere that fosters those qualities. Many children go through a rebellious period but will eventually grow into the role of parenting their own children with the same wisdom with which they were raised. In some states, with frightening government overreach, the states want to begin "home visits." This will set a terrible precedent for the rest of the states in the union. The government has, in many cases, replaced men as the head of the household. Even King Solomon relinquished spiritual headship when his wives swayed him to worship foreign gods, including Molech, the god who required the blood of babies:

> Solomon did what was evil in the sight of the LORD, and did not follow the LORD fully, as David his father

had done. Then Solomon built a high place for Chemosh the detestable idol of Moab, on the mountain which is east of Jerusalem, and for Molech the detestable idol of the sons of Ammon. — 1 KINGS 11:6,7

The saddest thing I see about the modern feminist movement is that it tells women the lie that children, a home, and a husband are not fulfilling. I think we all, individually, need to make that assessment for ourselves. What is good for one woman is not the same as for another. In the mid-1970s men were beginning to be scorned if they wanted to be homemakers and mothers. What previous generations valued; the next generation was taught to hold as insignificant. The media could make a homemaker feel that they were a "nobody" in the eyes of the world. I remember a television commercial that said a woman could "bring home the bacon" (meaning a salary), "fry it up in the pan" (be a homemaker) "and never, ever let you forget you're a man" (be a dutiful and loving wife). As millions of women found out, that was a lie. There are not enough hours in the day to accomplish all of that. In that mindset, many marriages began to fail with women feeling less worthy than ever. "What do you do?" became the first question people asked men and women in those days. Previously, it had only been asked of men. Being a "stay-at-home mom" automatically stigmatized women in the new culture. The result was that pregnancy and motherhood began to become a terrific burden and even an embarrassment. What was not told in the media, was that many of the women who promoted this new idea were lesbians who did not want a husband and children. These women selfishly stole the natural and historic pride of womanhood from the new female generation.

Those in the so-called "women's movement," are taking shrewd advantage of other women, in their attempt to convince them that they must give up their babies so that they may have a fulfilling, worthy life. Perhaps they try to convince others to justify their own lack of maternal feelings. Feminism can be beautiful, or it can be an aggressive ideology. It breaks my heart to see how many "feminists" try to deny one of the most important distinctions that set women apart from men and are the essence of our femininity. Even if a woman is, for some reason, unable to bear children, she still often has a beautiful, feminine, mothering instinct. While I believe there needs to be a healthy balance between child-rearing and a woman's vocational calling, it is best to read Proverbs Ch. 31 to learn how women can best fulfill the calling of being a woman. Of course, open communication with God through prayer will bring a woman a greater understanding of her purpose. God will guide her in how she can walk in His will as she cares for her family. Giving up motherhood for a career, flies in the face of reason, however, considering that women were designed to bear and nurse children. If a woman truly feels called to a career, she should have it, but if a woman knows that she was designed by God to be a wife and mother then she should be able to do so without being stigmatized. Modern feminists are also responsible for having put much of the whole present generation of children in daycare facilities. True feminists should encourage other women to excel in whatever they are called to do.

Goddess Worship

In my research, I was surprised to find out the prevalence of goddess worship. This is a "New Age" continuation of the ancient worship of Isis, Diana, Ashtarte, and others. Goddess worship includes the justification of a woman's right to use sex in whatever way she pleases. I have heard the testimony of many former abortion workers. They told stories about working alongside self-confessed witches who practiced "goddess worship." They spoke about women that used abortion clinics as places to quietly conduct child sacrifice as they worked. To satisfy Satan, they offer up dead babies straight from their mother's womb.

We are riding a turbulent wave. A crash on a rocky shore is imminent if we continue to turn a blind eye to the horrendous impact of the taking of millions of innocent lives in our country. Even from the moment of conception, the Bible shows us that **God has a purpose and destiny for each of us** if we follow His will for our lives. We will not get away with legal abortion for long. To continue this way is sure destruction, as we will discuss further in this book.

Be aware that if you dabble in Tarot cards, crystals, Celtic circles, or any practice which speaks of the "inner goddess," you are walking on the devil's turf. Any kind of practice, which diverts us from the One True God and takes our focus off Jesus, is satanic. The New Age movement seeks to divert us from the Bible. "New Age" practices and witchcraft of all kinds are attempting to control our country. Witchcraft is about manipulation and control. There is no formal New Age organization. Rather, it is a blend of Eastern mystic religions, yoga, many kinds of martial arts, earth worship, and any kind of spirituality which deviates from the Word of God. Jesus told us that He is the only way to the Father, but New Age beliefs teach that there are many paths to heaven. The devil, the "father of lies" works hard to keep people from God.[19]

"Get Dat Fetus, Kill Dat Fetus"

I saw a picture of one grinning woman who was holding up a sign on which the above words were written. That is just one example of thousands of disrespectful signs we have seen regarding the life of babies. New Age teachings lead us away from God and into spiritual darkness. Signs, chanting, vulgar costumes, and vulgar rants are all a sign that the spirit of Herod is angry and thrashing about in the streets of America. Young people are protesting with actual blood and fake blood on grotesque images they create to gain attention to their cause. When I was growing up, young people protested violence. They protested babies being killed in the war in Cambodia. Now some young people, some middle-aged people, and even some elderly people are violently protesting the right of babies to live.

If we look at the crazy mob protests that have occurred lately, with our spiritual eyes, we see the demon possession of the crowd. Unless one sees that there is a real God in heaven and an evil devil who works against God's purposes, that one will not be able to see the darkness of the spiritual realm. Demonic influence is real. Demons celebrate death, including the death of all preborn babies. The demonic realm is somewhat of a mystery, even though we know that it exists. When a non-Christian mob of the same ideals gets together, it is very easy for demons to influence every one of them. In fact, that kind of non-Christian, angry crowd, is just perfect for a situation of demonic mass hysteria — a kind of lunacy caused by demonic forces. If you have heard shrieking by protesters, you have heard sounds created by demons. When a United States President came into power, on a pro-life ticket, with a Christian pro-life vice-president, every demon working for the devil was shaken up. The spirit of Herod was shaken into a frenzy. It showed up in the streets of massive groups of protestors. I know that my politically liberal friends would not be among people that act like that, and I pray they will find a place of comfort away from the nonsense.

Reflection: Do the "ladies" involved in these protests represent American womanhood? Do the "gentlemen" represent American masculinity?

Where the Warfare Occurs

The Bible speaks of three heavens. The first heaven is what we can see in the sky, as far as we can see and that includes satellites with telescopes and beyond — whatever space and heavenly objects that are tangible. The third heaven is the realm of God. Paul tells us about this when He recounts the story of a man that he knew who had visited this "out of this world" place:

> I knew a man in Christ above fourteen years ago, (whether in the body, I cannot tell; or whether out of the body, I cannot tell; or whether in the body, or out of the body, I cannot tell: God knoweth;) such an one caught up to the third heaven. — 2 CORINTHIANS 12:2, KJV

While not everyone believes this, I think the second heaven must be where the spiritual battles rage and where the "prince of the power of the air" accomplishes much of his dirty work.[20] This is where demonic princes battle with God's warring angels as we learn in the Book of Daniel, Ch. 10, when Gabriel visits Daniel in response to his prayer:

> But the Prince of the kingdom of Persia withstood me one and twenty days: but, lo, Michael, one of the chief princes, came to help me; and I remained there with the kings of Persia. — DANIEL 10:13, KJV

When our prayers are not immediately answered, there may be a battle going on in the unseen realm that we know nothing about. In Daniel's case, a war between good and bad angels kept Gabriel from attending to Daniel immediately. The spiritual realm is a very busy place!

Gabriel is a very high-ranking angel. It was he that God sent to speak to Daniel, as well as Zacharias, the father of John the Baptist, and Mary, the virgin mother of Jesus. Michael is the only other named angel in the Bible, and he is the protector angel of Israel. We learn, here, about an actual battle in the heavenlies. The Prince of the Kingdom of Persia, which is modern-day Iran, is a very dark and powerful agent of Satan. It is very sobering to know that this prince is still battling the angel Michael over Israel. The Prince of Persia follows his master's will in trying to destroy the promises that God has made to Israel. Unrighteousness battles righteousness and love, in this domain. We do not know from the Bible the names of the angels or the demons that are battling over

America, but we know the battle rages and perhaps Michael also battles for America. The devil is a sore loser and wants to go down fighting. He knows his end is near.

Most of the Old Testament was originally written in Hebrew. The original Hebrew word for "host" means an organized regiment or army. The New Testament, originally and primarily written in Greek, also uses the word "host" for "army," as the night the shepherd's received the Good News of the birth of the Christ Child:

> And suddenly there was with the angel a multitude of heavenly host praising God, and saying, 14) Glory to God in the highest, and on earth peace, good will toward men. — LUKE 2:13-14, KJV

The heavenly host is an army, which is always ready to defeat an enemy force. The unseen enemies of God are organized but so are the host of God's warring angels. Perhaps God sent this host over Bethlehem to protect the Christ Child.

In Joshua Ch. 5, Jesus appeared to Joshua in what is known as a "Christophany," or a pre-incarnate vision of Jesus Christ. Remember that the Son of God always existed as the Second Person of the Trinity. We see here that Jesus oversees the angels. Joshua fell on his face in worship. Whenever someone encounters God in the Bible, we see them fall on their face. The King James Version says:

> And the captain of the LORD's host said unto Joshua, Loose thy shoe from off thy foot; for the place whereon thou standest is holy. — JOSHUA 5:15, KJV

The only way to bring America back to the moral and ethical place where life is valued is to bring Americans back to the God who made us and His Son Jesus Christ. Because God the Father values all our lives, He sent His only Son to save us. Calling upon the power of the Holy Spirit to help us, it is our responsibility to save the babies of God's creation. We grieve the Holy Spirit of God when we stand back silently without reaching out to help young mothers and fathers. When our spirits are not filled with the Word of God and we are not participating in the sweet communion of prayer with Him, then we can fall into apostasy and become open to the dangerous doctrines of demons.[21]

> The fear of the LORD is the beginning of wisdom, And the knowledge of the Holy One is understanding. — PROVERBS 9:10

Beatitude 6: "Blessed are the pure in heart, for they shall see God" (Matt. 5:8).

<u>Life suggestion</u>: Treat everyone with respect. Honor all human life. 1 John 4:7 says, "Beloved, let us love one another, for love is from God; and everyone who loves is born of God and knows God." We must remember we are all God's creation. Remember that Galatians 3:28 tells us, "There is neither Jew nor Greek, there is neither slave nor free man, there is neither male nor female; for you are all one in Christ Jesus." Jesus taught us equality in His ministry to all. Living a holy life requires us to be generous in our thoughts and treatment of others. 1 Peter 1:16 implicitly directs us: "'. . . it is written, "YOU SHALL BE HOLY, FOR I AM HOLY."'

Chapter Seven

Judgment

Righteousness exalts a nation, But sin is a disgrace to any people. — Proverbs 14:3

Will God Really Judge America?

Our Father's great and amazing love for each one of us includes His love for each preborn child of His creation. All babies are His; never mind the happenstance of their conception. God is righteous as well as loving and He will ensure that we receive our just reward as a nation, either for the good or for the bad, over abortion. We will receive righteous judgment, or we will be blessed. If we continue the path of unrighteousness, all the while knowing the truth, the Bible is clear that we will experience God's wrath.

> For the wrath of God is revealed from heaven against all ungodliness and unrighteousness of men, who hold the truth in unrighteousness; because that which is known of God is manifest in them; for God hath shewed it unto them. — ROMANS 1:18-19, KJV

America is in serious trouble. If we do not repent from the evil of abortion, we will regret it. I believe we are experiencing a lack of blessings and judgment even now. Look around at the terrible unrest in America. God obviously allowed Covid-19 to devastate our nation so that we would look upwards to Heaven. Please pray against the evil spirit that alienates precious babies from their mothers. We must cast this demon out from our country in Jesus' name.

> and I pronounced them unclean because of their gifts, in that they caused all their firstborn to pass through the fire so that I might make them desolate, in order

that they might know that I am the LORD.'" — EZEKIEL 2:26

I believe that prior to the 2016 Presidential elections, we had been falling into judgment for quite some time, over abortion and other atrocities. This country has become stunningly divided over racial and sexual issues, with abortion at the helm of the ship of division because we forgot that we are a nation under God. This gave rise, however, to an increase in prayer for our nation. God heard the humble and desperate prayers of His people and gave us a President who ran on a pro-life ticket. What is amazing is that, morally and politically, President Donald Trump was once pro-abortion! God has been doing a work in him. A trusted, famous Christian has said that he knows, without a doubt, that our President has turned to God. God has also shown me something similar in a dream. He showed me that President Trump is becoming a serious Bible student. The problem we had, however, was that we did not fully rise up as the Church and abolish abortion as we should have!

Chosen by God

God has shown me that President Trump was chosen directly by Him to accomplish His purposes in one of America's darkest hours. Not only were we thriving economically, employing more Blacks and Hispanics than ever before, but we were also beginning to turn the tables on abortion by putting pro-life judges on our Supreme Court. Because of his new faith and the leading of God, I believe that President was beginning to accomplish what the entire church in America had failed to do regarding the taking of innocent lives! He had been aggressively tackling human trafficking and pedophilia. Everything he was accomplishing was turned around with a new administration, but I am praying that God's will be done in the end!

The American church has lost its former influence and power, having lost some of its understanding of scripture and its closeness with God. We have been treating Jesus as only the Friend that He is but have largely ceased to acknowledge the majesty of His Deity. God is real and so is His love, but He is also, "a righteous judge, And a God who has indignation every day."[1] We must remember the work and sacrifice that Jesus gave at Calvary and we must not continue to appease the sinner and entertain the sin. We need to offer sinners reconciliation with the God of the Bible, and we cannot afford to be silent on the issue of the deaths of so many of His created beings. The church failed to fully support the president who was doing God's work!

What God is Showing Me About Covid-19 and how to Defeat It

The LORD showed me the following while I was down at our church altar, praying for guidance in preparing a Sunday sermon. While I do not believe God caused Covid-19 to invade our country, He allowed it! First, it is important to know that during this experience, if we are following His direction, God comforts us and says, "I am with you."[2] Without this perspective, we will have unnecessary fear. We can have confidence in His love and guidance.

Even before I knelt to pray, the LORD directed me to go to the altar and open my Bible. The LORD showed me that the model for the crisis event we are living through is found in the lessons of Haggai. This is the second shortest book of the Old Testament, but the message is huge.

Holes in the Bag

The period in which the events of Haggai occurred spiritually parallels our current age. While God did not create the coronavirus, which plagues us, He is using it to capture our attention now just as He captured the attention of backsliding Israel then — economically:

Now therefore thus saith the LORD of hosts; Consider your ways. 6) Ye have sown much, and bring in little; ye eat, but ye have not enough; ye drink, but ye are not filled with drink; ye clothe you, but there is none warm; and he that earneth wages earneth wages to put it into a bag with holes. — HAGGAI:1: 5,6, (KJV)

Did you ever put coins in a bag with holes? Did you ever put coins in a pocket with holes?

The scenario was that a remnant had returned to Jerusalem from the Babylonian captivity with the purpose of rebuilding the Temple of the LORD. They began the repairs but had gotten distracted by enemy interference. The Samaritans had attacked, keeping them from their work but when the attack was over, they never went back to the important task at hand. They were taking care of their own homes, which God had blessed them with, and they were paying attention to the affairs of this world, but the money started going into bags with holes. Because of Covid-19 restrictions, our booming economy quickly becomes one defective bag, and inflation is spiraling. Do you see what God is saying?

In 2016, we, through prayer, voted for and were given the most pro-Christian president in many years. President Trump also built our economy to incredible heights! Still, we continued to kill about 3,000 preborn infants a day. Still, our dishonor for Biblical marriage and ungodly perversion continued to grow. Still, many mainline churches championed ungodly values.

Haggai was a prophet who called upon the people of Israel to be renewed in holiness and faith and to continue the work of building the house of the LORD. Today the temple is our own body, which houses the Holy Spirit of God, but **we also have an obligation to rebuild the kingdom of God in our Christian-based country.**

Our LORD God said in Haggai 1:2 that the people were saying, ". . .The time is not come, the time that the LORD'S house should be built. He then said in v.4, "Is it time for you, O ye, to dwell in your cieled houses, and this house lie waste (KJV)?

"Cieled houses" refers to adornment or paneling. The paneled houses are reminiscent of God calling for the destruction of the ivory houses in the book of Amos. Ivory was, of course, very expensive and only used for the houses of the wealthy. God spoke of people inordinately concerned about the appearance of their homes. In other words, **they cared more about their own lives and neglected the things of God.**

In verse 5, God said, "Consider your ways!" He says it again in verse 7:

> Thus saith the LORD of hosts; Consider your ways. 8) Go up to the mountain, and bring wood, and build the house; and I will take pleasure in it, and I will be glorified, saith the LORD. 9) Ye looked for much, and, lo, it came to little; and when ye brought it home, I did blow upon it . . . (KJV)

The people looked for much, but God said that He blew it away! Then God gives the reason:

> . . .Why? saith the LORD of hosts. Because of mine house that is waste, and ye run every man unto his own house. 10) Therefore the heaven over you is stayed from dew, and the earth is stayed from her fruit. 11) And I called for a drought upon the land, and upon the mountains, and upon the corn, and upon the new wine, and upon the oil, and upon that which the ground bringeth forth, and upon men, and upon cattle, and upon all the labour of the hands (KJV.)

Our Drought is Covid-19

Our economy was blasting away, and we reveled in the economy, but did we revel in the opportunity to build the house of God — our bodily temples for the Holy Spirit and the

Kingdom of God on earth? Some did, but for most of the churches the answer is a resounding, "NO!"

When COVID-19 hit the world stage and moved quickly into our country, God blew our prosperity away. We cannot blame the communist/socialist agenda, although it is very real. We cannot blame the deep state, although it is very real. God can use whatever and whomever He chooses for any means and ends He desires.

President Trump was doing a marvelous job of containing the virus as best he could, and Vice-President Pence was leading the 2nd Chronicles 7:14 prayer of repentance. But WE the people are responsible for the heartfelt prayers of repentance. We the people of God's church are responsible to go down on bended knees and look up to the Heavens.

When the people heard the pleas of Haggai, the people responded!

> Then Zerubbabel the son of Shealtiel, and Joshua the son of Jehozadak, the high priest, with all the remnant of the people, obeyed the voice of the LORD their God and the words of Haggai the prophet, just as the LORD their God had sent him. And the people showed reverence for the LORD. — HAGGAI 1:12

The people became obedient. They repented. They turned back to God.

> Then Haggai, the messenger of the LORD, spoke by the commission of the LORD to the people, saying, "'I am with you,' declares the LORD." — HAGGAI 1:13

The only way to defeat COVID-19 and any other disaster is for the church to repent. We cannot call on nonbelievers to repent. They do not even know God. Our heartfelt repentance will spiritually clear the nation for a Great Awakening. The rebuilding of our own personal temples in holiness will bring about a new vigor for Kingdom-building in our land. This country was created by God to shine the Light of Jesus Christ.

God is getting our attention. He is blowing our wealth and stability away. Food prices have gone way up. The death rate of COVID-19 is terrible but so are the very much higher death rates of heart disease, cancer, and drug overdose. It took the shutdown of the nation for God to get our attention here in America. We must consider our ways!

We must not allow the enemy to divert our attention from the task at hand. The lesson is in Haggai, Ch. 1 — **Ignore the work of God and He will chasten us. Do the LORD's work and watch the blessings flow in.** He will be with us every step of the way.

Building with Bloodshed

There is no good future for citizenship that kills its young. The prophet Habakkuk wrote:

> Woe to him who builds a city with bloodshed And founds a town with violence! — HABAKKUK 2:12

Habakkuk was deeply concerned for the condition of his fellow man and his homeland. In anguish, he cried, "O LORD, how long shall I cry, and thou wilt not hear! Even cry out unto thee of violence, and thou wilt not save!"[3] Habakkuk witnessed the violence of his nation, and it was torturing his heart. Another word for violence in this passage could be "murder." Even more, than we do, God hates murder and violence. Imagine the pain of our Heavenly Father when His children hurt each other! Imagine God's pain when His created beings kill their own young!

I truly fear the eternal fate of the abortionist. If he or she does not repent they will literally have hell to pay for the violent destruction of each preborn child. Likewise, those who encourage abortions will be made to see the results of their evil when called to stand before the LORD, one day. God gives us all an open doorway to Him. Even the abortionist, as well as the mothers and fathers of aborted babies, have a Hope in Jesus if they choose Him.

It often seems as if God is sitting back allowing the violent to thrive. We should always remember that we all have the gift of free will, but we also should remember the opportunities He gives each one of us to repent. Amazingly, God is very patient and extends His time of mercy for all that will eventually turn to Him. Meanwhile, those of us who are burdened with the sins of our country are not so merciful and not so patient. We cannot bear the thought of injustice. Those who have a heart understanding of the reality of the grievous sin of abortion are suffering now, as did Habakkuk. We cry out to God for the murder and violence against the preborn to stop. Yet, we are responsible for at least letting others know what the Word of God has to say. God gives us the beautiful burden of sharing the Good News of salvation.

The Most Horrific Story I Have Personally Heard

About fifteen years ago I had the pleasure of meeting an older man who shared with me a few interesting stories from the past. He was the uncle of a friend of mine, and they had a close relationship. He was very likable and just as my friend did, I called him Uncle Mike. As a history lover, I enjoyed hearing him talk. Uncle Mike was considered "slow" from childhood. I do not think that he ever had a diagnosis but when I met him, he functioned well and spoke well. He was a little "different" from most people but could carry on a fine conversation. His stories were full of details.

Sadly, he passed away not too long after I met him. Even from beyond the grave, I got to hear one more piece of history from Uncle Mike. A few days before he passed on to Glory my friend took him shopping and he said that he had to tell her something. He told her that he had heard the angels singing to him, and, amusing to me, he said they sounded just like me! She told him that perhaps it was because he had been listening to me sing lately but it led her to wonder if he might be passing soon. He then began to question her and ask her if she thought he would be going to heaven. She told him, "Yes, Uncle Mike. Of course!" He cried, "But I did bad things." He then confessed that he believed that his first child was a stillborn baby because of the babies he had buried!

My friend came from a large, influential family. They donated heavily to a local church and all the children in the extended family attended the parochial school run by the parish. Uncle Mike told her that when he was a child because he was considered "slow" of mind, the authorities in that church thought that he would not be believed by anyone if he was to tell what he knew and what they made him do. He had various jobs to do around the church but the hardest job he would ever have in his life was the job he was made to do in the cellar.

On numerous occasions, he was given a shovel and told to dig a hole in the cellar for the babies that the leaders in the church, both men and women, would bring. (In those days, many of the older homes and buildings in our area had dirt floors and sandstone foundations.) After a newborn was placed in its cellar grave, Uncle Mike had to mix and pour cement over the baby to ensure that its cold, hard tomb would be hidden forever. Uncle Mike was clear in explaining who brought the babies down. He assumed that the pastors were the fathers of the babies.

After he shared this gruesome testimony, his niece assured him that he was innocent and that it was not in any way his fault. She was horrified but she offered peace to her suffering uncle. He never said, and we will never know if these were aborted babies or babies that were born and then died. Were their deaths natural? For their burials to be secret, these babies were not part of any honorable scheme.

My friend was very saddened by Uncle Mike's confession of his belief that his first child was stillborn as a punishment of God because of his participation in burying the dead babies. His marriage went on to produce two healthy children and my friend assured him that God did love him. Uncle Mike passed three days after this "deathbed confession" but as a believer in Jesus Christ, I know he is really talking with the angels and his large family in heaven. The Bible tells us not to judge, meaning that only God knows the heart and so we cannot determine the destination of anyone. We cannot know the destination of the church elders that abused this man with their gruesome tasks and caused this poor man so much torment for most of his life. We do not know if they ever confessed their sins to God.

Personal and National Responsibility

We need to be very careful about spreading indoctrination that is being promoted against God. Information has been abundantly disseminated that promotes murder. Webster's Dictionary of 1913 defines propaganda as ". . . any organization or plan for spreading a particular doctrine or a system of principles."[4] In this more modern era the popular definition has evolved to include false information spread through the culture to promote certain worldviews, which are usually dangerous to society.

Propaganda promoting abortion has done a great disservice to women. It has achieved its goal of bending the morality of genuinely nice, thinking people. I have heard many people say that they would never abort a baby, but they would not take away another person's right to do so. That has become the new moral high ground.

Let us look at that thought carefully. First, we must ask someone who states this idea, "Why would you personally not have an abortion?" That kind of delicate probing may allow the one being questioned to deeply explore their own convictions and, also, why they hold them. Hopefully, they will then understand that if murder is wrong for one person, it is also wrong for another.

That human life has intrinsic value is a logical as well as a Godly thought. That human life begins at conception is both Biblical and real science. To say otherwise is foolish and childish. Children often believe something simply because they want it to be so. They will sometimes lie because they want to believe that something that is false, is real. An adult doing that is deliberately lying with no fear of consequences. We must be very careful to keep from willfully sinning. When we do, we insult God. The Word says that if we do, we are trampling on Jesus!

> How much more severe punishment do you think he will deserve who has trampled underfoot the Son of God, and has regarded as unclean the blood of the covenant by which he was sanctified, and has insulted the Spirit of grace? — HEBREWS 10:29

That verse alone should call us to repent and ask God to check us for any sin! Likewise, as citizens of our country, we bear the responsibility to monitor our nation's sin! While we cannot always completely change our national moral landscape, we still have an obligation to speak the truth of the Bible. I notice that a lot of my friends on social media are beginning to express themselves more on their feelings about abortion. While it does upset some to look at what they call "political" posts, abortion is a subject that transcends politics because God has created life. It is not a Republican or a Democrat issue. While there are some Republicans that back abortion, most are pro-life. While there are many Democrats that back at least early abortions, some Democrats are adamantly pro-life. God does not change, and He is sovereign in all things, including matters of life and death.

Apathy Makes Jesus Want to Vomit

A large problem we have in this country, and even in the body of Christ, is that we often turn a blind eye to numerous kinds of sins. We often tire of dealing with our own problems and do not feel that we have the time to deal with the issues of others. Another problem we have is the fear of getting involved in issues that we do not feel concern us. We must remember, however, that Jesus told the church in Laodicea that he would vomit them out of His mouth because of their apathy.[5]

We must remember that when it comes to the righteousness of God, what God's Word says is more important for our own well-being than what we personally think or feel. Many people think that because God is loving and merciful, He will not judge us. Of course, He does not wish to harm any part of His creation. Let's consider, however, Proverbs 3:12, which says, "For whom the LORD loves He reproves, Even as a father corrects the son in whom he delights." God takes the time, because He loves us, to correct us and keep us from getting in deeper trouble. This verse is similar:

> FOR THOSE WHOM THE LORD LOVES HE DISCIPLINES, AND HE SCOURGES EVERY SON WHOM HE RECEIVES." — HEBREWS 12:6

He has plans for us that we may not always understand but they are always in our best interest. It is the same as a parent who has high goals for a child, when the child may not understand the parent's motives. For example, a son in college may want to major in a subject such as Sculpture, with no clear career goals. The parents may say that if the son wants to major in that subject and have them pay for it, then the child should also take some education or business courses. As in this example, God is loving and fair. His standard for us is established for our own good and written clearly in the Bible, although His mercy is great when we fail. If He did not set standards for us, then He would not be a righteous God. Only holiness can enter heaven and so we cannot bring unrighteousness there. Unrighteousness includes allowing the death of babies because of our apathy.

National Law vs. God's Law

We must take care not to become comfortable with what others are doing. Unfortunately, that is what has been happening in America. Some Christians have begun to accept the evil of abortion because it is the law of the land. Because it is legal does not mean that God approves of it. His law tells us not to murder! We sit under the severe threat of judgment from above.

Habakkuk's time was no different than today. We have all sinned and need grace. We are living in a land, which needs the mercy of God because of the violence and unrighteousness of its citizens. The widows and orphans still need our care, just as in the days when the Old Testament was written. This includes all the husbandless and those in single-parent homes. Let us look up and pray to be used by God to expose the sin of the times and to help bring a wave of Christian Revival across our great land!

National Guilt

As a nation, we have decided to take matters into our own hands by legally allowing the taking of human life. We have not only questioned God's authority, but we have shaken our fists in God's face! We will be held accountable. Romans 14:12 tells us, "So then every one of us shall give account of himself to God." Because our nation's backbone has historically been the church, we Christians have defaulted on our commitment to keeping this country a Christian nation. We must commit ourselves to our nation and God, glorifying Him, knowing that judgment begins with the church:

> Yet if any man suffer as a Christian, let him not be ashamed; but let him glorify God on this behalf. For the

time is come that judgment must begin at the house of God: and if it first begin at us, what shall the end be of them that obey not the gospel of God? And if the righteous scarcely be saved, where shall the ungodly and the sinner appear? Wherefore let them that suffer according to the will of God commit the keeping of their souls to him in well doing, as unto a faithful Creator. — 1 PETER 4:16-19

If America continues to tolerate abortion, we will continue to be under condemnation from God. As I write this, there is a feeling of hope, in the pro-life world, because many states are beginning to stand for life and are working towards outlawing all abortions.

Choose Life or Be Cursed

Because we want to see a new Great Awakening to God in America, it is important that we have an awareness of sin and a conviction that we are not adhering to God's standards of holiness and righteousness. **We must understand that all obedience comes with the promise of blessing and that every act of disobedience calls a curse upon us. This is especially true about the subject of life.** God's judgment is real and is a promise from God to the disobedient:

> "I call heaven and earth to witness against you today, that I have set before you life and death, blessing and the curse. So choose life in order that you may live, you and your descendants, 20) by loving the LORD your God, by obeying His voice, and by holding fast to Him; for this is your life and the length of your days, that you may live in the land which the LORD swore to your fathers, to Abraham, Isaac, and Jacob, to give them." — DEUTERONOMY 30:19,20

As we see in the above verse, God's blessings are all-encompassing and involve generations. Christians must be careful not to copy or compromise with the ways of our neighbors and the practice of child sacrifice, the "abortion" of ancient cultures. As the ancient Israelites moved into the Promised Land of Canaan, they were admonished by God, through Moses, to avoid copying the awful deeds of the heathen peoples that previously lived there. God told them not to sacrifice their children to foreign gods:

> When the LORD your God cuts off before you the nations which you are going in to dispossess, and you dispossess them and dwell in their land, 30) beware that you are not ensnared to follow them, after they are destroyed before you, and that you do not inquire after their gods, saying, 'How do these nations serve their gods, that I also may do likewise?' 31) "You shall not behave thus toward the LORD your God, for every abominable act which the LORD hates they have done for their gods; for they even burn their sons and daughters in the fire to their gods. — DEUTERONOMY 12:29-31

He then ended this passage with this solemn statement:

> "Whatever I command you, you shall be careful to do; you shall not add to nor take away from it. — DEUTERONOMY 12:32

God hates "hands that shed innocent blood."[6] I am reminded of World War 2 and Josef Mengele, the Nazi, eugenicist, "Angel of Death" during the Holocaust. He conducted horrific medical experiments on the prisoners at Auschwitz. He cruelly killed his victims without a thought.

The devil likes to claim there was no Holocaust. My Uncle Buster, a man normally of few words but with a mighty intellect, disagreed with a television program he was watching, shortly before he went home to be with the LORD. Someone in the program claimed the Holocaust stories were lies. A veteran of both WW2 and the Korean War, my uncle said, "I know it's true. I was there." He was present at the freeing of the

Holocaust prisoners in one of the concentration camps. My mother used to recall when he came back home from World War 2. She was still a young girl. She remembered his screams of terror during the night and would remark about what horrors my uncle must have seen during the war. She said he never talked about it, but it must have been very bad. The people of that time truly were "the Greatest Generation."

After the Western Allied invasion of Germany, Mengele escaped to Argentina, where he worked performing illegal abortions in Buenos Aires. Every abortionist knows they are killing babies. The paid abortionist, with his or her hands awash in the blood of babies, is in a terrible position before God as Deuteronomy 27:25a says, "Cursed is he who accepts a bribe to strike down an innocent person." If this is your present condition, please remember that God forgives those who are broken over sin when their hearts are turned towards His righteousness. Instead of the blood of innocent children, you can be covered from head to foot in the power of the blood of Jesus Christ. God's grace will allow Him to see the sacrifice of Jesus and not your sin. You truly will be washed as white as snow by the crimson flood. Jesus already paid your sin debt. Will you accept His atonement? I believe that God is very reasonable!

> Come now, and let us reason together, saith the LORD: though your sins be as scarlet, they shall be as white as snow; though they be red like crimson, they shall be as wool. —ISAIAH 1:18, KJV

As we mend our ways and pull away from the dedication to killing our nation's preborn babies, God will bless us more and stop punishing our nation. Those of us who have lived through the 1960s and 1970s have seen the striking contrast in our nation between those times and the times we are now experiencing. Even the dramatic societal upheavals of those days pale in comparison to the hateful divisions we see now. The godless ways are proliferating and have multiplied exponentially into the social and familial destruction we see today.

Cannibalism as Judgment?

Through the prophet Jeremiah, God warned the people about the consequences of their idolatry, which included the destruction of the family through male and female prostitution and killing babies. God is longsuffering and merciful but turns stubborn people over to their own reprobate minds after a time.[7] This is when God stops protecting them from the natural results of their own sin. The siege of Jerusalem was prophesied, and its accompanying horrors included the consequence of cannibalism. God warned them but they did not heed the prophets who brought them the horrific news of a macabre end. Jeremiah wrote:

> I will make them eat the flesh of their sons and the flesh of their daughters, and they will eat one another's flesh in the siege and in the hardship with which their enemies and those who seek their life will torment them. — JEREMIAH 19:9

> The hands of compassionate women Boiled their own children; They became food for them Due to the destruction of the daughter of my people. — LAMENTATIONS 4:10

God would never want people to eat each other, let alone their own children! He warned them what would happen when He took His hand off them; it was their choice. He was allowing them to go their own way, which was the course of disobedience that they chose. He allowed them the depravity they desired, turning them over to their reprobate minds. He stopped protecting them and their aggressive enemies pushed them into starvation. Cannibalism is an extreme example of what can happen when people go mad from hunger.

In the past, I read about archaeologists who have discovered jars of baby bones mixed with animal bones near a tower in southern Spain and in different parts of the world. In Spain, as mentioned before, there is a tower, which is approximately 2,500 years old. It pictures a child in a bowl, about to be sacrificially fed to a two-headed monster. These same kinds of jars containing infant's bones have been found in the ruins of the walls of Jericho. There are many rumors today about people who still perform child sacrifice to benefit from the blood of young children, as unbelievable as that sounds. I will write no more about it because I have no proof beyond watching a few documentaries with real footage of witch doctors in Africa who stole young children to murder them for their blood. Apparently, there is a belief that the blood of children is very powerful and helpful. There are many stories of people from other countries around the globe using fetuses and young children in various preparations to increase their energy, sexual prowess, and life.

Those who live in American culture may find it hard to believe that there are still witch doctors. The first I became aware of it was from the testimony of a Nigerian man in one of my congregations. He explained to me that some people where he lived were still very much caught up in practicing witchcraft and that Christians were active in doing spiritual warfare against the forces of evil brought on by the witches. He loaned me a couple of DVDs made in Nigeria that were very beautiful. Those filmed wore colorful outfits and the videos featured beautiful music and were very descriptive in showing the spiritual warfare they were undertaking. In another instance, a black woman in my place of employment shared with me that she was a pastor who had been training under another highly experienced woman pastor in deliverance ministry. She told me that while they were on a mission trip in Africa, a witch doctor looked her in the eyes and blew a powder from his hand into her face! Thank God she had the power of the living God living inside of her!

. . . greater is he that is in you, than he that is in the
world. — 1 JOHN 4:4

More Dreams

Two different women, who sometimes have prophetic dreams,
told me about horrific and realistic dreams they had, which
involved Satan worship and the murder of children. Both said
that in their dreams they saw blood everywhere and they both
recounted seeing it, especially on rocks. Neither of these
women ever consulted with each other and did not know that
the other had the same dream. Both of their descriptions to me
were very emotional and graphic.

The most gruesome dreams that God ever gave me revealed
horrors I could never have imagined. One was a dream about a
woman politician. In the dream, I saw blood dripping down
her tongue. I will not disclose the identity of this woman, but
she is very famous. In 2012, I had a longer dream that
disgustingly hinted at cannibalism, which I will describe next.

My Dream About Mary

When I was a child, I read morning, noon, and night
everywhere, and anywhere at all that I could carry a book. My
lifelong love of reading continues now that we have the
internet. Since my late teens, I have not been able to read any
fiction because I only pursue the facts! My reading obsession is
now often fulfilled with my smartphone, as I study Scripture
or Bible commentaries and news items. One day, as I was lying
on the floor of my den reading articles on my smartphone in
the middle of the day, just like when I was a girl, I fell asleep.
That is when I had the most disturbing and gruesome dream I
had ever had in my life.

I dreamed that I was walking down a hallway and I passed a
woman named Mary. She was wearing long, light-colored
robes and was very sad. She was obviously mourning. The
hallway was wide with tall ceilings and seemed dark and

ominous — like something out of a spooky movie. The building I was in seemed to be an eerie institution, that seemed to be a mental hospital. There was also another woman. The most horrible moment in the dream, and in any dream that I have ever had, was the point where I realized that there was human flesh in the mouth of the other woman. She began gagging, trying to spit it out. It frightened me awake.

The very first thing I did when I woke up was to turn on my phone to continue reading to try to forget the terrible dream. Amazingly, the very first email that popped up contained an article about a company that used aborted baby cells in actual taste testing for various products for human consumption! I had never heard of it before. God was trying to show me something in that dream and then directing my attention to the very upsetting article. The cell line of the aborted baby cells is called HEK-293, which stands for Human Embryonic Kidney cells. This information is real and available to anyone over the internet.

I then struggled to understand the dream. I realized that Mary, the mother of Jesus, is a precious and beautiful representative of motherhood. Just as Rachel spiritually mourned the loss of her future children, the dream represented the proverbial mother, Mary, mourning the cannibalism of today's babies. The mental institution, I believe, represented the insanity of using our own children for consumerism. To be clear, my understanding is that there are no actual human cells in our processed foods, but the aborted fetal cells were used for testing for flavor. I immediately began to boycott the products on the list that was supplied in that email. Since then, some businesses have separated themselves from that company. Many vaccines contain cells produced from a line of aborted baby stem cells. Many have an ethical problem with this, and it is wise to research every type of vaccine carefully so that we can make conscientious decisions regarding vaccine use.

Another abhorrent practice, which has been discovered, is babies being used as fuel for a factory in Oregon, Georgia, and the UK. I once read that a driver for an incineration company said that he met an abortion worker at a gas station to pick up frozen babies. He was morally convicted and left his job. Dead preborn babies are an actual commodity and part of our national consumption. How far have we sunk, America? **Where human life has no value, we can be sure that the spirit of Herod is busy at work.**

Filthy Lucre — Blood Money

In 1 Timothy 3:3, we read about "filthy lucre" or "dirty money." America and a few other countries in recent years have seen shocking reports about great financial rewards being had from the illegal sale of preborn baby body parts. If you have not seen them yet, do an internet search on this subject. A huge business is being done in marketing aborted babies for research. It is a grisly and bloody business. **We are a nation of hypocrites. We pretend to care for children and yet allow this gruesome practice to continue.**

The largest abortion provider in the nation was the subject of undercover videos, which exposed the true nature of much of their income. It has been widely reported that ninety-six percent of their income comes from abortion. They do not routinely give mammograms, even though they used to claim that they do. We know from published reports that even though this organization receives hundreds of millions of dollars in taxpayer money, it gives millions of dollars in campaign finance funds to pro-abortion politicians; many are presidential hopefuls. These same politicians are advancing and promoting third-semester abortions, even to the point when babies are capable of living on their own. From the undercover videos, we learn that larger and more intact organs can produce a much bigger income in body parts sales. Testimonies of abortion workers tell us that babies are often kept alive until their organs can be harvested. Selling little preborn baby parts (sometimes killing the baby out of the womb while its little heart is beating), has helped keep alive this bloody business of aborting babies.

I have read of teenage students in the Southwest using aborted babies from an abortion clinic for a summer camp course at a university. These students even dissected baby brains. Again, unless they have been taken down from the internet, many of the things I am sharing with you are factual circumstances that can be verified with a quick internet search. Try using various search engines to get a variety of information. It has come to light that many universities purchase aborted body parts for research, but a recent president signed a bill that no tax dollars would go to support research done with aborted babies. The present administration walked that back.

Can You Believe This Happens in America?

There is a tax-funded university that employs a doctor who has developed a technique to harvest perfect livers from late-term "abortions." In this procedure, however, the babies must be born alive so that the livers are completely healthy when they are cut out, so labor is induced with prostaglandin. The baby must be delivered intact and then transported. It is unclear as to whether the babies die in transit or if they die during the procedure. Many bank accounts continue to grow as the stuff of the most horrid nightmares converts into literal blood money. The love of money is the root of all evil.[8]

One customer of aborted babies may be the FDA! It is now being said that the US Food and Drug Administration is doing experiments to create actual human immune systems in mice! This is called transhumanism and goes against the creation order instituted by God. Instead, it lines up with Baal and Molech worship. Remember that Baal had the head of a bull but the bottom half of him was a man. You may remember that the pagan Greek deity, Pan, had the torso of a man but the body of a deer. Like Molech and Baal, he was a god of temptation and sexuality and he lured and tempted with his flute. Another Greek god, Dionysus, was also associated with various beasts, bull horns, wine, revelry, and sexuality and was the son of an incestuous relationship between Zeus and Persephone. Transhumanism is always mixed up with pagan, antichrist religions.

Transhumanism is a real problem today as scientists are doing experiments with pigs and other animals. I saw actual photographs, in a study that was posted online, of little aborted babies' scalps sewn onto the backs of mice. The experiment worked. The hair grew on the mice! The consequences of these Frankenstein-like experiments will be bizarre and sorrowful. These are unethical practices, and these mad scientists are opening us all up to a dangerous future as they experiment with things they do not fully understand. God stopped the building of the Tower of Babel for a reason such as this. Human beings were trying to obtain the knowledge of God. It would have ended in disaster because anytime we go against the created order or try to be like God, we end up failing miserably. Observe what happened to Satan when he aspired to be like God Most High. He ended up getting thrown out of Heaven. It was as quick as lightning. Jesus saw it all.[9]

Years ago, as youngsters, many of us read about Frankenstein's monster. We thought that dealing with human body parts was something that happened only on the pages of a creepy book and that it was only something, which could have been dreamed up in the bizarre imagination of some novelists. Today, we find out that grim fantasy does not even come close to trumping evil. It is a grisly reality, whether speaking of Frankenstein's monster, or the planned deaths of preborn babies that are full of life and promise! This is all part of Baal worship because it encompasses pride. These scientific experiments could lead to fame and fortune. The scientists are trying to be like God.

Worldwide Massacre

While God is the Creator of all life and Jesus came "that men may live," we are experiencing a worldwide massacre of preborn babies. It is not just the United States alone that is indulging in sacrificing its young. The United States and other Western countries have been pushing an abortion mindset, calling it "family planning," through the United Nations in places like Africa, where abortion is mostly abhorred. The massacre of preborn babies abundantly lines the pockets of many abortionists in countries around the globe. There are serious matters, which attract major news agencies and the resulting news reports create tremendous public uproar. The thousands of preborn babies being dismembered each day in the womb, in the United States, and around the world, however, attract very little attention.

Sadly, the state of New York passed a bill that extends abortion rights up to the very day a baby is due to be born. While many of our states are pushing to preserve the lives of the preborn, others are rushing to pass laws, which may result in the lives of healthy babies being aborted even up to the day of birth. I watched a video of a very sad display of callousness as the governor of NY and his supporters celebrated the event of the passage of their new law by cheering and clapping. Soon after, the state of Virginia narrowly missed passing a similar bill. I heard the author of the Virginia full-term abortion bill say, on a video, that passing her bill would provide the opportunity for the baby to be aborted, even as the mother was going into birthing contractions! Many governors of states have been provided with opportunities to vote for or against the "Baby Born Alive Acts," which required life-saving measures for babies accidentally born alive during an abortion procedure. Some who disapprove of these acts at the state level say they are unnecessary because the situation never happens. I have read and watched on video, many testimonies of former abortion workers who witnessed late-term abortions. Many women who have had late-term abortions, even in the ninth month, have stepped forward to talk about it. Recently in the news, it was widely reported that some doctors turn the babies over on their faces in saline solution to kill them. Other reports I have heard include strangulation and just letting a baby sit on a shelf until it dies on its own. Sometimes the spinal cord is snipped.

I do not believe that all the people who are "pro-choice" are evil. I have dear friends that favor open abortion laws, but I know they are misled. We must pray for the spiritual eyes of the nation to be open to the things of God and the importance and sanctity of life. I cannot count the number of times I have heard someone say that late-term abortion never happens, yet there is no restriction whatsoever on abortion in New Mexico, New Jersey, Alaska, New Hampshire, and Vermont. Many other states loosely interpret the laws which say abortions can only be performed for health matters.

Satan's Provocateurs

Satan lures and baits all of us to join with him in his ungodly realm. It is easy to slide into sin because of our own inherited sinful nature and the temptations the devil lays before us. Someone who enjoys bars, and the nightlife will find that their plans begin to revolve around going to the latest "hotspot" rather than a church. Once we commit one sin it is easy to commit another and before we know it, we are in league with the devil.

> "Woe to the rebellious children," declares the LORD, "Who execute a plan, but not Mine, And make an alliance, but not of My Spirit, In order to add sin to sin;"
> — ISAIAH 30:1

When alcohol fuels the party, we all know it is very easy to slip into unhealthy sexual liaisons. It is easy to commit the second sin of fornication after the first sin of getting drunk. When a woman finds she becomes pregnant after such an escapade, the easiest recourse is abortion. After all, how can she tell her family that she does not know the father? Now she has committed a third sin. When she is pregnant, she may begin lying about the entire situation, and the sins multiply, one on top of another. Meanwhile, there is a stranger somewhere that has fathered a child, but the child is now tragically dead. How much easier it would be for everyone to just stay out of the nightclub!

Another example of the multiplication of sin that begins with promiscuity is one when the fear of a lack of freedom, finance, and fun drives a mother and father to kill their young. Just like the pagan religions of history, they offer their babies on the sacrificial table of the root of all evil, which is the love of money. We should encourage our young people to stop worshipping the God of convenience, fear, and greed. We may not be comfortable with this, but fear is a terrible sin! It is the result of a lack of faith and trust in God. There is a consequence:

> "But for the cowardly and unbelieving and abominable and murderers and immoral persons and sorcerers and idolaters and all liars, their part will be in the lake that burns with fire and brimstone, which is the second death." — REVELATION 21:8

Notice that "cowardly" is listed first. The good news is that when we have a relationship with the LORD, He leads us to trust Him. Many high school and college-age girls believe that a baby will interfere with their education. It will be difficult, but the LORD will open doors when we put any matter to prayer. Helping in this situation would be a great ministry for those who wish to serve the LORD on campus.

Why Do the Heathen Rage?

> Why do the heathen rage, and the people imagine a vain thing? — PSALM 2:1, KJV

Recently, I saw a photo of pro-abortion protestors on social media. The scene was meant to shock, and it was very effective. A smiling woman in white and light blue robes, representing the Virgin Mary, stood in the street with her right arm raised in a show of victory. Her legs were spread, and what appeared to be blood was gushing onto the street as her "attendants" helped her to abort "the Baby Jesus." It was a gruesome mess. We can only guess as to what may have happened in this woman's life that opened her up to be led by Satan in such a way. This display is an example of what is meant by people raging and imagining a "vain thing" as we read in Psalm 2:1. These people put on a senseless, empty, demonstration that welcomed useless anger and disgust. A civil, adult conversation would have been more productive.

God will save even these people if they turn from their sins to Him. Any sinner with a truly repentant heart, that confesses past sins and seeks to live righteously before the LORD, will be cleansed! Whatever sin anyone has ever committed can be forgiven by God, except the one unforgivable sin. That is a final denial of the work of the Holy Spirit, which is faith in the death, burial, and resurrection of Jesus Christ. That would be taking your unbelief to the grave. The Word says, however:

> If we confess our sins, he is faithful and just to forgive us our sins, and to cleanse from all unrighteousness. — 1 JOHN 1:9

Those Who "Sacrifice Their Sons and Their Daughters to the Demons"

In Revelation 20:7-10, we read that the devil and his agents will be thrown into the "lake of fire and brimstone," which will be a direct result of their disobedience. While Hell was initially prepared for them, people can choose to go there too, because of their rejection of our Savior. God does not mince words when He speaks of the results of living in disobedience. These verses speak about the judgment of God against those who practice infant sacrifice. The same wrath of God is kindled against those who promote this today, in the name of "women's rights." Our land is polluted with blood.

> But they mingled with the nations And learned their practices, 36) And served their idols, Which became a snare to them. They even sacrificed their sons and their daughters to the demons, 38) And shed innocent blood, The blood of their sons and their daughters, Whom they sacrificed to the idols of Canaan; And the land was polluted with the blood. Thus they became unclean in their practices, And played the harlot in their deeds. Therefore the anger of the LORD was kindled against His people And He abhorred His inheritance. 41) Then He gave them into the hand of the nations; And those who hated them ruled over them. — PSALM 106:35-41

Abortion grieves God, causes severe emotional pain for women, causes babies to be robbed of their lives, and hurts our nation because of God's ultimate and inevitable judgment. America is in serious trouble; please reread verse 41. Please pray against the spirit that alienates these precious babies from their own mothers. Cast this demon out of our country in Jesus' name. Prayer warriors — do not fear. You are covered by the blood of Jesus. Perfect love casts out fear.[10] God uses us, the church, to be a witness to the evil spirits:

> . . . so that the manifold wisdom of God might now be made known through the church to the rulers and the authorities in the heavenly places. — EPHESIANS 3:10

Prepare to Meet Thy God

> . . . prepare to meet thy God, O Israel. — AMOS 4:12c

We must prepare for our future because no one knows what tomorrow may hold. Jesus told us to always be ready to meet

Him.[11] While it is important that we understand the wideness of the mercy that our Sovereign God has been extending to us, we cannot expect Him to ignore our sinful behavior. The same God that spoke our world into existence[12] will also execute righteous judgment.[13] He patiently waits, however, for us to see the truth, as God draws us to Him.[14] He waits for us to begin to make Godly decisions through our own free will. He will not wait forever.

"Free will" is a gift from God to every human being. We must be wise in using this gift. It is our free will to choose or reject Jesus and He respects our decisions. If we do not open the door, He will not come in. You may have heard it said that Jesus is a gentleman.

> Behold, I stand at the door and knock. If anyone hears my voice and opens the door, then I will come in to him, and will dine with him, and he with me. — REVELATION 3:20

The range of emotions regarding abortion is wide. I think that the most common is the nonchalant attitude. Those who do not carry a strong opinion about the mass slaughter of preborn infants feel very little remorse about the number of children killed. I would remind them of what Jesus told the church in Laodicea:

> 'I know your deeds, that you are neither cold nor hot; I would that you were cold or hot. 16) 'So because you are lukewarm, and neither hot nor cold, I will spit you out of My mouth. — REVELATION 3:15-16

The evilest deed is the taking of human life. In the United States, more people are murdered in the womb, than outside of the womb. This is cruel: injecting the drug Digoxin into the hearts of six to twenty-week-old infants in the womb, enabling the mothers to deliver them dead. Some mothers have horrific memories of seeing their little babies in the protective sac, which could no longer protect them. Some mothers have vivid memories of seeing little fingers and toes. We need to pray for peace for these mothers as they give their lives over to God. More people need to be informed about how abortion really works. It is a hard thing to present to people, but we need to make informed decisions on all matters and especially those that pertain to life and death.

Reflection: There is a story about a family that was discovered in 1978, living in the harsh wilderness of Siberia. They had lived there for forty years, having fled for their very lives from the terror of Communism because of their Christian faith. Their last name was Lykov, and they were members of a fundamentalist Eastern Orthodox sect called "The Old Believers." The father had witnessed his brother's murder by the Bolsheviks who were atheists. The family fled their home immediately with some seeds and eked out their own living, but it was hard. They were often hungry. In 1961 there was a late frost that killed everything in their garden, and they had to eat bark and even their shoes to stay alive.

Rather than see her children starve, their mother gave up her meager subsistence for them and perished. God has designed women to be nurturers. Do you think, perhaps, that something in society and culture has changed or has been broken to the point that women are no longer thought of as nurturing and self-sacrificing, as they were years ago?

The Prince of Peace

Before the prophecy of the most famous birth in all of history, the prophet Isaiah speaks of the confusion and noise of war by using the word "tumult":

> For every boot of the booted warrior in the battle tumult, And cloak rolled in blood, will be for burning, fuel for the fire. — ISAIAH 9:5

This verse speaks of the chaos of real battle with the ancient enemies of the Israelites, the Midianites, but it also describes the spiritual battle, and the way Satan plays his game. God promised, here, a cloak rolled in the blood (of Christ) and the cleansing, purging power of Holy Spirit-sent fire. God sent a child, who would eventually leave us the Holy Spirit, to restore the clarity of peace to the world:

> For a child will be born to us, a son will be given to us; And the government will rest upon his shoulders; And His name will be called Wonderful Counselor, Mighty God, Eternal Father, Prince of Peace — ISAIAH 9:6

Jesus is the final answer to the problems being discussed in this book and every problem this world can present. To avoid judgment, the importance of the blood of Jesus cannot be overemphasized. It is through His blood that we find salvation and are sanctified enabling us to live a life without the sin of our past when we lived without Jesus. His blood is all that keeps us from the punishment that we all deserve. Without the blood of Jesus, we would all be judged to condemnation. We must always remember that the blood of Jesus is a powerful cleansing agent!

> In him was life; and the life was the light of men. — JOHN 1:4

But Can't We Get into Heaven Because We Are Good?

I find that very many people struggle with this concept, so let us set the record straight. No one can enter heaven on their own merits. That is the basis of cults and false religions. No one can be that good. We can only enter heaven based on the righteousness of Christ and the work that He did on the cross for us! God gave us His Son with His grace. If we could enter Heaven because of our own works, then Jesus would not have had to leave Glory to die on a Roman cross to pay our sin debt. He provided our atonement. He redeemed us, delivering us from eternal punishment. The Bible is clear that we are saved by faith and "NOT AS A RESULT OF WORKS, SO THAT NO ONE MAY BOAST."[15] This eliminates the tendency of pride. It does not matter how much money we give to the church, although God does see that, and it is good. It also does not matter how much we help others, although God sees that, and it is good. It will not help us to be superstitious and wear a charm or a cross or anything at all. No one can pray us into heaven once we have passed. The Bible is clear. There is no work of man that can gain one entrance into the Heavenly Gates. The only thing that matters is that Jesus gave His lifeblood on the cross for us, who did not deserve a thing. But God is, oh, so good! We are saved by grace through faith alone:

> But God, being rich in mercy, because of His great love with which He loved us, 5) even when we were dead in our transgressions, made us alive together with Christ (by grace you have been saved), 6) and raised us up with Him, and seated us with Him in the heavenly places in Christ Jesus, 7) so that in the ages to come He might show the surpassing riches of His grace in kindness toward us in Christ Jesus. 8) For by grace you have been saved through faith; and that not of yourselves, it is the gift of God; 9) not as a result of works, so that no one may boast. 10) For we are His workmanship, created in Christ Jesus for good works, which God prepared beforehand so that we would walk in them. — EPHESIANS 2:4-10

Looking at verse 10, we can see that we are created for good works. We must do good works in response to our gift of salvation. It is not our works that provide our salvation, but our faith in what Jesus has done for us lowly sinners, by the grace of God.

God's Patience is Long-Suffering

Psalm 86:15 speaks of God's "gracious, longsuffering" (KJV). The word "longsuffering," in the King James Version of the Bible, is the old way of saying "patience." This verse also says that God's patience is abundant in "mercy and truth." In His mercy, God has been lovingly patient with the United States of America. Even though He has long witnessed our blatant disrespect and disregard for His creation — especially the treatment of our preborn babies who are unwanted — I believe that He is giving us a window of time to turn back to Him. God is love[16] but He is also righteous.[17]

If we look at 1 Corinthians 13:7, which was quoted at the beginning of the Preface of this book, we can see what great love He has shown us, considering our treatment of human life. Our country has continued to support and normalize abortion for decades, even though God's Word is clear in that He desires us to protect life. Would a loving God expect otherwise? He wants to save all lives.

> For God did not send the Son into the world to judge the world, but that the world might be saved through Him. — JOHN 3:17

Jesus went to Calvary, died, and rose again out of His great love for us.

> "Who was delivered for our offences, and was raised again for our justification" — ROMANS 4:25

We should always run to Him who will receive us in His love. It is the souls of those who live past the age of accountability (whatever God has determined for them) that we must pray for, while they still have time to accept Jesus as their LORD. When any of us leave this earthly sphere, we move on into life eternal, but our eternal destiny depends on whether we choose the wide or narrow path while we are alive and are still able.

Our God never changes, and Jesus is the same yesterday, today, and forever.[18] He always stands for truth and love. He is always ready to forgive and share heaven's blessings. I love the poetic feel of Psalm 85 as written in the King James Version:

Surely his salvation is nigh them that fear him; that glory may dwell in our land. Mercy and truth are met together; righteousness and peace have kissed each other. Truth shall spring out of the earth; and righteousness shall look down from heaven. — PSALM 85:9-11, KJV

Anything we have ever done wrong can be covered by the blood of Jesus. He sacrificed His life for us on the cross. He was the Sacrificial Lamb. In the Old Testament days, a perfect, unblemished animal was required as a blood sacrifice. Jesus came and took that old system away and brought us into the age of grace.

"Behold the Lamb that taketh away the sin of the world," were the words that John the Baptist cried out just before He baptized Jesus in the River Jordan.[19] Sincere repentance and belief in Jesus Christ and His work on the cross saves us from our sins for eternal life in glory! We must believe in our hearts and speak with our mouths that Jesus Christ is Lord:

> that if you confess with your mouth Jesus as Lord, and believe in your heart that God raised Him from the dead, you will be saved; — ROMANS 10:9

None of us have lived a perfect life and how wonderful it is that we can call on the LORD! It is sad, however, that some of those in power, political places and others that have access to popular platforms seem to know very little about God's righteousness and salvation. Let us face it — we all need Jesus!

Beatitude 7: "Blessed are the peacemakers, for they shall be called [daughters and] sons of God" (Matt. 5:9).

Life suggestion: Plan for the future of your ministry. If you are a Christian who advocates for life, not everyone in your church or family is going to agree with you. You may not have help and so must be particularly strategic in seeking alliances and perhaps, financial support in advancing pro-life work in your immediate community.

<u>Life suggestion</u>: If you are pregnant and wish to keep your baby, against the desires of others close to you, keep the peace for the sake of your baby. Do not argue. No one can force you to have an abortion. You may want to seek help from various agencies and your church or pregnancy center for medical and financial resources. Do everything you can to preserve the health of your baby. Be prayerfully diligent.

Chapter Eight

Hope and Forgiveness

As for me, I have hope. — Psalm 74:1

God's Restorative Power in Broken, Childless Women

Already mentioned is the importance of Biblical genealogies. Even though the genealogies of the Bible were traditionally listings of the male lineage, in the genealogy of Jesus we find five important women. For the most part, they had no worldly importance, but it was their brokenness before God that is highly significant. They emerged from their tragedies victoriously through the grace of God and His redemptive love.

Ruth, the Moabitess, lost her husband and was left childless. Her people descended from a union steeped in the sin of incest between Lot and his oldest daughter.[1] Ruth left her pagan land, where child sacrifice was practiced and followed her mother-in-law, Naomi. By committing herself to the God of her deceased husband's people and obediently following Naomi's instructions, she was blessed with marriage to a Godly Hebrew man, Boaz. The Hebrews were prohibited from marrying Moabites,[2] but God extended His grace. Her faithfulness saw her through. Ruth became the great-grandmother of King David, and an entire book of the Bible is dedicated to her story.[3]

Tamar lost her first and second husbands, who were brothers, to death. Their father Judah, by law, was obligated to give her another of his sons to wed. When he failed to do so, Tamar disguised herself as a prostitute to become pregnant by her father-in-law. It was trickery but he admitted he was in the wrong. It was his duty to give her a husband so that she could have the blessing of a child. In reading the dark story of Tamar, it is difficult to believe that the line of the Messiah would come through her and Judah, but God's grace prevailed. As the Bible says, she was "with child by whoredom." She gave birth to twins, one of which was Pharez, who was in the ancestral line of Jesus! [4]

Rahab was a Canaanite prostitute in Jericho, a place of idolatrous sin, but she bravely sheltered the Hebrew spies Joshua had sent out. Her new faith in the one true God led her to protect these men. Her life was spared in the battle at Jericho. Although the Bible called her a harlot, she was redeemed by the grace of God and married Salmon, of the house of Judah, who was one of the spies. She gave birth to Boaz, who married Ruth, thus putting her in the royal family line from which our Savior was born.[5]

Bathsheba was called for by King David to sleep with him. David then had her husband killed to try to cover up his moral failure. As punishment for adultery, her first baby born of that marriage was taken to heaven, but God gave her another son in her marriage to David — King Solomon.[6] She was redeemed, and a bad situation became transformed into a marriage.

Mary, the mother of Jesus, as one highly favored of God, was made pregnant with child by the Holy Spirit. She could have suffered shame in her pregnancy as she was not yet a married woman, but she trusted God. She was the willing vessel to birth Jesus Christ, the Savior of all the world.

These stories reflect the glory of God and His mercy, transforming power, and goodness to restore broken lives. He will do the same for any of us, including childless women who became medically sterile because of abortion.

Reflection: What would have happened if the Messiah, our LORD Jesus Christ, had been aborted? Mary was a virgin, but would abortion have helped her to be spared the embarrassment of being pregnant without being married? If abortion were available to her, what do you think she would have chosen? What would have changed?

A Letter of Hope from the Heart of an Old-time Sunday School Teacher

In the days when it seemed the people of America walked more closely with God, a certain Mrs. Passmore, a Sunday School teacher in Hammonton, NJ, and a dear Christian lady, wrote to my great-grandmother, Emma, in the time of her greatest need. When Emma was about seven months pregnant with my grandfather, her youngest baby girl became extremely ill and passed away. The postmark on the envelope is dated December 11, 1891. Great-grandfather Joshua was a South Jersey cranberry broker and farm manager. In those days that meant living in the woods, far from a town. They were far from medical help and other people, especially in the late fall and winter when the farm trade slowed down. Part of Mrs. Passmore's letter read:

> *Mrs. Norcross had told me the dear little one was gone, but the day Belle told me how she was swollen, I felt there was hardly a hope left. And from that day I have prayed that her sufferings would be as little as the dear Father thought best, & that when the hour came He would help you all bear it.*
>
> *I wanted to write you then but did not want to alarm you, because there is always hope while life lasts. I have copied some lines for you, which have comforted others, & I trust will do the same for you. You are a Christian, & know where to look for help . . .*

Mrs. Passmore wrote more words of comfort and copied some lines of others, one of which is this piece, "written by Helen Hutch Jackson on the death of her own loved baby":

Lifted Over

As tender Mother's guiding baby steps,
When places come, at which the tiny feet
Would trip, lift up the little ones in arms
Of love, & set them down beyond the harm:
So did our Father watch the precious child,
Led o'er the stones by one, who stumbled oft
Myself, but strove to help our darling on:
He saw the sweet limbs faltering, & saw
Rough ways before us, where my arms would fail,
So reached from Heaven, & lifting the dear child,
Who smiled in leaving me, He put her down
Beyond all hurt, beyond any sight & bade
Her wait for me. Shall I not then be glad,
And thanking God, press on to overtake?

When times are desperate and it seems no other soul is there to help us carry the burdens of life, we may say, as in the words of the old song, "Where could I go but to the LORD?" In this lady's time of desperation, God allowed her great insight into how the Father lifted her dear baby girl into Heaven, where she would wait to see her momma again on one sweet day. She found hope in that truth.

> Looking for that blessed hope, and the glorious appearing of the great God and our Saviour Jesus Christ — TITUS 2:13, KJV

The word "hope" in the original New Testament Greek is a word that means "an assurance." Jesus is, assuredly, the answer to life's every problem. Today we may say we "hope" we may get the job, or the assignment, or whatever is important to us, but with the word comes lingering doubt. **The Bible tells us that Jesus is the assured answer and the only Hope for all of mankind.**

All Babies Are with the LORD

I believe that all babies and preborn babies who have lost their lives are with the LORD. Scriptural confirmation of this can be found in 2 Samuel 12:23. After King David and Bathsheba lost their first child, David expressed confidence that he would see him again when he said, "I will go to him, but he will not return to me" (KJV).

Young children and babies, although born with a sinful nature, are innocent and have not lived enough to be taught the things of God. While we all need salvation to enter Heaven, the LORD is merciful. In His mercy, He prepares a place for those who are not allowed to live their normal life spans because of Satan's wicked devices. Our merciful Father would not condemn innocent infants to an eternity without His loving presence. The Apostle Paul said, for Christians, to be absent from the body is "to be at home with the LORD."[7] Satan desires each soul. That includes our children, but we do not need to fear their eternal destiny. When babies die, they go to a land of Glory and Light. We know that their souls are safe. Remember at the beginning of this book, I shared that the LORD told me that the babies of abortion are safe with Him.

As Christians, our spirits immediately go to heaven when we pass over from physical death.[8] The unsaved spirits go to Hades (Sheol, in the Old Testament) until after the Millennium Reign of Christ when they must stand at the Great White Throne of Judgment. The resurrected unsaved will find their eternity will be in the lake of fire with the devil and his angels, which is called the "second death."[9] We will all be judged. At the Judgment Seat of Christ, we believers will be judged separately for our deeds done in the body (2 Corinthians 5:10) and will receive rewards based on our works. (Please read 1 Cor. 3:11-15 and 4:5.) Believers will not be condemned (Romans 8:1). Many Christians work so hard at evangelism because we do not want to see anyone in hell! Those who are not telling everyone about the great mercy of

God and the love of Jesus need to start sharing! We do not want to be "ashamed before him at his coming" (1 John 2:28 KJV).

Abortionists cannot take away the eternal lives of these infants; if it were possible and there was money to be had from it, they surely would. How can I defend that statement? I do not need to. A person who has no moral standing in saving or preserving the earthly life of an infant cannot be very concerned about anything that happens with that baby. I believe that all babies and children, as well as mentally underdeveloped adults, have not reached a place of responsibility for their eternal destinations. They are not yet accountable to God for their choice of salvation. Their souls already belong to Him. God, in His mercy, allows everyone time and room for understanding. Luke 12:48 explains the concept of God requiring much from whom much is given, but not so much from those to whom little is given. We do not understand why God allows some babies to pass on to Him. That is one of the questions that will be answered for us on the other side of eternity.

Is God Capable of Making Mistakes?

The spirit of Herod also discriminates against the less-than-perfect because it has no compassion. This spirit, working through people, deceptively seeks to destroy what may seem useless. This spirit glorifies self and selfishness. In this modern era, babies with congenital problems, which are not genetic, are singled out in the womb for termination. Parents who feel they are not up to the task of caring for a handicapped child are given the option to abort. This is deception about the purpose of life.

We need to consider if we were put on earth to put our own best interests forward, or those of others. The Bible says that God created us for His pleasure. He takes no pleasure in our selfishness but rather in our selflessness and our open giving.

We need to understand that God allows challenges in our lives. Hard times give us opportunities to grow beyond immaturity into a place of peace and confidence in God. Many of the children born with disabilities have given those that are caring for them a new capacity to love and nurture that they never thought they had. When I worked with disadvantaged and troubled children, I found a deeper ability to love those who may, on the surface, seem unlovable.

You may have heard it said that God does not make mistakes. That is true. He created the Garden of Eden as a place of purity and perfection. The devil tried to destroy Paradise because of his own pride and will. Sometimes people are convinced of the devil's lie that God is mean and will then blame Him for things that they cannot personally control. We must remember that many birth defects are simply the result of living in a fallen world where creation was marred by the original sin in Eden. Others are caused by medical malpractice, automobile accidents, drug, and alcohol abuse by the parents, etc. These things occur within the realm of what God allows but it is never His intention to do harm to innocence. At these times, we may ask God, "Why?" Often, the answer lies on the other side of eternity, but we need to put our trust in Him. Our Father in Heaven knows all our cares.

When coping with the stress of caring for a handicapped person, it helps tremendously to ask the LORD for His strength. I had to do this when I was the sole caretaker for my father, who had slipped into a declining condition with Alzheimer's disease. He had "Sundowner's," a condition that causes a victim of dementia or Alzheimer's to become sleepless and aggressive at night, beginning around the time when the sun starts to go down. I barely slept for more than fifteen or twenty minutes a day for over a year. He rarely slept and I was the single mother of teenagers. I also had to guard the door because he was prone to wander. Sometimes, caring for a helpless person can become a spiritual battle but God can ease the difficulties and give us emotional peace. I know very well the difficulties as it somehow fell to me to have full and partial care of four elderly people until they passed.

Jesus Christ, our LORD, calls us to lay our burdens down before Him. He will exchange our heavy cares for an easy load. In the old days, the yoke was a wooden farm implement that would lie across the shoulders of the beast of burden and would carry the weight of the farm tool, like a plow or tiller. Two beasts of burden may be yoked together. Jesus calls us to trade our heavily burdened yokes for His that are easy and light. He said:

> "Come to Me, all who are weary and burdened, and I will give you rest. Take My yoke upon you and learn from Me, for I am gentle and humble in heart, and YOU WILL FIND REST FOR YOUR SOULS. For My yoke is comfortable and My burden is light." — MATTHEW 11:28-30

The first sentence in the previous passage is the Vision Statement for our church. Jesus wants us to know that if we give our troubles over to him, our load may not go away, but He will carry our hard and heavy problems. Some things on this earth are too hard for us to deal with alone. It is when we learn to give everything over to the LORD that we will learn to fly unfettered by life's troubles.

Our Imperfections and Handicapped Babies

We know that King David was not perfect. The Bible records his victories, his righteousness, and his failings as well. We cannot count the many thoughts God thinks of us! King David wrote:

> Thine eyes did see my substance, yet being unperfect and in thy book all my members were written, which in continuance were fashioned, when as yet there was none of them. 17) How precious also are thy thoughts

unto me, O God! How great is the sum of them! —
PSALM 139:16,17, KJV

We are living in an imperfect world, and nothing will be
perfect until Jesus comes again, but God loves each one of us
and thinks of us constantly. This is a good reason to talk to
Him all day. Paul tells us to pray "without ceasing."[10] Not one
of us has been born perfect. Some have greater and/or
different problems. We do not have the authority of God to
take the life of one who does not measure up to our standards
of perfection. This is a dangerous precedent and a slippery
slope. Just how perfect must we be so that we may earn the
right to live? We need to do what we can to make life better,
more tolerable, less painful, and to show more compassion; we
are given the task to strive to do our very best in this world.
The Bible also tells us that there was only one that was perfect
and that was Jesus. We can never measure up to His standard
of perfection without Him. We all need a Savior. God, in His
mercy, allows us time to get things right spiritually, no matter
our imperfections. By His grace, He gives us a place to live
beyond our natural lifespan in a place of glorious beauty. He
offers us the opportunity of Eternal life with Him, through His
Son, Jesus!

**When babies are aborted, abortionists are placing
themselves on a level with God, deciding who may live
and who may die. Have they been ordained as the
givers and the takers of life? Are they to judge who
may live and who may die based on convenience and a
warped standard of perfection?** Jesus said about the
woman taken in adultery, "He who is without sin among you,
let him first cast a stone at her."[11] I ask, which of us is perfect
enough to judge as to whether to commit the life of an unborn
baby to death?

It is possible that a severely handicapped child might be
allowed in our lives to teach us how to love without limits.
Does God the Father not exhibit limitless love to each of us?

We all have handicaps — physical and mental. We live in a fallen world. There are different kinds of imperfections and imbalances. Not one of us will get through our lives without problems, and that is okay. We grow spiritually through our trials as we learn to lean on the goodness of God.

Problems

Others I have known have encountered very serious medical obstacles in their children's lives. They have held on to God to get through each day. One of my sons was born with an undetected heart defect that was about to kill him, but God intervened and led us to a wonderful doctor. This is life in a fallen world. Nothing is perfect on this side of eternity. There are going to be hardships along the way. Who are we to say what problems we encounter, that God will work out for the good? We should not concern ourselves with physical perfection but with holiness. He may use the hardship He allows in our lives to grow us into a more holy perfection, as we take our grief to Him. If it were not for my hardest trials, I would not have the spiritual strength and courage that I have today. As the old saying goes, "I'm not where I'm going, but I'm not where I have been." Thank you, Jesus! Grief and trials give us an opportunity to see what Jesus will do when we feel powerless.

Is Life Only for the Privileged and the Perfect?

Should we have the power to eliminate the imperfect? If we, as a nation, allow babies to be aborted because of imperfections, where do we draw the line? Every human life is a gift given by the Giver of Life, with whom there is no shadow of turning. Our Father God is the giver of every good gift, which comes from above.[12]

> God created man in His own image, in the image of God He created him; male and female He created them. — GENESIS 1:27

Our country's family sizes began to drastically shrink with the

"Baby Boomer" generation. It seems as if having children is becoming more and more like a trip to a department store. First, we check our pockets. Do we have enough money? Next, we check our calendar. Do we have the time? Are we able to pay for maintenance? What about colors, sizes, and the ability to store information? Gene selection is being experimented with now and there are people who want to utilize this science. Why can we not just simply accept the blessing of a child from God — a gift of His choosing?

Is it only right to bring children into the world when our bank accounts are large, our homes are full of furniture, and our employment is assured? If our parents and grandparents thought that way, many of us would not be here. It is right to plan well for our offspring, but many of us were born to parents who were just starting out and had very little. I had a crib and a bassinet as a baby, but I do not think any less of someone whose first bed was a padded bureau drawer. My parent's first house was so small that guests literally had to sit on top of the kitchen sink when eating dinner!

Many of our early ancestors had log cabins and dirt floors when they pioneered this land. The settlers out West had sod homes until wood could be purchased. Sod was dug out of grassy mud and buffalo dung. How many people today would be willing to work that hard, using sod as a building material, to create new homes for their families? Both sets of my grandparents never had an indoor bathroom. Since we lived nearby, my sister and I and all our cousins grew up that way when we were at our grandparents' house, which was often. We drank water out of a pitcher pump. We were happy! We had great childhoods! Life is what we make it. Many of us who lived through the materialistic 1980s learned from our culture to lust for wealth. We yearned for bigger houses to live in with our smaller families. Larger families of generations past could only dream of the modern, large homes we have today. We are living in abundance, yet many of us do not even recognize it. We have the ability today to choose many kinds of lifestyle options.

Our choices have also expanded in reproduction. I recently saw an internet advertisement in which a woman seeking "the perfect family," with equal distribution of the sexes wanted to exchange her "healthy female embryo" for a male one. They already had a girl, but they also wanted a boy. She wanted to direct the course of her life and family. She wanted to play God. It is good to be proactive in one's life but there are things best left to the One in charge.

One might even say, "We don't want a baby with defects!" There are those who are fanatical about having the perfect child, but God gives us challenges in our lives. Many parents and caretakers of children born with disabilities have found within their hearts a new, deep capacity to love and nurture. We learn. We grow. As I grow older and become more experienced with disadvantaged and troubled people, many mentally and emotionally, I find an ever-growing and deeper ability to love those who may, on the surface, seem unlovable. We need to try to look at people with God's eyes. Here is a privilege — to love.

Less Than Perfect Circumstances with Amazing Outcomes — Illegitimate Children

Every child is created in the image of God and is, therefore "legitimate." The child who is born to unwed parents is not at fault. Below are some surprising instances of children born to single moms, who became famous because of outstanding ability:

Jenny Lind, the "Swedish Nightingale," was one of the most gifted opera singers ever to have lived, but her parents were an unmarried schoolteacher and a bookkeeper.

Steve Jobs, the co-founder of Apple, was given up by teenage parents and raised by adoptive parents.

Leonardo da Vinci was only raised by his peasant mother until the age of five but lived the rest of his childhood with his wealthy father and grandparents.

William the Conqueror, who unified France and conquered England in 1066, was the product of an illicit relationship between the son of Robert 1, Duke of Normandy, and a tanner's daughter.

Billie Holiday, an American jazz singer, was the daughter of unwed, teenage parents.

Tim McGraw, a famous Country music star, was the son of the famous Philadelphia Phillies baseball relief pitcher, Tug McGraw. His teenage mother was a waitress in Jacksonville, Florida, and raised Tim in Louisiana.

Eartha Kitt was fathered by the White son of a South Carolina plantation owner who raped her Black mother.

These are only a few examples, and I am sure you know many others in your own family and circle of friends.

Unwanted Children

Today's abortions are sometimes gender-selective, especially in other countries where having a male baby helps the family economically. In China, children have been rationed in forced abortion policies for nearly four decades. In India and China, male children are usually preferred over female, as males are expected to help support aging parents. Males now dominate the population in these countries, making it difficult for men to find wives. In some parts of India, a female child is said to be a curse. China and India are dangerous places to be female as many baby girls are killed in the womb and even newborn girls are even killed by their families. Forced abortions and sterilizations often occur without the use of anesthesia. The

United States is also experiencing some gender selection. I have read of incidents where parents have selected the sex of their child and aborted those who were not of the desired sex. Every nation that welcomes abortions is a nation separated from God.

Communism and China's One-child Policy

Forced abortion and even infanticide have been common in China for decades because of that country's notorious "one-child" policy. Recently China moved from a one-child policy to a two-child policy for certain citizens and now allows three. It is still illegal for an unmarried woman to have a baby. If a couple is married traditionally, but not by the Chinese government, they are not considered legally married.

Female genocide is still being practiced in the country, even though females are vastly outnumbered by males. It is not usually the women who make the decisions to do gender-selective abortions. It is often the husbands and the families. The despair of living with the memory of forced abortion will follow the women who were victimized all their lives.

Sadly, there are proponents of this extreme policy in the Western world. This view belongs to some who believe the world is overpopulated. I once read an article espousing that view. When I began to read the entire piece, I thought it had to be a joke or a parody of communism. Much to my dismay, the writer wrote genuinely on the virtues of the one-child per family rule. I was under the illusion, apparently, that even non-Christians in the West believed this policy to be barbaric. It made me more aware of the fact that we are living in evil days.

Christians in China, who were never given the ability to worship freely, are now even under more scrutiny and danger. We must realize that Communism, and its sister, Socialism, will never allow us the freedom of religion that we were guaranteed in the First Amendment in our country. Not everyone believes in freedom. These political ideologies disallow the freedom of choice and moral free will. We must pray to free all those under communist and socialist oppression.

The United States is moving closer to full socialism and eventual communism. That we are even in a moral place in our country where partial-birth abortion is debatable is an indicator of how far we have declined spiritually in the past one hundred years. An indicator of our openness to godless communism is that fifty years ago, killing a baby while part of its living body was already out of the womb would have been deemed unthinkable!

Killing human life, at any stage, is always indefensible. Some people believe in a zero-population rate, even to the point of mandatory abortion. Many environmentalists believe that every living creature, except humans, should be preserved. They believe that abortion will keep the population rate down, which will somehow be better for wildlife. We need to pray and lovingly seek God's guidance as to how best to minister to those environmentalists so that they will understand the importance of a baby's life over that of plants and animals.

When a government like China rules our child-birth rates, we will have lost all our rights as citizens and will no longer be living in a free nation. Look for more insane ranting of this "one-child policy" vein in the future in this country. The problem is that the noise starts out small, but the volume grows.

We need to be aware of global conversations. There is always the threat that those from other countries, as well as ungodly voices from within our own country, will have an undue influence on our legal system. The United Nations has been very aggressive in trying to institute abortion in countries that resist and loathe it. Our basic human "right to life" is at serious risk as this evil rhetoric from the vocal few travels out of the

USA and other countries that devalue life, into lands where family and children are seen as blessings. Recently the United Nations expressed concerns that many of our states have been passing new laws limiting abortion. Instead, they should be pleased that we are working to advance the human rights of babies, not only in the United States but also around the world. The United Nation's values are not based on an understanding of God's Word.

Why We Need a Born-alive Protection Act Until We End Abortion

Remember that even after Roe vs. Wade is overturned, life issues will still be left to be decided by individual states. Each state needs a "born-alive protection act." When Rome ruled the known world, it was uncommon to find a Roman family with more than one daughter. Both abortion and infanticide were widely practiced. As mentioned before in this book, unwanted babies were left out in the elements to die of exposure. During excavations, there were many babies found in the sewers of ancient Rome, where they had been disposed of because they were an inconvenience to the family. The fall of the Roman Empire was no accident. While there were other mitigating factors, I truly believe that its decadence and lack of respect for God and man led to its demise. We are on the same track as the Ancient Roman Empire in America today, leading to a sure case of national demise if we do not return to our LORD God.

The following verse speaks of infanticide by infant exposure:

> "As for your birth, on the day you were born your navel cord was not cut, nor were you washed with water for cleansing; you were not rubbed with salt or even wrapped in cloths. 5) "No eye looked with pity on you to do any of these things for you, to have compassion on you. Rather you were thrown out into the open field, for

you were abhorred on the day you were born —
EZEKIEL 16:4,5

Rubbing with salt and olive oil and washing with water were all sanitary procedures and standard care for a newborn. God was speaking of the compassion he had for His people and was alluding to their helpless condition. Similarly, many aborted babies who survive abortion are left unattended, uncared for, and unloved. They are left to die with no comfort, which is why we need a Born-Alive Abortion Survivors Protection Act. It would help to end infanticide in those states that hold onto abortion rights, continuing to kill babies in the womb, after the demise of Roe vs. Wade. Some babies live through the ghastly experience, only to die of lack of love, neglect, and exposure. At the end of this book is a long letter, written by a friend of mine who is an abortion survivor.

The prophet Jeremiah speaks to us even today and tells us that the LORD forbids the shedding of innocent blood. He forbids any deed, which takes advantage of the ones who are vulnerable in society:

> Thus says the LORD, Do justice and righteousness, and deliver the one who has been robbed from the power of his oppressor. Also do not mistreat, or do violence to the stranger, the orphan, or the widow; and do not shed innocent blood in this place. — JEREMIAH 21:3

Reflection: There is a practice called "selective abortion," which happens in cases where there are two or more infants in the womb. The parent chooses how many children will be born. What could be the prolonged effects of selective abortion? What will the child who survives think of the situation where they survived but their parent(s) chose to kill his or her sibling(s)? Will the parent reflect negatively upon the decision in the future?

Spina Bifida and Down Syndrome

There was a twenty-one-week-old preborn child, I read about, whose parents had opted to abort him because he was diagnosed with Spina bifida. This is a birth defect that damages nerves because part of the spine is left exposed when the spinal bones do not completely close to form a circle, as they should. Even though this condition is more treatable than in the past, with operations available in the uterus, the parents of the twenty-one-week-old chose to abort. In a disastrous set of circumstances, the abortion procedure failed, and the baby survived enough to cry for an hour in his mother's arms until he was dead. This baby may have been saved. I have known of people that have lived their full lives with Spina bifida, although it is very painful.

There was another baby in the news with the same condition. This baby was operated on in the womb and is doing beautifully! The country of Iceland brags that it is nearly free of Down Syndrome kids. This is because most people in Iceland elect to abort those babies. The United States is not too far behind that record. I remember having to have a test for Down Syndrome when I was pregnant with my last child. I did not want to test but my doctor's office insisted on an amniocentesis. I did not understand why because I told them that I would not abort if there was a problem. Later, I found out that the test has the risk of miscarriage and other problems, and I was upset that they had put my baby at risk when I had already told them that I would not abort. I think there is a serious moral problem in a country where abortion seems so reasonable and acceptable in the medical community.

Three Reasons Why It is Wrong to Abort a Child with Physical Handicaps

1. The taking of any innocent life, a life just like yours and mine, even with known physical problems, is still murder.

How many handicapped adults are thankful for their lives despite their handicaps?

2. Parents that take "the easy out" are robbing themselves of the chance to grow in the strength of the LORD. When we are faced with life's strongest demands, we may grow by leaps and bounds if we depend solely on the LORD. Maturity does not come without a price, but the reward is fantastic. Special needs children can help us to mature spiritually.

3. By aborting a baby, parents are robbing themselves, and God, of more love in this world. This world surely needs more love. When we are young, many of us lead a rather selfish life, given to pleasure-seeking and self-interests. It is not until we must care for someone else that our true capacity for love and generosity is tested. How big is a human heart? Can love ever be measured? There are no statistics — just experience and the testimony of others. There is a certain experience and journey of love, to which only the parents of children with disabilities can bear witness. Special needs children often help us to realize a love of which we never thought ourselves capable.

I have an inherited condition of migraine headaches. Many days are spent in horrible, torturous, nauseating pain. On my good days, I live life to its fullest. On my bad days, I am incapable in many areas. Yet, I finished college, held many jobs, ministered to many, have raised four wonderful children, and am helping to raise my grandchildren while running a full-time ministry. God is using me despite my life-long ordeal.

What if my mother knew ahead of time that she would pass her migraines on to me and that I would suffer even more than she had suffered because I have them much more frequently? Should she have aborted me for my life-changing disability? I have a sister who has them occasionally. Of my four children, three suffered from migraines. Two of them are healed, praise God, but the other is not. Still, I never once considered not having children because of the possibility of migraine showing up in them. As I write this, I am thinking of two of my darling grandchildren that have already experienced migraine. Where do we draw the line on just how able and healthy one has to be to be allowed to live?

There is a touching story in the Bible about King David. He once searched to bless a descendant of the House of Saul to honor Jonathan, his dear friend. Mephibosheth, a cripple, was found. David made sure that he was fed all his life:

> So Mephibosheth lived in Jerusalem, for he ate at the king's table regularly. Now he was lame in both feet. — 2 SAMUEL 9:13

We are living in an imperfect world, but God cares for each of us. There is no one that is a perfectly formed individual. If everyone were happy with their appearance, plastic surgeons and doctors would be out of business. If everyone were healthy, we would have no need for physicians and surgeons. There would be no death. The certainty is that we are living in a fallen world of imperfection. Death and decay are assured. With God, however, we may look forward to that glorious day when this world and our physical bodies will be restored to the beauty and perfection of Creation.

What if They Believe they are Gay, or Other than God Has Designed Them?

One time I was working as a substitute aide in the same classroom where I had previously taught Fine Arts. Two of the students, whom I knew well and loved very much, were self-professed homosexuals. They were both very large young men, seventeen and eighteen years of age. The classroom was isolated because it was in a separate building unto itself, away from the main school, attached to a few other classrooms on the other side of the building.

I was sitting at my desk, and the other teacher had just left the room when I found myself alone with these two students. I normally would not have been apprehensive, however, when the time came to change classes, instead of leaving as they should have, these two somehow seemed to be instantly at my desk in what appeared to be a preplanned verbal attack on me! They towered over me shouting at me that God hates gays! I never found out what they had been discussing previously or why they happened to come to me at that moment. It was not a subject I had ever discussed with them or anyone else at that school. I believe it was simply because they knew me as a pastor and a strong Christian. I always left my Bible on my desk as an open invitation for anyone that wanted to speak about the LORD.

I did not think that I was in any danger with these two boys, even though one of them had told me that he had previously stabbed a teacher in another school, but the situation was alarmingly out of control. I slowly rose, praying quietly for Godly strength and wisdom, as they both simultaneously continued their ranting and raging. I did not take my eyes off them and addressed them by name, even as they tried to shout over my voice, which I kept low and calm.

"God loves you both, and you both know that" I countered. "He loves you with an everlasting love and nothing can change that." Of course, I wanted to diffuse the situation, but I also wanted to remind them of God's abounding love for them. I continued, "He loves you enough to let you know that He wants His best for you. God's best for you is better than you can think of for yourselves. He wants what is good and right for you."

As I spoke, I walked to the door, and they walked along with me. "Would you like to pray?" I asked. They agreed. We, all three, bowed our heads in prayer and I prayed over these boys in the love of God. I asked God to help them with decisions and asked God to bless them in every way possible. We all said, "Amen!"

The next semester one of those young men called me over to him as he was sitting on a bleacher in the gymnasium. He was very excited to tell me about an amazing experience he had when he was alone, praying in his room. I was able to share with him that what he had experienced was the work of the Holy Spirit. I opened my Bible and showed him the mighty rushing wind in Acts Ch. 2. He had felt and heard that mighty rushing wind occur in his room, alone, with all doors and windows shut. He had been praying, "Lord, make me a pastor, make me a missionary, send me anywhere You want." He had totally yielded himself to God in that moment before the Holy Spirit wind blew. I told him, "The LORD let you know that He was there!" I had experienced that same mighty rushing wind when I was fifteen years old and at the time, I had no one to explain it to me. I was thankful that I had time with this young man to speak with him about the miraculous nature of God as joyous tears filled both of our eyes and ran down our cheeks. I felt God's presence and was thankful for that prayer I had shared with him many months earlier. I do not know how he is doing now, but I pray for God's best for him wherever he goes. Sometimes, as it did with me, Christian growth comes later in life.

If I had spoken to those two young men in anger, the day they verbally attacked God and me in the classroom, I doubt I would have heard about the miracle that occurred during the one young man's prayer time. Love builds the bridge. "Love never fails."[13]

> Beloved, let us love one another, for love is from God; and everyone who loves is born of God and knows God.
> — 1 JOHN 4:7

If you know your children would at some point identify as gay, would you still give birth? While "the least of these" cannot defend themselves, we are responsible to help the oppressed, the sick, the mentally challenged, the poor, the abused, and the preborn infant. We are responsible for our neighbors and that includes the "hard-to-love" ones and the preborn. We have the obligation to help people and save lives. Abortionists, mothers, or any other human beings, do not have the spiritual authority to take life. That authority belongs to God.[14] He can use any life for any purpose.

Reflection: How do we measure handicaps? Do we have the capacity to measure perfection? Can we really judge if one is perfect enough or not perfect enough to live, or die? We are not God. Which handicaps and genetic "defects" are acceptable or unacceptable? Do you or I really have the authority to make that choice?

Powerful Love and Our Great Hope

The reason that many non-Christians are conflicted, concerning abortion, is because their hearts are full of sympathy for the mother, as they should be. We all need to treat the mother-to-be with love and we need to "put ourselves in her shoes." As we explain to the mother why her baby's life has dignity, we need to respect hers. We also need to have love and understanding for those who are pro-abortion! They need our love too!

> If I speak with the tongues of men and of angels, but do not have love, I have become a noisy gong or a clanging cymbal. — 1 CORINTHIANS 13:1

I have read the words of a certain group of pro-life activists who shout and call the young women who come out of abortion clinics "murderers." With that approach, these young women are not going to listen to anything they say. That is not how we should treat people. Without love, we are just making a lot of noise! As Christians, we know that we need to present the Gospel in love because the power of the blood of Christ resides in the love, with which He shed His life's blood. We need to offer our love in the name of the One who represents all Hope — Jesus Christ.

> For God so loved the world, that He gave His only begotten Son, that whoever believes in Him shall not perish, but have eternal life. — JOHN 3:16

A true change of heart changes any sinner from one deserving of death to one deserving of life, by the power of the Living God.

> There is therefore now no condemnation to them which are in Christ Jesus, who walk not after the flesh, but after the Spirit. — ROMANS 8:1, KJV

Repentance

Jesus was concerned with the innocent, but He also preached a Gospel of repentance and forgiveness to the guilty, as we see here:

> Take heed to yourselves: If thy brother trespass against thee, rebuke him; and if he repent, forgive him. And if he trespass against thee seven times in a day, and seven times in a day turn again to thee, saying, I repent; thou shalt forgive him. — LUKE 17:3-4, KJV

In Jeremiah 32:38, we read ". . . And they shall be my people, and I will be their God: 39) And I will give them one heart, and one way . . ." God forgives His people. He makes this promise to those who call on the name of Jesus. In John 14:6 (KJV), we read of Jesus speaking to Thomas: "Jesus saith unto him, I am the way, the truth, and the life: no man cometh unto the Father, but by me." Everlasting life was promised in scripture long before Jesus was born as a baby in Bethlehem. Our God of grace and mercy had a plan to gather His people unto Him and not let them slip away. He sent Jesus to fulfill that plan. Is the Father calling you home today? May He give us each "one heart, and one way" which is unified in Him and His love!

Who Cannot Be Forgiven?

Forgiveness is available to all who seek the LORD. The only

unforgivable sin is denying the work of the Holy Spirit.[15] This would be denying the work of God. If anyone is fearful of having committed this sin, then they have a heart awareness and Holy Spirit conviction and so are not guilty of this sin.

Forgiveness is available to those who have participated, in any way, in the sin of abortion. Jesus tells us that at the end of the age, ". . . the righteous shine forth as the sun in the kingdom of their father."[16] How wonderful it is that even the most unrighteous may be forgiven of sins and become righteous. When Jesus began His ministry on earth, His very first words were, "Repent: for the kingdom of heaven is at hand."[17] Before He left this earth to ascend to His Father on high, some of His last words were, "All power is given unto me in heaven and in earth."[18] Jesus has the power to redeem your sins. In fact, He already paid the price. If you believe and accept His sacrifice on the cross then you do not have to pay the price of the sin with your own spiritual death. Jesus did that for you.

The Gospel of Jesus Christ is available to all. Among all the world religions, only Christianity stands alone on the death and resurrection of Christ. He was made sin so that we may be righteous in front of God when we believe on Jesus. The power really is in the blood of Jesus. The Apostle Paul wrote, "Christ died for our sins according to the scriptures,"[19] "and that he was buried, and that he rose again the third day according to the scriptures; 5) And that he was seen of Cephas (Peter) then of the twelve: 6) After that he was seen of about five hundred brethren at once; of whom the greater part remain until this present . . ."[20] When Paul wrote these words, many were still alive who had seen the Risen Christ!

The Holy Spirit is given to all believers to guide us in following the ways of God. "For to be carnally minded is death; but to be spiritually minded is life and peace."[21] This means that we must stop following the ways of the world and our own desires, but we should, rather, allow ourselves to be led by the Spirit of God into righteous thinking and actions. The Spirit of the Living God that dwells inside all believers in Jesus Christ, bears witness to this. True believers know that God loves us and delights in us in many ways when we live our lives in acknowledgment of, and obedience to, Him. Our delight, when living in obedience, is magnified when we realize God's magnificence! We can never experience true joy and peace until we come fully to Christ in true repentance and a turning from worldly ways. It is not something that can fully be explained. Experience is the best teacher! By living in the LORD's presence, and walking daily with Him, we can stop thinking carnally regarding abortion and choose, instead, to be Spirit-led.

We must remember that Jesus said, "Suffer little children to come unto me, and forbid them not: for of such is the kingdom of God."[22] This was a very important message from the Lord Jesus. We must have faith like that of a little child. 1 Peter 2:2, KJV tells us, "As newborn babes, desire the sincere milk of the word, that ye may grow thereby." 1 Cor. 14:20, KJV says, however, "Brethren, be not children in understanding: howbeit in malice be ye children, but in understanding be men." This means that we are to not only repent and be converted unto Christ, but we are to learn and grow in the Word, not forsaking our childlike faith and gentleness. Anyone can be set free from the guilt and pain of abortion by renouncing their sins and turning to the LORD of all. Redemption is real when we repent and reform. Jesus lives today.

> O give thanks unto the LORD; for he is good: for his mercy endureth for ever. — PSALM 118:1, KJV

The Hope of Salvation

The spirit that worked through King Herod tried to kill the Hope of Salvation, but he could not. The devil will never win. God had a plan. His Way is always higher than the ways of man and the ways of demonic forces. Jesus Christ is the Hope of all. With a confession of faith from the heart, we invite Christ to be the LORD of our lives and of our hearts. When we have the Spirit of Christ, which is the Holy Spirit, living inside of us, we do not lack strength or power in all things spiritual. Praise God!

The Good News is that Christ died for all. He came to set the captives free. Will you receive salvation today? Receive your freedom from whatever is keeping your soul hostage. Receive Jesus as LORD of your life and let Him take control. You will never want to look back! Prepare to be persecuted by those who do not understand your new faith but rejoice that your reward is great in Heaven! Those of us who are pro-life understand that we will be attacked for our Christian faith.

Beatitude 8: "Blessed are those who are persecuted for righteousness' sake, for theirs is the kingdom of heaven. Blessed are you when people insult you and persecute you, and falsely say all kinds of evil against you because of Me. Rejoice and be glad, for your reward in heaven is great; for in the same way they persecuted the prophets who were before you" (Matt. 5:10-12).

Life suggestion: Go to the LORD for your strength and peace. Every Godly person suffers persecution from the ungodly. Those who support abortion are often shockingly cold or vicious towards those who value the life of the preborn. If you are in a church, you may want to ask your pastor for suggestions and prayer. If you participate in a pro-life march or demonstration, go with a friend for protection. Sadly, I have seen many videos of violent pro-abortion activists taunting and physically assaulting pro-life activists. This is one of the reasons pro-life advocates shy away from making a public protest. We must remember — "Do not fear!"

Chapter Nine

Light Dispels the Darkness — The Church

. . . let us walk in the light of the LORD. — Isaiah 2:5, KJV

How Many Christians Have Abortions?

Because abortion is so prevalent in our society, we need to be prepared to address abortion in the church. Of course, in the same way, Jesus has offered us forgiveness, we need to offer our hands of help sensitively and lovingly to our congregations, on this matter. **I know many women who have had abortions who refer to themselves as Christians and attend church.** Many are sorrowful and repentant and have found God's forgiveness. Many are unrepentant but, I suspect, also sorrowful. We cannot ignore the fact that abortion is touching many Christian families. At the same time, we must honor the fact that God condemns taking the lives of infants.

> Moreover, this they have done unto me: they have defiled my sanctuary in the same day, and have profaned my sabbaths. 39) For when they had slain their children to their idols, then they came the same day into my sanctuary to profane it; and lo, thus have they done in the midst of my house. — EZEKIEL 23:38-39, KJV

Attack on the Pulpit

A very long time ago, I had the occasion to attend a Sunday morning church service when a young, professional woman loudly disagreed with the pastor as he was speaking from the pulpit! He had spoken freely about his pro-life position. I was astonished. I had never seen anyone confront a pastor before!

It was especially shocking to see this happen in public during a church service! A few weeks later, another professional woman, a teacher, verbally exploded in anger at the pastor about a short and truthful comment he made about a political candidate that she apparently favored, who was cheating on his wife. On this occasion, he was also preaching from the pulpit! When, in response, he mildly gave a brief, two-sentence defense of his position, her teenage daughter seemed to instantly turn into a bully and joined in on the angry, verbal assault against him. This woman and her daughter were usually kind and friendly.

After the service, she attempted to get my ear and my sympathy. I suppose she thought that I, as a young, modern woman, would agree with her. "I don't know why he has to talk about politics in church," she said disgustedly. Then she continued talking about his previous comment about abortion, a few weeks before. I defended him. "This is not about politics." I responded, "This is about God." I explained to her that God is the Creator of all life. When we talk about abortion it is primarily a "God issue" and secondarily political. I was not prepared to see the anger displayed by these two normally very nice ladies in that little country church.

I have been shocked and surprised at the number of venomous, verbal attacks by women of childbearing age, against those of us who highly value life. Just as the young women in that church seemed to have unnatural anger for a pro-life pastor, many women today have an unnatural hatred for those of us who are in the pro-life movement. These women proudly proclaim "the right" to end the life of any baby that is nourished in the womb. In certain progressive circles, it even appears to be the mindset that if a young woman has not had an abortion, she may be at a loss of having fully come into her own as a true feminist of the twenty-first century They want to see the practice of abortion protected without any thought of the protection of the preborn child. They are blinded to the fact that these little ones need protection. They ask, "Why?" To that, I can only say, "Why not? These are human lives!"

Be Known to Those Who Inherit Hell

Hell was originally created for the devil and his angels.[1] Anyone who refuses to accept the gift of salvation offered through Christ will find an eternal home with them. There are people in churches who have not yet accepted Jesus as their Savior. Isaiah 29:13 speaks of people who honor God only with their mouths but not with their hearts. Their church attendance and Christian practices consist of things they learned by tradition, but God wants our hearts.

We honor God when we give him our lives — not idle talk and actions. An evil spirit once said to a group of people who were trying to work in deliverance ministry, ". . . Jesus I know, and Paul I know, but who are ye (you)?"[2] These exorcists were exposed as ineffective and, in fact, were run out of the house hurt and naked! They did not have a personal relationship with Jesus. Imagine being exposed as a phony by a demon!

If we are empowered by our strong faith and obedience to do the work of Christ on earth, we will not need tee shirts to advertise ourselves. People will know our fruit and the devil will know our damage. As far as the subject of baby's lives, we, the church, have not been fulfilling our job of sharing the true meaning of the Gospel that Jesus came so that all might have life, and that abundantly!

If we clearly advocate for life, people will not be so quick to compromise with the world's views but would align themselves with the Word of God. **Our culture has devalued the sovereignty of God because many of our churches have slid into the deception of too often relying on rationalism.** To be rational is good. To rationalize away faith will lead to heresy, spiritual darkness, and powerlessness.

There are modern churches with modern worship times that compete with God. Instead of allowing room for the glory of God to enter, they create smoke and fake glory cloud effects. Fancy lighting tricks and the like sometimes inhibit the true light of God from entering the hearts of worshippers. If the Glory Cloud of the Spirit of God enters the room, how will we see Him? We need to stop playing church and be the church. We need to be known in Hell as disturbers of the agenda of Satan.

Power in the Blood

There are some churches and preachers that preach "another Jesus."[3] These preachers deny and devalue the reality of miracles. God is considered "cool," but He is no longer Sovereign in these churches, which are compromising with the secularism of the world. The reality is that many churches and their lack of solid Biblical teaching have contributed to the great slaughter of preborn babies in America today. Jeremiah 33:15 tells us that Jesus will "execute judgment and righteousness in the land." We need to be aware of what God says about the matter of life. Until we all get back to the Bible and are educated with a knowledge of God's Word, this madness will continue.

The blood on the abortionists' hands and in their lives can be covered by the blood of Jesus if they will only repent! There is power in the blood of Christ. We need to preach the blood that saves and sanctifies. Bloodless teaching is powerless preaching. I once heard a choir director say that she did not like the songs that spoke about blood. Another young lady and I immediately started singing, "What can wash away my sins? Nothing but the blood of Jesus . . ." Always remember that life is in the blood.[4] Prayer warriors — do not fear as we come up against abortion. You are covered by the blood of Jesus. Perfect love casts out fear.[5]

Mary and Elizabeth Encouraged Each Other

As we examined earlier, after Gabriel delivered the news of her pregnancy to Mary, she ran to her cousin to share her joy, and they rejoiced together.[6] It has been said that there are no "Lone Ranger" Christians. Colossians 3:16 says, "Let the word of Christ dwell in you richly in all wisdom; teaching and admonishing one another in psalms and hymns and spiritual songs, singing with grace in your hearts to the Lord." In Luke 1, we see how two women who are related to each other have stronger bonds than their family ties because they are bonded in their joy in the LORD. Our greatest spiritual ties may often be found with our Christian brothers and sisters instead of with our natural families.

As we go about our daily business, let us be aware of the presence of God, His call on our lives, and the miracles with which He reveals Himself to us. As we witness these miracles, let us encourage each other in love. While a life filled with miracles is common to a Christian, it is also a life with much to overcome. In fact, there will be much tribulation in the life of a Christian. Let us stop concentrating on faults and failures and lift other Christians in prayer with words of encouragement and grace. Mary had companionship in her pregnancy with her cousin Elizabeth. They shared their good news of the expectancy of the births of their babies. Mary also had company in her grief; she was joined by other Godly women at the foot of the cross on which her firstborn Son, our Savior, Jesus was crucified.

Standing in Agreement — Christian Unity

Uniting in prayer over the holocaust of abortion is one way that the body of Christ can come together as one. In John 17:21, Jesus prayed for his disciples, "That they all may be one; as thou, Father, art in me, and I in thee, that they also may be one in us: that the world may believe that thou hast sent me" (KJV). It is imperative that we work together to advance God's

Kingdom on earth. In so doing, we are better able to help bring others to a saving knowledge of Jesus Christ.

We need to work and serve together, especially taking care to lift each other up. As we do this, we operate in the ministry of helps, as found in Acts 6:2-7 and 1 Corinthians 12:28. Those operating in this gift, in a very real sense, are often part of the glue holding the fabric of the church together. When all members of the church work in a spirit of unity, the Holy Spirit of God is more apt to flow with signs and wonders following. As I read the history of the church, it is evident that when the supernatural manifestations of God are witnessed, the church always grows. We have seen that false manifestations also sometimes occur because the devil does not like to stay out of the mix. We need to exercise discernment. True growth occurs, however, when people sense and see the real presence and power of the LORD. We need to come together and encourage those who often serve without much public acknowledgment. We know that the last shall be first in God's Kingdom.

We need to fulfill the commandment that Jesus taught us in Matthew 7:12, "In everything, therefore, treat people the same way you want them to treat you, for this is the Law and the Prophets." Denominational differences keep us at odds with one another. We are not always going to agree. The Apostles Peter and Paul had a disagreement until God revealed the facts to Peter in a vision.[7]

Reaching out across denominational lines will grow our love for one another. We need to come together in set times of prayer. Unity can be expressed in this way. I will never forget that it was the Catholic Church's passion for the sanctity of life that brought me to an awareness of the reality of babies being killed in the womb. No one has talked about it in any church I have ever attended. I talk about it.

How I Learned About Abortion from the Catholic Church

I remember the first time I ever heard the word "abortion" and the impact that it had on me. It was one of those life-changing moments. I was twelve years old and in my cousin's bedroom. She went to a Catholic School and the nuns at her school had given her an 8 1/2" by 11" black and white paper copy of a poster on the subject, which was hanging on her bedroom wall. I asked her what "abortion" meant. She explained it by saying, "That's when a mommy kills the baby when it is still in the mommy's tummy." I was shocked and deeply troubled. How could anyone do such a thing? I am thankful to the Catholic Church for the stand they so often take on issues concerning "life."

The subject left my mind for a while and surfaced later when I heard stories in high school. I am sure that you have heard the rumors about girls who had abortions, including gossip about whose boyfriend paid for whose abortion. The language was not compassionate. The word "abortion" had somehow become the subject of a whispered business transaction between girlfriends and boyfriends. Although they were not married, the trauma of abortion had intertangled them in what was their first major economic transaction. Of course, none of these tragic relationships that I saw lasted. They had been darkened by death. I remember being silently dismayed. What could have been loving, permanent relationships ended with the deaths of innocent babies.

Pastors

The cry for life needs to be bellowed from our pulpits because God is the Grantor of life and no matter what the quality, it is God-given and therefore sacred. We need to speak about this in our private conversations. When in the pulpit, we can word our messages well, so as not to upset young children. I am saying things in front of and to my children now, however, that

I never would have years ago. They are hearing terrible things elsewhere and as parents and grandparents, we need to inform them. At some point, they need to know that there are mothers and fathers that really do kill their babies. Parents can decide when their children can handle such information. Exposing the evil will help to destroy it. We must examine atrocity to deal with it properly.

Pastors and church leaders — let me encourage you to tackle this major and sometimes volatile issue. Remember that your Father will not fail you when you are doing His work.

> Be not afraid of their faces: for I am with thee to deliver thee, saith the LORD. — JEREMIAH 1:8, KJV

> And David said to Solomon his son, Be strong and of good courage, and do it: fear not, nor be dismayed: for the LORD God, even my God, will be with thee; he will not fail thee, nor forsake thee, until thou hast finished all the work for the service of the house of the LORD. — 1 CHRONICLES 28:20

Pastors also need to be in touch with their local pro-life pregnancy centers so that they will be equipped with good resources when the need arises. It is also good to connect with other pastors in their area concerning this issue. Preborn babies who die in abortions do not get a second chance to speak for themselves, but we Christians have been blessed with the ability to affirm and assert the importance of the lives of our most vulnerable. We must affirm the needs of a young mother, who is caught in the grip of confusion over an unplanned pregnancy. Pastors, you must cry "Life!" from your pulpits. The LORD God has allowed us to retain our freedom of speech in America! Let us use our freedom to advance the importance of heeding God's Word in honoring all life, or God will take our freedom away! It is already threatened. We need to share this important message in every congregation. We must eliminate our modern equivalent of infant sacrifice on the ancient altar of Molech. We must encourage and celebrate all life, as that is God's will.

My Experience with Adam and Eve

In the late 1970s as an art major at Rutgers University, I took one semester on the Old Testament and one semester on the New Testament as elective classes. My professor was a Methodist pastor. He was a gently spoken man and I was a naive and shy 19-year-old. We were a very large class, but I remember that he often singled me out by telling me to speak up when I participated because he could not hear me well. I regret that I was so timid and did not speak up more because he shook up my faith on some very important issues!

These classes were intense with information and our tests consisted of writing down our memorized classroom notes. I am not sure that the classes were designed to be theologically instructive but many things I believed about the Bible were challenged. On our very first day of class, we learned that our God had the same name as the false gods of the neighboring Canaanites because they were all named "El." It seemed to me that the professor was deliberately putting the One True God on the same level as false idols. It gave me a sickening feeling, even though at that point in my life I did not have a doctrinal understanding of deity or even salvation. I did believe in God and His Son Jesus Christ. We were taught that the story of Adam and Eve was made up about five hundred years before Christ by the Jews who were in Babylonian captivity; it was supposedly allegorical and meant to persuade the Jewish children to stay with their parents' religion instead of following the lewd Babylonian gods. Therefore, we were informed, that the story could not have been written by Moses. In my heart of hearts, I knew this was wrong! I had believed in Jesus since I was four years old, and I now know that I had the Spirit of the Living Christ living in me and rejecting these strange ideas. We were taught that there was not just one man of God that wrote the book of Isaiah but that there were three Isaiahs. We were also told that John the Baptist was an Essene, which would mean that he was a member of a mystical sect that lived in the desert and practiced baptism. While there are similarities, we were not shown the significance of the differences between John the Baptist and the Essenes, such as the fact that John's following was organized and that he had a unique and historic relationship with Jesus Christ. In these and many other topics, it seemed that the goal of the class was to take away any pre-conceived idea about the authority of the Bible. I had to write all this new and strange information down in my tests!

Most shocking and upsetting to me was what we were told about Adam and Eve. That was foundational and rocked my theological world! In later years, I discovered the truth that Moses was verified by Jesus as a prophet and the writer of the Pentateuch — the first five books of the Bible, which includes Genesis. Genesis begins with the story of Creation and Adam and Eve, as written by Moses. If verification of the truthfulness of Genesis by Jesus was not truthful and valid, then how could Jesus be valid? The whole of the Bible, including answered prophecies and His testimony, shows us that Jesus is Who He says He is — the Son of God, the Word made flesh, and Co-Creator as part of the Holy Trinity. The Trinity is the Godhead, which consists of God the Father, Jesus the Son, and the Holy Spirit. Jesus is Deity and God cannot lie. Many pastors have been taught liberal theology which has changed their Biblical lens of the world and has contributed to abortion being accepted in mainline denominations. It is heresy.

When Jesus Visited Me in the Night

I thank God that He allowed me a visitation by Jesus when I was eight years old. Like Thomas, I saw the Risen Christ. I did not feel the wounds in His sides, but I saw Him with my eyes, and He spoke to me. I had no room for doubting the existence of the Son of God. At the age of nineteen, I had never been truly educated in the Bible other than through simple Sunday School lessons. During my experience in these college classes, the Bible became a thing of great mystery! Rutgers was one of our country's first colleges, instituted as a place of education for our first ministers of the Gospel. The change in the belief of the Bible by our educators over the centuries is even causing doubt of the veracity of the Bible in young people who are attending seminary for training as a pastor. Later, when I first began walking seriously with God, He blessed me with books written by some of our greatest theologians across the denominational spectrum. They enabled me to refute all the things that disturbed me in my college Bible classes.

Responsibility of Watchmen and Watchwomen

God knew our gifts and calling before we did. **His plans for us stem from before our conception and His call on our lives is set while we are still in the womb.** God told the prophet, Jeremiah:

> Before I formed thee in the belly I knew thee; —
> JEREMIAH 1:5a, KJV

The prophet, Isaiah, said,

> . . . The LORD called Me from the womb; From the body of My mother He named Me. — ISAIAH 49:1

We honor God when we walk in the gifts the Holy Spirit has given us. As we disciple others, we should also take care to encourage them to minister to the body of Christ with them because it is a community concern. It is heartwarming to see bands of pastors from all denominations working together to reach the community. Pastors that are proactive in faith are the ones that give the most support in any situation.

As church leaders, we must always stand for the disenfranchised and this includes our children, and even adults, who have been the subject of physical, emotional, mental, psychological, spiritual, and sexual abuse. The trauma of abuse can only truly be healed by the touch of Jesus Christ as we minister in the Word.

Ezekiel 33:1-9 gives a stern warning to pastors about their responsibility to relay the truth of God's Word. It has been my experience that some pastors have gone over to the way of the world in objectifying reason over faith, and rationalization, over belief. Many pastors do not believe in Biblical miracles or the truth of God's righteous judgment. Ecumenicalism is a marvelous means of reaching the world with Christ but not when we back down from what we know is Scriptural. If at the altar of reason, we sacrifice our belief in the Deity of Jesus and in His miraculous virgin birth, then we have unduly compromised with the world. God is building His church through us and if we are obedient, "the gates of hell will not prevail."[8]

Intellectualism is often very good when paired with God-given wisdom. God created us with the intelligence to be stewards of our planet. It can be dangerous to our immortal souls, however, when we elevate our "head knowledge" over faith. Reason, without faith, is one of the problems that leads to aborted babies and women who are emotionally scarred. It is reasonable to say that a young woman cannot afford a baby. It is reasonable to say that caring for a baby will affect her schooling and her chance to lead a good life. It is faith on the young woman's part, however, that says, "God will get me through." He always will when we walk in faith and obedience.

Our faith is also reasonable because we know what God has done for us in the past. We draw upon our experiences where God has saved us so that we may look forward to seeing what He will do in our present circumstances! It is reasonable, then, to say that He will attend to any of our needs in the future. A lot of people like to say, "He did it before and He will do it again!" This is the message that we must share with young men and women that are facing an unplanned pregnancy crisis. As watchmen and watchwomen, we have a responsibility to share the full counsel of God and give warnings, when necessary. It will serve our young people better, in the end.

Blobs of Tissue and the Holy Ghost

A pastor's word is held in high regard by many and so the pastor's importance in "life issues" cannot be overstated. Many pastors today believe that abortion is a political issue or are even of the opinion that it is a "woman's choice" and are fearful of upsetting a congregation. They may believe the anti-science lie that a preborn baby is just a blob of tissue. There are many verses in the Bible that tell us that the Lord is our Creator and forms us in our mother's wombs. We were created with purpose and for a purpose. He would never make a senseless "blob of tissue," a phrase some still use as an excuse to abort a precious life. Every life has a purpose, even if we do not understand what that purpose is.

Pastors, please consider the following verse, which speaks of when John the Baptist was filled with the Spirit of God:

> For he shall be great in the sight of the Lord; and shall drink neither wine nor strong drink; and he shall be filled with the Holy Ghost, even from his mother's womb. — LUKE 1:15, KJV

We cannot predict when and where the Holy Spirit of our Lord may move.

> The wind bloweth where it listeth, and thou hearest the sound thereof, but canst not tell whence it cometh, and whither it goeth: so is every one that is born of the Spirit. — JOHN 3:8, KJV

Finally, I would like to add a verse that clearly shows that we human beings, unlike animals, which only have body and soul, are composed of body, soul, and spirit.

> And the very God of peace sanctify you wholly; and I pray God your whole spirit and soul and body be preserved blameless unto the coming of our Lord Jesus Christ. — 1 THESSALONIANS 5:23

Just when does the soul and spirit join with the body? If the Lord filled John with His Holy Spirit even before his birth, and we know that man already has a spirit before being indwelt with the Holy Spirit, and that there is no valid reason to think otherwise, then we can assume that God creates all three from the beginning. God created us in His image. "Our image," as you read below, refers to His triune nature. We are created in His triune image.

> And God said, Let us make man in our image, after our likeness: and let them have dominion over the fish of the sea, and over the fowl of the air, and over the cattle, and over all the earth, and over every creeping thing that creepeth upon the earth. — GENESIS 1:26

Pastors know that we cannot predict anything at all about what God will do except for the fact that He always moves in His great love, mercy, holiness, and justice. If we try to predict at what time and day life begins, other than the moment of conception, we are trying to be like God. Please pray with me for a peaceful solution and an end to the chaos and nonsense that revolves around the central, important issue of life.

> Follow peace with all men, and holiness, without which no man shall see the Lord — HEBREWS 12:14

Many are blind to the damage that devaluing life has done to our cultural and historic way of living in the United States. While not perfect, America has always been a beacon of light, goodness, and righteousness when compared with other lands. Look around and consider if the "right" to abortion has helped our nation. How many children, with a promise of great things, have died under the knife or in a chemical bath, by an abortionist? How many possible

Christian leaders or prayer warriors have been taken from the Christian army of love before they could take their first breath? Amongst the missing, was there even a possible Christian President who would have done the will of God? Who have we lost? What have we lost?

Why I Left My Pastoral Ministry in a Mainstream Denomination

One year after I began pastoral ministry as Senior Pastor of a small and loving mainline denominational church, I was moved to a wonderful, very large church in the same denomination to serve as Assistant Pastor. Both churches were a great blessing to me. I loved both congregations and while God helped me to accomplish a lot for the Kingdom in my short time in the first church, I was able to preach to many more in my second church. Four hundred came to at least one of the four services we held each weekend at the second church, and I felt privileged to teach two well-attended Bible study classes during the week. Both churches provided me with beautiful offices and my salary was great for only having served for two years. Everything was going fine.

There was just one problem. I was against the church's ambiguous stand on abortion and many within the church were radically pro-abortion. Money was being filtered into an ecumenical organization, the Religious Coalition for Reproductive Choice (RCRC), that actively promotes abortion here and abroad. Ecumenicalism is when a variety of religious organizations work in harmony with one another, which often can be very productive. In this case, it is dangerous to babies. Thankfully, long after I left, my former denomination's stand was changed by vote in a world general council meeting and the church officially reverted to a Biblical position, although this is being fought vigorously. Votes from more conservative representatives of the general world council are helping to keep the denomination in line with Biblical teaching. Most laypeople had no idea about any of this until a call for a real split in the church began last year over Biblical beliefs.

When I first got called by God into the pastoral ministry in that denomination, I had serious reservations, but I heeded the voice of God. I was aware that many in my denomination had shifted away from Biblical teaching, yet I reasoned that I could be a voice within the denomination. After all, God had called me, and I wanted to walk in obedience.

When I went to Pastor Licensing School, before I entered the pulpit, I almost had my world upended. It was held at a college, which was supported by the denomination at the time (although that is no longer the case). I remember how excited I was to have a chance to explore the library at that college. I love to study and had amassed quite a large theological library at home. In my heart, there was wonderful anticipation of the time I imagined that I would have studied in that library, but it was not to be.

On the night I expectantly entered the library, my eyes were immediately drawn to a large, life-sized metallic catastrophe of a statue that was standing in the rear right corner of the large room. I walked over to it and as I focused on the grotesque monstrosity, I saw a crudely written sign hanging around the bulging stomach of this human-like creature. The words on the sign sank my spirit. Stunned, I made my way closer to the corner to examine the sign to see if I was reading it correctly. The sign read, "Abortion Rights."

My head reeling, I walked back across the room towards the receptionist's desk when I saw another woman pastor who was attending school with me. She was about to leave. I admired her faith very much and I said to her, pointing at the statue in astonishment, "Did you see what's over there?" Her wide-eyed response was, "Yes! And wait until you see what's over there!" as she pointed in the other direction.

Before checking out what was "over there," I approached the counter in trepidation. "Can you direct me to your Christian book section?" I asked, thinking that as a Christian College there must be a vast array of Biblical books, perhaps in a separate room. I was pointed in the same direction that my pastor friend had indicated, when she had said, "over there." I walked to where I was directed and had another shock. The Christian book section was so meager that my library at home surpassed it in every way — content, quality, and size. (I had obtained all my books practically for free because of God's outlandish and generous miracles but I will share that testimony another time.) There was very little there for me to use to write my sermon assignment. That was not the worst shock. As I moved to leave, I noticed what was attached to the end of the bookcase with small pieces of transparent tape. It was a newspaper clipping, which featured two men embracing and kissing each other on the lips. There was a chair close by and I literally had to sit down, feeling as if the floor was being pulled out beneath me. The sign and the picture were obvious attacks on those of us who were there for Local Pastor Licensing School and read the Bible literally. Some of us believed in the Bible and the full counsel of God, but there were those attending who did not! I wondered if I should speak up, but to whom? I prayed and considered the situation. If I gave up, I would lose my opportunity to share Bible truths with many others. I reasoned that God could use me as a voice within the denomination. In the end, I listened to God, and He was leading me to stay.

For the duration of the classes, I kept my mouth closed except to those with whom I knew shared my Biblical values. I squirmed when one of our instructors taught us that when we prayed in front of a congregation, we should never call God "Father" as it might offend someone! I wondered what she would say to Jesus if she had the chance. After all, he taught the disciples to pray, "Our Father . . ."

Because I was elected by my class to lead the preparation of our final service in the college sanctuary, which was to be on our last night of class, I thought that some of the other pastors, many of whom were progressive, did not really know my literal understanding of the Bible or they would not have chosen me. I found out later that I was more transparent than I thought, in my Biblical views, at least to the pastor who was my group's main instructor. In my final review, he mentioned that he sat squarely on the fence when it came to liberalism versus conservatism. "I'm somewhat to the right of that," I said. "Oh, I know you are!" he replied. Then I recalled a conversation that I had with a young Korean pastor as we entered the elevator one day. He was sharing with me that he had been on the phone with a young lady back home trying to convince her, unsuccessfully, not to have an abortion. He and I had a short, but intense, discussion and I was so wrapped up in this subject, that was so near and dear to my heart, as well as in our mutual grief over the loss of the little one, that I hadn't realized my instructor was in the elevator until it was too late. He must have heard our whispers. While I was trying to be discreet in my Biblical worldview, so that I could get my license to preach, I still did not stand down in my advocacy for Biblical truth. How sad it is that I felt I had to be covert in my belief in the true Word of God so that I could be licensed in my Christian denomination.

We have allowed many churches to be ruled by the world rather than honoring Jesus Christ as the Head of the Church, as scripture says. Many churches today preach a "social gospel," aiding the needy, as we should, but neglecting the long-term care of eternal souls. We do not share the true Gospel when we ignore the Biblical teachings on repentance, Heaven, and Hell. Many churches have bought into the world's ways and the world has bypassed the church of true believers. Now we have come to the place where our young people favor the very things that they have been taught outside of our homes and it is all our fault! We have let it happen by allowing our children to be raised by societal norms instead of our own common sense and Biblical values.

Taking Every Thought Captive — Destroying Strongholds

Many of our churches are experiencing declining memberships. It is sad that many churches are being sold and turned into hoagie shops or historical societies. A dead church dishonors Jesus. The building is not to be worshipped, however. Some fall into the trap of allowing the building more respect than the congregation and the unsaved. My experience has been that when we reach into the community with the love of Christ, our churches tend to thrive. When we keep to ourselves and do not fulfill the Great Commission of going out into all the world,[9] we lose our energy and become stagnant. How can we expect the unsaved to act like Christians? No matter how nice they are, they still are open to the devil's direction because they lack the Holy Spirit of God. More Christians need to be taught how God gives them the ability to overcome sin through the Holy Spirit.

In some places, God's Word has been replaced with microcosms — feel-good phrases that wet the whistle but never quench the thirst for God and all that He is. We must get back to the Bible and start living out our witness and depending wholly on His Word. If we take care of God's house while following His Word, the doors will stay open. **The Christian church is the backbone of our country. If the back is broken, nothing can move. The Bible says that "judgment must begin at the house of God."[10]** God wants to purge His house of sin and so sometimes declining church memberships are a result of judgment. We cannot follow God straddling the fence of indecision.

> Does a fountain send out from the same opening both fresh and bitter water? — JAMES 3:11

We need to give our nation over to God to stop the divisiveness over abortion. We also have the situation that not many Christians understand that they have the Holy Spirit of God to empower them over sin. **Abortion is the largest scourge on the Christian church today.** We cannot call ourselves Christians and support the mass killing of preborn babies. The job of every Christian is to submit to the will of God. He gives us the resources to destroy the strongholds of abortion and every antichrist spirit.

> Finally, be strong in the Lord and in the strength of His might. 11) Put on the full armor of God, so that you will be able to stand firm against the schemes of the devil. 12) For our struggle is not against flesh and blood, but against the rulers, against the powers, against the world forces of this darkness, against the spiritual forces of wickedness in the heavenly places. 13) Therefore, take up the full armor of God, so that you will be able to resist in the evil day, and having done everything, to stand firm. 14) Stand firm therefore, HAVING GIRDED YOUR LOINS WITH TRUTH, and HAVING PUT ON THE BREASTPLATE OF RIGHTEOUSNESS, 15) and having shod YOUR FEET WITH THE PREPARATION OF THE GOSPEL OF PEACE; 16) in addition to all, taking up the shield of faith with which you will be able to extinguish all the flaming arrows of the evil one. 17) And take THE HELMET OF SALVATION, and the sword of the Spirit, which is the word of God. 18) With all prayer and petition pray at all times in the Spirit, and with this in view, be on the alert with all perseverance and petition for all the saints, — EPHESIANS 6:10-18

To evict the spirit of Herod, which is the spirit of abortion, we need to pray against every vain imagination and idea that is not of God. We must cast down every false idea that abortion is a woman's right. We must rebuke the lie that a preborn baby is not a person worthy of life.

> Casting down imaginations, and every high thing that exalteth itself against the knowledge of God, and bringing into captivity every thought to the obedience of Christ. — 2 CORINTHIANS 10:5

I Saw His Mugshot! We Must Be Careful to Vet

We also need to evict the spirits of pedophilia and incest out of America, as well as abortion. Child trafficking needs to be confronted in the spiritual realm. These people need Jesus, but we need to be vigilant in protecting our nation's children. Recently a large internet retailer was persuaded to stop selling child "sex dolls"! These dolls were relatively inexpensively priced at eighty-five dollars and had different and shockingly provocative poses and clothing. It is almost unbelievable that any of these things even exist, but we need to face the truth of the evil that pervades our nation so that we may bring the enemy down. Recently, while online I saw promotional details for a library drag queen educational program. The graphic sexual instructions for children were disgusting. The actual photos of the presenters, as could be seen on their personal web pages, were demonic. Subjecting kids to this kind of evil and confusion is child abuse. A recent movie was deceptively presented as sharing an important message against child exploitation. Instead, this movie sexually exploited young girls by featuring them in sexual dance routines and clothing. It also served to sexually entertain pedophile voyeurs.

Another problem is that the many websites and cellphone apps that are commonly available to children are popular tools for sex predators to lure children. Predators are EVERYWHERE. If your child has access to a smartphone, perverts are available at fingertip's length in the hands of your little one. They prowl online just as they prowl in the streets.

I recently talked to a man, during my travels, who was clerking at the front desk of a hotel in a Southern state. He said he was studying to be a Christian counselor and that he wanted to come to hear me preach. He also wanted me to commiserate with him about the troubles he was having. His marriage was going through a difficult time, he said, and he complained that his wife would not let him see their kids. He relayed that the stress of a possible divorce made him quit his job of being a gym and history teacher and that was why he was now working at a motel.

Something seemed "off" with him so on a hunch I looked up his first name, which was all I knew, but it was unusual. About seven newspaper articles came up on the internet, which were dated from last year. He is a sexual predator of children! I saw his mugshot! I believe the Holy Spirit was nudging me to see the whole story of this man. It is better to be informed than to be in the dark.

He had been arrested because of a police sting operation and was out on bond for meeting a child on the internet and for going to meet this "child" with the intent of sex. Eight different men fell for this trap — the "child" was a police officer! This was great police work! Not only did the articles say that the man in the motel was a married man with kids, a vice-principal, and a gym and social studies teacher, but he was very active in his church and community! I had been talking to a pedophile!

We must be alert! Someone may be targeting your neighbor's child or yours. The old-fashioned neighborhood watch is one of our best defenses to evil in our society. The police cannot be everywhere. We need to be vigilant about our own backyard and we should protect our neighbor's children as we protect our own. To this motel clerk, I would say, "You can come to hear me preach but you will be under surveillance. Do not think for one minute you will ever be out of my sight or the sight of responsible members of my church!"

Does he need forgiveness? We all do. Would I ever trust him near children? Never. We need to be so careful! One of the lessons learned here is that even if somebody claims to be a Christian, their claim may be false. Perhaps, also, they may be backslidden.

Evil spirits seek to destroy the promise of the future as they sicken our society. We must be very careful to vet all childcare workers in our churches. We must test the spirits. The spirit of Herod influences child abusers just as it works through promoters of abortion. When someone sexually molests a child, either physically or verbally, he or she is destroying that child's optimum future. Those who callously seek the destruction of children will burn in the hot fires of hell and will do a great amount of gnashing of teeth.[11] Those who allow themselves to be the vessels of evil, without repentance, will suffer the fate of this loathsome spirit.[12]

> Their feet run to evil, and they make haste to shed innocent blood: their thoughts are thoughts of iniquity; wasting and destruction are in their paths. — ISAIAH 59:7, KJV

Anyone who would entice a child to do evil is not following Jesus. In the same way, anyone who would approve of the death of an innocent preborn child is not following Jesus. God speaks strongly about those who would harm others.

> Whoever sheds man's blood, By man his blood shall be shed, For in the image of God He made man. — GENESIS 9:6

Decision

If we are to move on into God's heavenly home of love and bright glory, then each one of us must make the decision to walk the Heavenly highway, which is the Way of salvation with Jesus. The devil stalks each one of us, Christian or not, looking to see "whom he may devour."[13] He tempts each of us in the ways where we are the weakest. Our temptations will not injure us spiritually, however, if we remember where our strength lies. No matter what our weakness is, when we rely on Him and He strengthens us, God gets the glory. In 2 Corinthians 12:9, KJV, Paul says that God told him, ". . . My grace is sufficient for thee: for my strength is made perfect in weakness." Paul used this information practically, as we all should. Paul then said, "Most gladly therefore will I rather glory in my infirmities, that the power of Christ may rest upon me. 10) Therefore I take pleasure in infirmities, in reproaches, in necessities, in persecutions, in distresses for Christ's sake: for when I am weak, then am I strong." When we work through the strength of Christ, our strength is magnified. Without Him, we are nothing.

Prayer

We must take the time to meet Him in prayer as the body of believers gathered, in one accord, at Pentecost. Our travels in evangelism should always bring us back, with new believers, to the gathering of the saints. Meeting for prayers, singing, sharing, and expounding upon the Word is a part of the healthy life of the Christian. It seems today we are pretty good at singing and sometimes the preaching, but the gathering for prayer is hardly seen at all. The only way to bring the change that is needed for our churches, as well as for this country, is to wait upon the Lord, in one accord, with increased times of intentional prayer. When we wait upon the LORD, in earnest expectation of His divine Spirit, He will always show up.

Preborn babies need our love and commitment to their health, safety, and well-being. A great part of that commitment needs to be time spent in prayer. There needs to be a heart change concerning abortion and not just a legal change. As I like to say, "Change will not come just through legislation; it can only come through a praying nation." Those prayers need to be not only in our own time with the LORD but prayed in the church. God will respond to our praying churches and our praying nation. Christians need to continue to pray for the babies, mommas, and all of those who need Jesus.

This is how I often pray:

> LORD God! send Revival to your Church and to your nation! LORD, your arm is not shortened that it cannot Save! Rend the Heavens and show us Your glory!!! Turn the hearts of America! In Jesus' Name, Amen!!

Compromise with the World

Church, the days are evil, but we must remember to walk in holiness and be a pure church. God will hear our prayers as we walk in holiness while living in a place of cultural evil. There are those that would say that individual "human rights" supersede morality. **Without morality and a strong sense of decency, based on a biblical worldview, however, our entire society will collapse and slide into the sewer.** There are many who will say that it already has. This affects each one of us who is raising a family. One person's demands for "rights," which are against God's standards, tramples on the rights of each member of society who is struggling to hold on to the beautiful, Godly sense of family we have traditionally enjoyed in our country.

One day I drove through the downtown area of a once beautiful and historic city. There was a church on every corner! I pictured what it once must have looked like on a Sunday morning. In my mind's eye, I watched churchgoers, dressed in their "Sunday best," pouring out of the front doors of homes. I saw church doors opening and welcoming parishioners into the houses of worship as the sound of church bells filled the air. I am praying for an America that looks like that again.

We have let the secular world cultivate a strong culture of death. As the body of Christ, we need to cultivate the family of faith into a culture of life and invite others in. I am sure there are those who preach the truth in small hamlets where they may be under the radar, so to speak. We need to preach about the value of life as well as sin and judgment.

> Woe unto them that call evil good, and good evil; that put darkness for light, and light for darkness; that put bitter for sweet, and sweet for bitter! — ISAIAH 5:20, KJV

Reflection: *If a young lady were to approach your pastor or another church member in anguish over an unplanned pregnancy, how would she be helped? What resources does your church offer? Many mainstream churches refuse to support crisis pregnancy centers. If you are a member of such a church, perhaps you may want to pray about personally helping through volunteerism or donations.*

The Church and Masculinity

The culture around us is devaluing and denigrating masculinity. This is wrong. **It is the job of the Christian church to encourage young boys to grow into Godly men.** With fatherless homes being a leading factor in the delinquency of boys, even many in secular society will admit that boys need male guidance.

All children need to grow up feeling positive about the way they were created by God and the specific attributes that are generally either male or female. We know that males are physically stronger because they have more muscle mass. We know that women are often stronger emotionally. Why women are often able to handle hardships easier is a bit of a mystery to me. Perhaps we grow stronger emotionally because of the childbearing and childrearing processes. Perhaps it is because we are more encouraged to allow our emotions to show. The important thing to note here is that males and females are created very differently by our Sovereign God.

Toxic Masculinity?

The "buzz word" today, concerning masculinity, is the word "toxic." We hear so much about toxic masculinity that the concept has been normalized, but that phrase comes from the lips of Satan. It tends to demean and generalize all men. We can say that King Herod acted with toxic masculinity, but masculinity, as God intended it to be, is anything but harmful. By God's original design, males are usually larger and stronger and are therefore built to protect females. Even so, due to heredity and genes from different parts of the world, in America, we have a wide variety of sizes. I know men who have a physically short stature but who are large in God's Kingdom because of their spiritual strength and Godly character. It was a shameful day in Israel when Barak refused to go into battle unless Deborah went along. Deborah was a prophetess and the Judge of Israel, which was the top leadership position in the land at that time. Under enemy attack, she agreed to go along but warned Barak that the enemy would fall into the hands of a woman and the journey would not be for his honor.[14] The woman who was distinguished for extinguishing the enemy was Jael who struck a tent nail through their leader's temple with a hammer.[15] Judges 5:24 says, "Blessed above women shall Jael the wife of Heber the Kenite be . . ." (KJV).

Sunday schools need to teach about Jesus, but we need to stop making Him effeminate. Effeminacy is a sin.[16] Jesus was very strong. He endured scourging and His time on the cross with little to say. He gave no answers to his accusers in self-defense. He was a leader of men and women. Very manly men looked to Him for guidance. The Apostle Paul, while merely a man, had great strength. He walked the known world, endured severe beatings, and was shipwrecked, but it took more than that to kill the mighty man of God. We need to teach our little boys these things. We need to teach them how King David, as a boy, killed lions and bears in defense of the sheep he cared for before he killed Goliath, the Philistine giant, all with the help of God. My little grandchildren enjoy the following verse:

> David said moreover, The LORD that delivered me out of the paw of the lion, and out of the paw of the bear, he will deliver me out of the hand of this Philistine . . . — 1 SAMUEL 17:37

This verse shows children that God will always help them through the difficulties of life. We need to teach them the strength of Samson and the battle stories of the people of Israel who had to fight off enemies who sought to destroy them. I am not suggesting we teach them war, but that we teach them the Bible stories of defending one's home and nation. Boys rightly seek masculinity.

King Herod was not a protective or honorable man. He acted selfishly and violently as an aggressor towards — not the defender of — the weak. He did not protect his family but aggressively destroyed his own heritage. He left a legacy of death so that even he knew he would not be mourned at his funeral. He had others killed so there would be mourning in Judea at the time of his death! What a manipulator!

He's a Boy!

One day, when I was younger and my oldest son was not yet two years old, I took him for a walk in a park. First, let me share some background. He was a big, strong boy, and I was a "stay-at-home-mom" giving my firstborn all my motherly attention. His dad worked a lot of hours, often out of state, so we did not see him much. As a natural teacher, I gave him lots of lessons but was not too concerned with my son's "maleness" or sports or anything of that matter. By two, he not only knew the entire alphabet but also the name of every American President. One thing he did not know was guns. We did not have any in the house, and he never had a toy gun. The only television programs that I allowed him to watch were Sesame Street and Mr. Rogers.

That one memorable day, when we were walking in the park, my son noticed a certain stick. He was used to picking up sticks and stones and exploring with me in the woods, so that was not unusual. What was unusual was that, when he picked up this stick, he began to pretend to shoot it like a gun. It was, in fact, shaped like a big revolver. It was astounding. I really do not know where he would have seen one. He had never been left with a babysitter, and we were usually home and alone in those days.

I was not afraid of guns. My childhood home often literally had a gun in every corner, and I was a pretty good shot, myself, having years ago asked my dad to teach me to shoot when I was a teenager. For some reason, I had been trying hard to make my son the perfect child and to keep him away from every kind of violence. At the age of two, however, he looked like he was very familiar with guns, and he even looked like he had perfect aim. My ignorance got knocked out of me that day. I said to a friend who was with me, "He's a boy!"

The Pediatrician

Years later, when my fourth grandchild was born, I was in the hospital room with my daughter when the pediatrician came in for his first visit. As he examined my sweet little grandbaby, he made a remark that in the past would have seemed like just a social pleasantry or a remark in passing. He said, intensely, but with a smile, "He's a boy and you can't change that!" Then he looked straight at me.

His words hit me like a ton of bricks. It seemed like he was intent on making an important statement. If so, I knew what he was saying. I was stunned into silence as my brain tried to calculate why he made that statement. It seemed he was intentionally saying that he was against the current trend to make children "gender-neutral." How sad that we can no longer say "It's a boy!" or "It's a girl" without someone protesting what God has created! How sad that a pediatrician must deal with unbalanced parents that want to change their children's genders! How sad that there are pediatricians who are driven by perverted ideologies and money, to forever mutilate a child surgically with hormones and hormone blockers to change the child's sex! How sad it will be on Judgment Day for all who harm a child!

Godly Masculinity and Parenting

The church needs to change the culture instead of allowing the culture to change the church. When the world dictates the conscience of the church, the church loses its power and its potency. Pastors must stand upon the fact that God created two genders as His ideal for this world. The lies that the world spouts about this subject and other moral issues are the direct lies from the "god of this world," who blinds the minds of unbelievers.[17] We need to stop remaining silent in the fear of adversity.

Children have been taught by the media to disrespect their parents. Families pictured on television and the movies were once decent, but today's children watch depictions of other children making their fathers out to be laughingstocks, and they copy that poor behavior. There is nothing funny about demeaning men.

The welfare system has enabled fathers to shirk the duty of providing for their families. They are not expected to live up to be the men they were created to be. We know by the Ten Commandments that God ordains that we honor our parents:

> Honor your Father and your mother, that your days may be prolonged in the land which the LORD your God gives you. — EXODUS 20:12

This promises a special blessing of long life if one honors one's parents. Children cannot honor a father who is rarely or never present. Our culture has not encouraged the respect of parents and even has gone so far as to actively push euthanasia. These verses in Malachi tell us about a curse if there is not mutual respect between the generations:

> Behold, I will send you Elijah the prophet before the coming of the great and dreadful day of the LORD: 6) And he shall turn the heart of the fathers to the children, and the heart of the children to their fathers, lest I come and smite the earth with a curse. — MALACHI 4:5,6

We have been cursed because of a lack of true fatherhood and Godly male leadership. American cities are filled with violent street gangs. There are many adolescents craving a sense of belonging, and the violence is part and parcel of the package that a gang gives them. Many young ladies are also falling victim to the promise of the closeness that a "gang family" will give them and, without fully realizing it, the promise of love from a pimp pushes them into prostitution. Many males also become prostitutes with the promise of their next "high" from the drug at hand coming from the coffers of the pimps. The skyrocketing use of heroin and other drugs, despite the well-publicized dangers, tells us that something is deeply wrong in America. Fathers are not acting as true fathers in many homes. Broken homes or homes where fathers are addicted to drugs or alcohol often produce children who have problems with addiction, street crime, theft, and worse. Of course, the same is true for mothers and possibly more so. Young parents need to be guided to decide whether the false gods of Satan or the Living God will rule the house before they establish a home together. Joshua made a decision. He said, ". . . as for me and my house, we will serve the LORD."[18]

Women and Men Expect Less

Males brought up with no Godly leadership may not understand the honor and responsibilities of fatherhood. It is not always because they are selfish, although that does come into consideration, they are often not equipped to handle the full responsibility of manhood and manliness. They often have a lack of knowledge about Biblical roles in the home and in society. When presented with the news of a pregnancy, many become rebellious. After all, the culture has glamorized sex without commitment and responsibility. It has taught young men that sex for entertainment, without emotional involvement, is their right. They feel entitled to it without the bonds of the marital covenant. They sometimes exist in a culture where "self" is all that matters. Meanwhile, our culture has taught women to expect this degrading treatment as somehow "normal." If a woman expects less than the Biblical institution of marriage, a man may deliver less than he can, and should, give. This enables a man to fall into irresponsibility. For an irresponsible man, abortion is a wonderful choice. A man that manipulates a woman into abortion often finds intimidation is necessary to convince her. This scenario is very common. It is rebelliousness against the authority of God. We need to remember what the Bible tells us about rebellion:

> For rebellion is as the sin of witchcraft, and stubbornness is as iniquity and idolatry. — 1 SAMUEL 15:23

This is because, when we rebel, we manipulate in order to get what we want, and we ignore what God wants. Anything in the spiritual realm outside of God is of the devil.

The young man in this situation does not even realize that he is practicing witchcraft, but obviously manipulating a young woman into killing the life inside her is evil. If he is not a Christian, he will have no understanding. It is not even enough to simply tell a young man, "Man up!" Years of lack of guidance and manly encouragement cannot be fixed in one short imperative or even one discussion. The whole culture needs to change. Our young men are victims of a culture that does not encourage them to be men. They often do not have high expectations for themselves regarding honor and integrity. They have been taught to subdue their manliness so much that it interferes with their design of being the protector of the family, even though they are built larger and with greater bone mass and strength. This low expectation of manhood is all by the design of Satan. The church must help strengthen the male identity of men and boys.

The Male is the Protector

Once I watched my one-and-a-half-year-old baby son plow into the shins of my teenage son because he was lightly teasing their sister. My little one saw the situation as being of a very serious nature and went to his five-year-old sister's defense. Of course, we all laughed, but it gave me wonderful insight into my baby's male identity. I was very moved by his protective stance. This was not learned behavior; it was nothing he had been exposed to before then. It was innate and God-given. I was a proud momma, but really it had nothing to do with me. That was how God made him. That was his God-given response. I believe a lot of male children tend to push that innate protectiveness down because our culture is teaching them to stop honoring women. Many women get angry if a man holds a door open for them because the feminist culture teaches that polite action is somehow insulting. Many women feel that to be an honoring gesture. It is.

In this culture, women are encouraged to act in a more masculine way to get ahead in their careers. I once read an article that encouraged women to brag about their accomplishments even though that may seem unfeminine. The point of the article was that men very naturally brag, which often provides them with advancement opportunities in their positions of employment. I am old enough to remember when females broke into the newscasting field on television. They were encouraged to speak with deeper, more masculine voices in order, it was thought, to be taken seriously. I can remember the female broadcasters sounding very rough and unnatural. We need to encourage our nation's "daughters" in Godly femininity. The church needs to find ways to nurture and encourage Godly masculinity and femininity if we are going to stop the downward spiral of the destruction of the family.

Reflection: How many homes in America lack a father with a Godly moral compass? The moral compass of the father sets much of the atmosphere of the home.

Our God Restores

Our weak notions of what constitutes a Biblical family, and our moral fabric can be restored in America. God is so good and merciful. Although His children in the Old Testament were practicing the evil of the religion of their pagan neighbors in the days of Jeremiah, He still offered them restoration in the future — even after their impending punishment:

> Behold, I will gather them out of all countries, whither I have driven them in mine anger, and in my fury, and in great wrath; and I will bring them again unto this place, and I will cause them to dwell safely: 38) And they shall be my people, and I will be their God: 39) And I will give them one heart, and one way, that they may fear me for ever, for the good of them, and of their children after them: 40) And I will make an everlasting covenant with them, that I will not turn away from them, to do them good; but I will put my fear in their hearts, that they shall not depart from me. 41) Yea, I will rejoice over them to do them good, and I will plant them in this land assuredly with my whole heart and with my whole soul. 42) For thus saith the Lord; Like as I have brought all this great evil upon this people, so will I bring upon them all the good that I have promised them. — JEREMIAH 32:37-42, KJV

Three points out of this text that the Lord wants us to know are:

1. Nothing is too hard for God!

2. He will give us a heart for Him — one heart and one way. Jesus is the Way.

3. Even in His just anger for our sins, He stands willing and ready to forgive; that is His promise.

We need to allow our hearts to accept God's forgiveness, which He will give in response to our true repentance. Sorrow over sin will be rewarded with supernatural comfort because God will wipe away every tear.[19] In John 16:20 (KJV), Jesus says, "Verily, verily, I say unto you; That ye shall weep and lament, but the world shall rejoice: and ye shall be sorrowful, but your sorrow shall be turned into joy."

Let It Be About Love

Nearly one million aborted babies in the USA alone, per year, means nearly one million women in need of Jesus. When we turn our lives over to God the Father through Jesus, our LORD, and Savior, we realize that God is LOVE. The Holy Spirit will bring the truth and conviction of abortion when there is real repentance. He will also comfort us through, and with, the love of God.

We must remember we are NEW creatures in Christ, "Where there is neither Greek nor Jew, circumcision nor uncircumcision, Barbarian, Scythian, bond nor free: but Christ is all, and in all."[20] Christians belong to the family of God, and He is our Heavenly Father. We must all get along. Even if we have historically voted Democrat, Republican, or Libertarian it does not mean that we can carry hate in our hearts for anyone. If someone is "going under" because of sin in any way, he or she absolutely needs our sincere prayers. It is wonderful for sin to be exposed because that is when it can be checked and dealt with accordingly. If that one is a Christian, we must pray to restore that one. If that one does not know the LORD Jesus

Christ, then we must witness His love and God's mercy and forgiveness.

To move forward as a country under God, we must be a country about God and in Him, as well. All our sins were nailed to that cross at Calvary 2,000 years ago. Living in unforgiveness ignores what Jesus has done for each one of us — no matter our differences. As Christians, we are one in Christ. Remember the old song, "Jesus loves the little children, all the little children of the world. Red and yellow, black and white — they are precious in His sight. Jesus loves the little children of the world."[21] Pray for a move of God that unites believers as one in Christ Jesus, our LORD, and Savior.

Jesus prayed for our unity, and when He ascended into Heaven, He left us the Comforter, the Holy Spirit, to equip us for all good works. He enables us to love without question. 1 Corinthians 12:13 says, "For by one Spirit are we all baptized into one body, whether we be Jews or Gentiles, whether we be bond or free; and have been made to drink into one Spirit" (KJV). Our children and future generations may be blessed or cursed, as a nation, according to our acts of love today.

> Let nothing be done through strife or vainglory; but in lowliness of mind let each esteem other better than themselves. — PHILIPPIANS 2:3

In his 1738 hymn, "And Can It Be That I Should Gain," Charles Wesley wrote these words: "Amazing love! How can it be, That Thou, my God, shouldst die for me?"[22] When we reflect on the length at which our LORD, Jesus Christ, went to pay our sin debt, it is hard to fathom, but He died for each one of us. He died for those preborn babies, as well. He did it all for love.

It is an act of love to tell the girl who wants an abortion that God condemns the taking of life. It is love that drives us to tell the abortionist that God offers forgiveness of sins. It is love that carries the message of life. We cannot continue to sit silently by the wayside while the slaughter of the innocents continues. We cannot continue to lie to young women and tell them that it is their choice. We must not fear to speak out and stand up for Jesus. God is perfect love. Perfect love casts out fear.[23]

Loving somebody means telling him or her the truth about God's Word and helping to seek healing and restoration. Scripture urges us to speak the truth in love. Condoning sin is the most hateful thing we can do. The church in the US may splinter over this and abortion. Membership continues to shrink over these issues, while the more Biblically grounded churches overseas watch their numbers grow. Life is precious to those who survive! Life should be precious to all of us. The big question is — will America and the American church survive abortion?

Prophetic Message to the Church from Amos 3

In December of 2017, God gave me this message to share with the worldwide church:

"God is giving me this Word to deliver to the CHURCH of all of you who say you are Christians. Read Amos 3 and find out about the houses of ivory (v.15). You who live in palaces now will find your homes diminished to nothing if there is no change of heart.

CHURCH — while you decorate for Christmas and practice singing Christmas chorales, you are allowing God's innocent babies to be murdered in the safest haven of all — the mother's womb. A baby that should be nourished is being slaughtered in the time it takes to read this.

CHURCH — What are you doing about it?

You say you worship the Christ Child? You bring gold and frankincense and myrrh to the manger bed and yet cease to hear the crying of the babies as their necks are being slit?

Does this make you uncomfortable? It should!

"For they know not to do right, saith the LORD, who store up violence and robbery in their palaces (v.10)." The abortion industry is bloody and lucrative.

We, in America, have been given a reprieve of religious freedom. It is time to exercise this freedom and woe to them that hear these things and ignore them. Judgment is coming upon those who tolerate the violence against the innocent and who do not open their mouths to defend the voiceless.

Verse 11, "Therefore thus saith the LORD GOD; An adversary there shall be even round about the land; and he shall bring down the strength from thee, and thy palaces shall be spoiled."

CHURCH — will you continue to let the babies die and remain in defiance of God? Will you continue to participate in murdering defenseless children by voting into power those who seek to kill babies by calling abortion "a right"? If so, the judgment of verse 11 is nearer than you think.

CHURCH — the time to repent is now and the time to seek God's Glory is now. We must all line up together in solidarity as Christ-followers and protectors of the innocent. "Can two walk together except they be agreed?"

Revival and Turning Over Roe vs. Wade

There is currently a groundswell of praying Christians seeking an outpouring of the Holy Spirit in this land. Many Spirit-filled Christians are sensing this will happen. Some of us believe we are on the threshold of a great national revival, which I believe will affect our brothers and sisters to the North, in Canada, as well. I would like us to remember Canada in our prayers, as I believe we are spiritual sisters. Our foundations are very similar. Abortion also has a stronghold on their land.

As we pray, we are getting closer to the turning over of Roe vs. Wade. The year 2022 marked forty-nine years of bondage to legal slaughter. 2023 is the Jubilee Year for Life! In God's divine plan, we will see the return and restoration of the value of life and family! We must separate that year to the holiness of God in a special Jubilee Celebration!

> So you shall consecrate the fiftieth year and proclaim a release throughout the land to all its inhabitants. It shall be a jubilee for you, and each of you shall return to his own property, and each of you shall return to his family. — LEVITICUS 25:10

Please join me in praying that God will release the latter rain of Holy Spirit anointing[25] to bring in an end-time harvest of souls to the Kingdom in a Great Awakening. Please pray that the Holy Spirit fire will fall, that God will get the Glory, and that the latter rain will water us with the Living Water.[25] Pray that the fire will refine us, our impurities will be removed, and the pure gold of truth and righteousness will remain in each believer. Please pray that we will all have a new fiery passion for God and His will for us.

Jesus Lesson: _"You are the salt of the earth; but if the salt has become tasteless, how can it be made salty again? It is no longer good for anything, except to be thrown out and trampled under foot by men . . ." (Matt. 5:13)._

Life suggestion: _Salt is a preservative and stimulates our taste buds. Christians are responsible to preserve the word of God. As each of us lives out our Christianity, our witness should be incorruptible and appealing to create a hunger in people that will only be satisfied with a life in Christ. Salt is pure. Christians are called to the purity of holiness. We should live no other way. If we fail in our witness, men will indeed want to trample our Christianity underfoot and call us "hypocrites." We are of no use to the Kingdom when we exit the "Highway of Holiness."_[26]

Chapter Ten

Winning the Victory

Open your mouth for the mute, For the rights of all the unfortunate. — Proverbs 31:8

Marching for Jesus

The March for Life in Washington DC has been spectacular! Streets filled with energetic pro-lifers of all ages cause great excitement about the increasing number of young people who are advocating for life! We are raising a generation that is becoming more sensitive to the issue of abortion. We need to continue sharing the truth that all life has intrinsic value. We need to pray for and raise up a generation of spiritual giants who will take on the evils of our times. Hundreds of thousands walk this annual, historic march, often in freezing temperatures, so we know this country has hope.

Onward Christian Soldiers

One of my favorite songs, when I was a little girl, was Onward Christian Soldiers.[1] Perhaps it was a favorite of yours, too. I do not think I grasped the true depth of its meaning when I was a little girl. We had record players in those days and my mother had bought my sister and me some little yellow records, including a 45-rpm disc of that precious old hymn. I can remember us sitting on the floor and listening while watching the turnstile spin round and round as the needle etched out the precious, uplifting words, "Onward Christian soldiers, marching as to war, with the cross of Jesus going on before!" Sometimes, I sang along. I am glad to say that I still sing that old song and march along in my spirit.

We are in a spiritual war for the lives of God's babies, and we will not lose because the cross goes before us! The relatively new, annual Women's March in Washington DC a few years ago, purposefully scheduled a week before the annual March for Life, can be an interesting show. It was organized by those who hate the pro-life movement. While I am sure many attended with pure motives, those motives get lost behind contrived, demonic displays that do little to cause anyone to sympathize with their cause. Nothing screams louder that you do not want to be taken seriously than screaming obscenities. The Women's March looks like a painfully bad joke. It is an anti-life march mixed with heavy doses of anti-American ideologies. I do not know if it will continue.

> Do not be deceived, God is not mocked; for whatever a man sows, this he will also reap. — GALATIANS 7:7

When We Didn't March

Prayer was taken out of public schools in the early 1960s because one atheist, Madalyn Murray O'Hair, railed against the nation and won her case in the Supreme Court. No one did anything to stop her. The same situation occurred again with Roe vs. Wade. The church, again, was silent. This nation and the church now stand accountable for tens of millions of aborted babies.

This is what happened: against God's admonition in Ephesians 4:27, we gave "place to the devil" and we grieved the Holy Spirit of God. We allowed Satan to come in and take over territory that was rightfully ours. Being "politically correct" was a problem then, although not as much as today. Still, it was considered impolite to speak about politics or religion. Another problem we had in Christian churches was that we became complacent and were afraid to be out of step with the world. We gave up without attempting to battle spiritually. We cannot walk in bitterness because that type of heart condition will also give room to the devil. Rather, we should walk in faith, allowing God to fight our battles as we live obediently if we want to achieve the goal of saving the lives of innocent ones.

Why Do the Heathen Rage?

Those of us who deeply respect the sanctity of life have often been perplexed by the lack of concern of those who do not value life the way we do. We find it hard to understand why human beings cannot see the importance of preserving the life of all children — those already born as well as those who have been conceived but are still in their mother's womb. We wonder and are alarmed by those who promote abortion passionately and angrily. We witness indescribable violence in the streets and mobs of people screaming over God's plan for life.

What is the source of this kind of anger? What is the source of the venomous screaming and disrespect, complete with vile costuming and profanities that we see and hear from pro-abortion protesters? It is hard to understand why anyone would want to appear in public wearing vulgar hats and carrying vulgar signs and it is hard to comprehend the desire to kill babies in the womb. God showed me that we need to look beyond natural reasoning to get an understanding of why the abortion massacre continues in a seemingly civil society. We need to get a spiritual understanding of the people who are adamantly pro-abortion.

> Why do the heathen rage, and the people imagine a vain thing? — PSALM 2:1

The heathen refers to the ungodly nations and people that are plotting schemes that go against the truth of God, but their plans are in vain. These plots will fail. Even people that claim the name of Christian join these ranks. Hosea 8:7 says, "For they sow the wind, and they shall reap the whirlwind." God speaks of even His people following the foolishness of false idols (sowing the wind). In doing so, they will find they reap the whirlwind of God's judgment.

The source of their anger is demonic. It is only in the spiritual realm that the battle can be fought against this demonic anger. Reason has not made an impression on them, and they have no real understanding. Abortion is a tool that the devil uses to counter the good purposes of God. Anger and intimidation are weapons that abortion activists use against those who value life. I have personally felt the brunt of this anger and have been maliciously, and verbally attacked. Once, I was told an abortion supporter was donating $100.00 to an abortion clinic just because she heard that I was about to lead a small women's conference. I never let their anger take control. It is through prayer and the demonstration of God's love that we can finally change hearts and end the slaughter of almost a million babies a year in America.

It was shortly after the annual Women's March when we saw New York State government officials smiling and cheering for the death of babies when the vote passed that would permit babies to be killed after they are born. The circumstances where this would be allowed would be in the cases of failed abortions. These legislators will reap the judgment of God. There is no question that the Bible is clear on how He exacts vengeance on murderers. Amazingly, God is so forgiving that they can change right now and be free of their sin! I pray they will. That bill gives a wide pathway to abortion — even when the baby is perfectly healthy, but the mother is emotionally unhappy. If they do not turn back, God will give them over to their reprobate minds and their fate will be sealed. A reprobate mind is a mind that is depraved and godless.

> And even as they did not like to retain God in their knowledge, God gave them over to a reprobate mind, to do those things which are not convenient; 29) Being filled with all unrighteousness, fornication, wickedness, covetousness, maliciousness; full of envy, murder, debate, deceit, malignity, whisperers, 30) Backbiters, haters of God, despiteful, proud, boasters, inventors of

evil things, disobedient to parents, 31) Without understanding, covenant breakers, without natural affection, implacable, unmerciful: 32) Who knowing the judgment of God, that they which commit such things are worthy of death, not only do the same, but have pleasure in them that do them. — ROMANS 1:28-32, KJV

Other states are following suit, but God does not tolerate sin forever. At some point, He will turn us over to the deviousness of our own minds, in His wrath against ungodliness.

Babies in NY may now be killed by the mother for almost any reason, but when an abusive father kills the baby in the womb through violence it means he will no longer be charged with a felony because the baby is not recognized as a person, all the way to his or her birth. This miry pit just keeps getting deeper and deeper. What happened in New York was also attempted in Virginia. These are desperate acts by legislators because they fear that Roe vs. Wade will be overturned. I believe it will be and, obviously, so do the lawmakers.

We are now in a place where the evil of man's heart is being exposed through the desire to kill preborn babies up to birth and even by the endorsement of infanticide (allowing a baby to die after birth) if he or she is not wanted. Is it any wonder that, as a nation, we often feel God's distance? The ancient civilizations that allowed and encouraged infant sacrifice are all gone today. They have been replaced with new and modern approaches to infant sacrifice in the US and other countries. In the face of evil and ungodly ignorance, we need to stand firm with joyful and loving patience:

> Strengthened with all might, according to his glorious power, unto all patience and longsuffering with joyfulness. — COLOSSIANS 1:11

A thorough reading of Romans Chapters 1 and 2 gives us a deep understanding of righteousness and the judgment that is a result of deliberate sin. Even those who do not know the laws that were written by God are responsible before Him because He has written a moral law on every heart.[2] No one has an excuse to abort a baby. We all know, deep inside, that it is wrong.

As much as God loves us, the Bible is clear on all life issues. He is also clear about the judgment that we shall receive, should we choose to ignore His commandments. The penalty for infanticide was harsh in the Old Testament laws. God takes killing infants very seriously:

> . . . 'Any man from the sons of Israel or from the aliens sojourning in Israel, who gives any of his offspring to Molech, shall surely be put to death; the people of the land shall stone him with stones. — LEVITICUS 20:2

God is Longsuffering and Has Had Patience with America

Our country has moved so far from God that it is a wonder He has anything to do with us! We are drowning in illegal drugs. Any choice that we make to deliberately change our senses is a gateway to the devil and this includes being drunk or high on any drug. We are exposing our children to pedophilia by flagrant and open sexualization of children through media, including music, clothing, and even classes in school that legitimize promiscuity. Children are exposed to things that are way beyond their years and level of comprehension. We also allow convicted pedophiles the freedom to harm children again as they leave prison because of light sentences. We are the first people in the history of the world to legitimize what God calls an abomination through same sex "marriage." Instead of loving the confused enough to take the time and patience to help them through their personal torture, we lazily condone the sin. There are media reports of pastors that gather to "bless" abortion clinics. The Bible tells us, however, that, "The wise man's eyes are in his head but the fool walketh in darkness . . ."[3]

God is not done with America yet. By looking at the Nation of Israel, we can see that God remained faithful to those who are called by His name. They had a relationship with Him. He chastised them by allowing their dispersion over the years, but He allowed them to return home seventy years later as prophesied.[4] Miraculously, in 1948 He allowed the Jews to fully return home as Israel was restored as a nation. Although they sinned and turned from God, as shown in the Bible, God was patient. The King James Version uses the word "longsuffering" for His patience towards us.[5] I like that. It illustrates how God looks at His erring children. Loving parents can identify with "longsuffering" patience!

Preach the Gospel in Love — Speak Words of Life

The LORD's Army must spread the Gospel across America and to the ends of the earth, ensuring that all who are unsaved hear the Good News of salvation. Whatever we do in the name of the LORD, we must do prayerfully in love. As we minister to mothers-to-be and fathers-to-be, we need to speak words of assurance and understanding. The enemy of our souls does not offer love, but false fulfillment, or even a false love in the treachery of hidden hate.

We can also access the supernatural power of God's holy angels to surround us, protect us, and free us from harm. In Acts 5:19, the angel of the Lord even opened the prison doors for the apostles. The angel also delivered a message to them from God:

> Go, stand and speak in the temple to the people all the words of life. — ACTS 5:20, KJV

When God frees us, He does so to speak on behalf of His kingdom. We cannot keep the Gospel to ourselves! It is meant to be shared, for Jesus came that all the world would be saved.[6] Salvation is free to all who will accept. We cannot be politically correct and remain silent because of fear of others. Peter said, "We ought to obey God rather than men."[7] We must compassionately share with women who have had abortions. After an abortion, a woman needs healing, and the best answer for an empty womb is the empty tomb. Jesus can show everyone how to live life fully because He came so that we can be reborn and live new lives. These women can be resurrected in their faith and hope for the future.

Reflection: A few years ago, there were horrific forest fires in the state of California that swept through many communities, destroying thousands of homes, and killing many. Hospitals and many residential centers had to be evacuated. I read a story about a young woman who had just given birth at that time. Hospital employees placed her newborn in her lap and began to evacuate them as the deadly fires moved rapidly. It was common knowledge that many had already been killed elsewhere in these fires. It was reported that this brave young mother, still awkwardly hooked up to an IV, told those evacuating her to leave her behind and save her baby if necessary. She survived, but I will never forget this story of a mother's love. I do not know if she is a Christian. I do know she is a living testimony to the selflessness that God has placed in every mother who has not had maternal instincts broken. What would you do? I believe if that baby were a day younger, there are many who would consent to abort that baby.

Be Filled with the Spirit

It is humbling to know that we can help others achieve the "abundant life" that Jesus came to give us. To be effective in our pro-life work, we must be filled with the Holy Spirit, and not wine.[8] In the battle between good and evil, we need to stay on the winning side and allow no room for sin and debauchery. Ephesians 6:10-18 directs us in putting on the full armor of God for spiritual protection. Jesus came to set the captives free; as His disciples, we are to help others get free from bondage. As an army of believers, we are responsible for spiritual defense and spiritual warfare. We are an army that battles in love and for love.

The "sword of the Spirit" is the Word of God and not a physical sword that draws blood. The only blood we deal with is Jesus's shed blood on Calvary to cover all our sins. The "shield of faith" includes no physical barriers but is a defense system built solely on belief in the LORD. In the Roman army, the shield that each soldier carried was interlocked with the shields of the soldiers next to him, in front of him, and behind him, over their heads, as a covering. Christians need to lock their shields together in unity and faith and stand as one against the onslaught of the enemy, as we have a covering by the blood of Jesus as our protection. I pray that you are excited as I am to know that God gives us the tools to defend ourselves in spiritual battle while we stop the enemy from destroying life. **As we go up against the spirits responsible for killing preborn babies, we need to cover everyone involved — the preborn babies, the parents, grandparents, and even the abortionists — in prayer.** It is wonderful to hear about abortionists and those in the abortion industry that have turned their lives over to Jesus after repenting of their sins.

Be Prepared

If anyone should come to you, your church, or your organization for help with a crisis pregnancy, are you prepared? We need to be proactive in preparation for all the needs we may encounter in a church or social organization. If you are reading this book, God may be preparing you to spearhead a group that will minister to these needs. Perhaps there are members of your church or group that are willing to receive volunteer training at a local pro-life pregnancy center.

Anyone who comes to your church or organization looking for help needs deserves privacy. In the following types of cases, however, proper authorities must be contacted:

Talk of suicide.

Minors who may be "runaways."

Possible child abuse, including sexual abuse.

Possible dangers to others, such as threats.

Statutory rape.

These are all situations where common sense and the law dictate that reports be quickly made. In statutory rape cases, state laws vary so you must be aware of those particular to your state.

Strength through Humility

Back in Chapter 3, we discussed that Beatitude number three is, "Blessed are the meek: for they shall inherit the earth."[9] This does not make sense in the way that the world often teaches about success. Being "meek" will not get one too far, in the way that most of us think both of success and the word, "meek." In this teaching of Jesus, however, the word "meek" seems to mean a humble strength that we can only draw from God. Unger's Bible Dictionary says that "meekness' is "first a meekness with respect to God" and "the face of men."[10] Unger also holds that it is an "inwrought grace of the soul." Meekness requires a work of grace by God, then, in order to face, with resilience, those who will taunt or ridicule us. There is a gentle strength in meekness, but it is not weakness.

Even in the face of false science and hateful pro-abortionists, God wants us to draw upon His strength to be strong but gentle in the face of opposition, while not surrendering the cause of life. There are two ways to exercise meekness when it comes to the issue of abortion:

1. We meekly submit to God's will, concerning the issue of life versus abortion, when we are personally involved, because He is God, and we are His people. If we face the devil as he tries to convince us that abortion is the right "choice" for a given situation, we should draw upon the strength and peace that only God can give and direct the issue back to His will according to His Holy Word.

2. As we face opposition — some of which is violent — from pro-abortionists about life matters, we still can draw upon the strength and peace of God. While speaking in love to those who do not understand this, we must draw upon the strength of love for others, through God's love, to be meek when others come against us.

To sum up — we must love God first and then our neighbor, even when that neighbor is a pro-abortionist! It is by prayer, love, logic, and the power of the Holy Spirit that we will help win them over to "life." We must exercise meekness while defending the lives of the preborn.

> AND YOU SHALL LOVE THE LORD YOUR GOD WITH ALL YOUR HEART, AND WITH ALL YOUR SOUL, AND WITH ALL YOUR MIND, AND WITH ALL YOUR STRENGTH.' "The second is this, 'YOU SHALL LOVE YOUR NEIGHBOR AS YOURSELF.' There is no other commandment greater than these." — MARK 12:30-31

Power to Win in Jesus' Name

It should be obvious that assembling with the saints[11] should not be neglected if we want to be effective in helping deliver this nation from the widespread sin of abortion. In Matthew 18:19, Jesus says, ". . . if two of you shall agree on earth as touching any thing that they shall ask, it shall be done for them of my Father which is in heaven." There is power in united prayer. There is power in the assembling of Christians together:

> Let the word of Christ dwell in you richly in all wisdom; teaching and admonishing one another in psalms and hymns and spiritual songs, singing with grace in your hearts to the Lord. — COLOSSIANS 3:16, KJV

We cannot go down without engaging in the battle. The body of Christ will win every battle because victory is ours in the name of our LORD and Savior, Jesus Christ. Consider the following passage:

> And Jesus came and spake unto them, saying, All power is given unto me in heaven and in earth. 19) Go ye therefore, and teach all nations, baptizing them in the name of the Father, and of the Son, and of the Holy Ghost: 20) Teaching them to observe all things whatsoever I have commanded you: and, lo, I am with you alway, even unto the end of the world. Amen. — MATTHEW 28:18, KJV

When Jesus was preparing His disciples to move out into the world as His apostles, He began by stating His authority: ". . . all power is given to me in heaven and earth." The next thing He said was, "Go ye therefore . . ." Jesus was saying that He was leaving, but first had to commission His servants to continue His work. The power that He had, He bestowed upon them. Jesus still bestows this power upon every believer.

This is the message from the Cross: Christ died for all! He also can empower anyone at any time to bring the message of freedom in Him to the masses. **Any one of you may hear the voice of God calling you to stand up and be heard for your generation. The eyes of God are upon us now and always. Who will take a stand to free the little ones from death?** As believers in Jesus Christ as the Son of the Living God, we also may bind and loose the evil spirits of this world. He gives us the authority in His name to bind strongmen, cast out demons, and release people from demonic oppression. In John 16:7, KJV, we learn that when He was preparing the disciples for His departure, He told them that it was good that He was departing because if, ". . . I go not away, the Comforter will not come unto you; but if I depart, I will send him unto you." The Comforter here refers to the Holy Spirit of God, who indwells every believer. In Acts 1:8, Jesus said, "But ye shall receive power, after that the Holy Ghost is come upon you" Sometimes we need to unwrap the Old English of the King James Bible. The previous verse simply says that after the Holy Ghost (Spirit) comes upon you, you will receive power from above. Philippians 4:13 tells us that we can get through any situation with Christ: "I can do all things through Christ which strengtheneth me." Christ does strengthen us, but we must not forget that He also calls on us to exercise our authority and power in Him. In Luke 10, the seventy that Jesus sent out returned in surprise:

> And the seventy returned again with joy, saying, Lord, even the devils are subject unto us through thy name. 18) And he said unto them, I beheld Satan as lightning fall from heaven. 19) Behold, I give unto you power to tread on serpents and scorpions, and over all the power of the enemy: and nothing shall by any means hurt you. 20) Notwithstanding in this rejoice not, that the spirits are subject unto you; but rather rejoice, because your names are written in heaven. — LUKE 10:17-20, KJV

Believers need not fear the devil or his devices! As we go out into the world in pro-life work the devil will always be on the prowl seeking to devour us. He or his many minions will be seeking to trip us up. Focusing on Jesus will keep us grounded in the work. Focusing on the work of Satan will bring us down.

If we are wearing the full armor of God as found in Ephesians 6, we will never go down in failure while engaging in spiritual warfare. We can only be defeated if we lose our focus on Jesus. When Peter focused on Jesus, in faith, he walked on water. When he allowed himself to get distracted with fear, he quickly sank.[12]

Ministering to Young Mothers with Love and the Spiritual Gift of "Helps"

The church needs to get more involved in helping young mothers and dads both financially and spiritually. This could mean offering a young man opportunity for employment. "The ministry of helps" is essential to the great body of Christ. In this type of ministry, we reach out to others with the love of Christ. Those who operate in this office, however, are often undervalued in the order and workings of the church. It means to be anointed to help others. Those who are helping others, though, also need to be helped and encouraged.

> And God hath set some in the church, first apostles, secondarily prophets, thirdly teachers, after that miracles, then gifts of healings, helps, governments, diversities of tongues." — 1 CORINTHIANS 12:28, KJV

The Greek word, "helps," is interestingly placed in the middle of 1 Corinthians 12:28. Helping others is in the middle of everything we do in the church. We cannot exist as a true, Biblical church without ministering to others. We all need help in some way! Incidentally, there is nothing better than helping others to get your mind off your own troubles! As children of God, when we are filled with the Holy Spirit, we are all given a measure of God's grace to love others and treat them as we would want to be treated.[13] This includes ministering to needy and/or unwed mothers and fathers and hard-working young families that are just starting out and could use a "hand up." In an ideal world, every young family will have already made financial preparations, and not every young family has parents or grandparents helping these days. When we work together in one accord, we strengthen the body of Christ. Since the ministry of "helps" is one of the gifts of the Spirit,[14] we can also pray to ask God for a special anointing in this area.

Every life has a purpose. Every call from God needs to be answered for us to fulfill God's plan for our lives and those of others we may influence. Recognizing that God uses the humble, we should speak encouragement into the ears of our fellow laborers in Christ. Many of us are fearful. We are usually afraid that we will not measure up to His expectations, but God knows who we are before He commissions us!

Many who serve often do not receive much public acknowledgment. Friendly, loving support is vital to strengthening the local body of Christ and the great, universal, Church of God today. Ephesians 4:16 says, "from whom the whole body, being fitted and held together by what every joint supplies, according to the proper working of each individual part, causes the growth of the body for the building up of itself in love."

If each of us is faithful to serve in whatever capacity the LORD leads us, our rewards are in Heaven. We are equally important to the body of Christ and the Kingdom of God if we remain faithful to the Word and prayerfully wait on God. The ministry of helps is very important to the function of the church. It is a ministry that covers a large area of services and is extremely important to the Church. The Church cannot operate properly without the office of helps.

God Gives His People Victory

Time is short. Jesus is coming back, but not for a sin-stained people. When He returns on the clouds in glory, He is coming back for a church without spot or wrinkle.[15] This means that He is coming for a pure and holy church, such as a bridegroom comes for a pure and virginal bride on their wedding day. He is not coming back for a complacent church that tolerates sin. He is not coming back for a church that compromises with the world, especially over the issue of abortion. All Christians need to be proactive in faith by uniting in prayer, sharing our faith, and gathering with other Christians in prayer meetings that are intent on calling down the power of God.

While we have the victory over Satan in Jesus Christ, we are still called to bring as many into God's Kingdom as possible. Tackling the important, yet difficult, issue of abortion in the twenty-first century involves saving the lives of babies while also encouraging Christian growth in those contemplating abortion. We must also minister to and disciple those who have already been involved in taking the lives of their babies, and we must share the Gospel message of forgiveness and salvation with abortionists. It is very humbling to realize that, without the grace of God, none of us are worthy of Heaven.

A Call to Holiness

First, we need to recognize that, as Christians, we are a kingdom of priests.[16] Rather than concentrating on the honor that such a title brings, we must concentrate on the duties of the office. In the book of Leviticus, we read that priests were directed to be purified in order to be qualified to enter the LORD's service. God explained in detail how the priests were to sanctify themselves.[17] There is no strength or power in God's work without being sanctified (separated from the worldly system). Living like the world opens us immediately into sin. Sin is the opposite of holiness. Sin is ugly but holiness is beautiful to behold.

> Give unto the LORD the glory due unto his name; worship the LORD in the beauty of holiness. — PSALM 22:9, KJV

The Apostle Peter directs us into holiness and sanctification, in his first epistle. He reminds us of the LORD's directive to "Be ye holy as I am holy."[18] Most of us wonder if we can reach God's standard of holiness but God would not give us this direction without first equipping us to do so! Even in the secular world, a good manager does not send his workers into the field without the necessary training and tools! God gives us His Word, which clearly states His position and what He expects of us.

We are expected to be separate from the world. That is why we need to accurately understand the concept of sanctification. We cannot battle with the god of this world if we are still on his spiritually dark team. James tells us that a fountain does not "send forth at the same place sweet water and bitter."[19] In our world today, we might call it "straddling the fence." Like Joshua, we must choose whom we will serve. Jesus says that we cannot serve two masters.[20] We will have no strength to serve the LORD while holding hands with the devil.

We must ask the LORD to sanctify us, and we must sanctify ourselves. We must remove ourselves from sin-infested, worldly concerns, and we must remove any ungodly, tangible elements from our homes. Burn them if the LORD leads you to. Sinful movies, music, and revealing street clothing must go. Tarot cards and Ouija boards need to be destroyed. Remember that the spirits who influenced Queens Jezebel and Athaliah, as well as King Herod, were involved with witchcraft in their pagan religion. We must stay away from horoscopes and mediums. These things are all condemned by God. (Read Deuteronomy, Ch. 18 for a full list of condemned occultic practices.) When we retreat from holiness, we are not able to work effectively for Jesus.

We are in this world, but we are not to be of this world.[21] We Christians are on a pilgrimage to our final destiny. "I go to prepare a place for you," Jesus said. "If it were not so I would have told you.[22] As we travel through this world, while raising our children, the best we can do is to work towards the advancement of the Kingdom of God, as best we can, while preparing the way for our grandchildren and future generations. As Jesus prepares a place for us, we pave the way for His return through service, worship, evangelism, and prayer. This is how we bless God. We do this all for His glory!

Children raised in Christian homes already know about the love of Jesus. Even they, however, may decide later in life that they really do not need the LORD. They may feel that they are just too smart to believe in what they cannot see. After all, they learn in school that scientific fact is to be held in higher esteem than what some call "old folk tales or stories." These kids then go the way of the world and forget the guiding hands of those that loved them and taught them about Jesus. It is hard to bring them back. We need to be on the frontlines doing spiritual warfare for all our children, our friend's children, and the children of our nation. The devil seeks to devour them.

Intrinsic Value of All Life

It still amazes me that there are people that condone abortion. A greater understanding of the Bible has shown me why there are seemingly nice people who believe in their hearts that abortion is a good and necessary practice! They are practicing self-deception. **The Bible tells us that we are living in the days when good is called evil and evil is called good.**[23] There are many other areas and situations where what God has ordained has been completely abandoned or else twisted by demonic lies.

Not everyone recognizes this, but there is value in all life that God has created. The life of every single human being has intrinsic value. As we read the first few verses of the book of Genesis, we see the delight that God has in His creation, which He called "good." Babies are precious gifts from above! Life is beautiful and to be cherished.

If the mother's womb is the safest and most comfortable place on earth for any baby and this miracle home is designed to nourish and protect, then **abortion is akin to a violent home invasion where the legal occupant ends up being brutalized, tortured, dismembered while alive, and then slain.** How does this honor God, who created us in His goodness?

> You are worthy, our Lord and God, to receive glory and honor and power, since you created all things, and

because of your will they existed and were created! —
REVELATION 4:11

There are many ways that abortion advocates undermine the value of preborn babies' lives and demean pro-lifers. We must remember that many of the remarks are demonically inspired, so there is no real answer to their accusations. This is a verse that we need to keep in prayer, concerning our country:

> He who justifies the wicked and he who condemns the righteous are both alike an abomination to the LORD.
> — PROVERBS 17:15

The strangest argument I have heard is that we who advocate for life are only pro-life until the baby is born. Since most pro-lifers are Christian, we know this is a false accusation. We care about the mothers and the babies. This is a serious accusation based on prejudiced conjecture. It is not possible to win a verbal argument with a pat answer, so, while we must be honest, the only way to win over pro-abortion-minded people is with our consistent love. This will help the truth to be revealed to them.

God is love. We must love the least among us, or we are not of God. We must choose sides. Either we are on the side of the abortionist, who is ruled by the spirit of Herod, or we are on God's side, praying against the evil bloodbath that has been taking place in our country, on a tremendous scale, for decades. There is no middle line. There is no gray area. Jesus told the complacent, lukewarm church of the Laodiceans that He would spit them out of His mouth.[24]

Adoption

As Christ-followers, we are compelled to tend to the orphan and widow, feed the poor, and clothe the naked. American churches are better at caring for those in need than we are at many things. Because we were founded on God's Word, the US is more generous than any other country in the world. We have shared our many blessings, which were given to us because of our Christian roots, which honored God. We are decidedly pro-life after the birth of babies.

When family members are unwilling or unable to care for a baby who was born because of unintended pregnancy, adoption is available. I have personally known many beautiful couples who were unable to conceive yet longed for a baby to complete their families. I have read that Christians are more likely to adopt than any other group of people. There are adoption websites that explain the differences between open and closed adoptions and answer any other questions. According to reliable information I have heard, practicing Christians have adopted more than twice as many times as other people groups, so finding a Christian family for a baby should not be difficult. Abortion costs are lightly touched on elsewhere in this book.

Will You Pray?

Preborn babies need our love and commitment to their health, safety, and well-being. A great part of that commitment needs to be time spent in prayer. There needs to be a heart change concerning abortion, not just a legal change. As I like to say, "Change will not come just through legislation; it can only come through a praying nation." We need to pray for state lawmakers to declare that no taxpayer funds should in any way be used to pay for abortions. Time is of the essence. Will you help our nation by praying for a resolution that is in God's will? As we lay it all down at the foot of the cross of Jesus, we know that God reigns supreme, and He will not tolerate evil forever. He has promised us Hope in Jesus. God is with us as we stay close to Him. Please ask God to show you where He wants you to serve. Serving in the place where God wants you is part of the abundant life that Jesus came to give us.

Please pray for those contemplating taking the life of their preborn babies. In abortion clinics across the nation, there are young mothers who are scared and uncertain about the future. Please pray that they will turn to Jesus and answer His call for Life. Please pray for abortionists across the land to lay down their tools of death and to turn to Jesus and accept His work on the Cross and ask for forgiveness.

Pray Against the Spirit of Herod

Please pray against the spirit that drove Herod the Great, and others, to slaughter the innocents. This spirit still drives the abortionist's knives and scissors today. It drives the males who force their wives and girlfriends to kill their unborn children. It drives the grandparents that force their daughters to kill their grandchildren. It is more subtle when it convinces a young woman that her "rights" are more important than that of her child. It is more subtle when it tells a parent to abort a Down Syndrome baby or a baby with other issues. It is more subtle when we tell a rape victim that it is alright to kill her baby. An abortion for that reason, however, is just as much a murder as is an abortion by a woman who willingly had relations that resulted in conception. **All life is sacred because God created us.**

Please pray for a change of heart for all those, across our great land, who believe that abortion is acceptable. We need to pray for all those that support abortion to come to a spiritual understanding of God's gift of life and an understanding that innocent blood is being shed daily in huge numbers. Please pray for the post-abortive women, that God will calm their troubled souls as they turn to Him for safety and forgiveness. Please pray for Life in America.

Preborn Babies Dream

Did you know that babies dream before they are born? Years ago, I read about sleep studies that proved that babies show rapid eye movement during REM sleep. This means that they dream! We may surmise that their dreams consist of sounds, light, and movement, and most likely the mother's voice, the father's voice, and the voices of others, such as siblings. Babies come into the world knowing their families. Perhaps they may even dream of music they hear while in the womb. We should consider the quality of the sounds to which we expose the preborn infant.

It is the dream of every Christian, pro-life advocate that each preborn baby will grow up to realize, not only his dreams but also the plan that God has for his life. As we spread the news of the great love of Jesus Christ, more people will be led by the Holy Spirit to understand the depravity of abortion. When He was preparing the disciples for His departure in John 16:7, KJV, Jesus told them that it was good that he was departing, because if, ". . . I go not away, the Comforter will not come unto you; but if I depart, I will send him unto you." The "Comforter" is the Holy Spirit, the Third Person of the Trinity. He is sent to help us and is also our Teacher and Guide in spiritual matters.[25]

Reflection: _What would have happened if Herod had succeeded in killing the baby Jesus? A dying world would have been deprived of the ministry and the salvation of Jesus Christ!_

Deposit the Love of Christ into the World Bank

The world economy is a subject of interest to many, and it is an important subject. We need to sustain ourselves and others. Our moral condition is also important in God's eyes. Because of our current lack of Biblical moorings, we, as a nation, have become increasingly morally bankrupt. For example, we allow violent and sexual movies to assault our eyes and ears. We also have been persuaded to compromise our Christian values when they conflict with secular mainstream thinking, which Jesus would never do.

Our eyes and ears should be receiving the things of Christ. Our lips should be speaking only Christ-like words. Our hearts should be filled with the love of Jesus as we minister to others in this dark and dangerous world. We should make daily deposits into the bank of love, which will benefit all people, including our elderly, our children, and our precious preborn.

Jesus Lesson: "You are the light of the world. A city set on a hill cannot be hidden; nor do people light a lamp and put it under a basket, but on the lampstand, and it gives light to all who are in the house. Your light must shine before people in such a way that they may see your good works, and glorify your Father who is in heaven (Matt. 5:14-16)."

Life suggestion: Talk with others. Ask God to show you the way to share the truth of life. This is one of the life purposes of every Christian. Matthew 29:19 describes our "commission." Our light should shine so brightly that it draws others to the Light of Christ.

Conclusion

While out walking one day, near the top of a mountain in the Southern Appalachian Mountain range, I stumbled upon a small, old graveyard. As I explored the area near the rear of the yard, where the older graves lay, I noticed two headstones that were highly decorated — obviously, the graves of small children. As I inspected the site a little more closely, I saw that one grave was of a baby who was less than one month old when she went to be with Jesus, and the other was possibly a stillborn as she was born and had died on the very same day.

What struck me most profoundly was the love put into each little resting place. I had seen such love displayed before in other cemeteries, in other states, far away from where I was that day. What was evident about these, however, was that the gravestones were handmade. One was a cross cast in cement. Since it did not look professionally made, in my mind's eye I pictured some grief-stricken father laying a wooden form and pouring wet cement into the wood as a labor of love. I pictured the heartache and the holding back of tears as he worked to mark the grave of his little one.

The other headstone was in the shape of an arch, as is common to headstones, but it was rugged and hand-hewn of native rock, with the child's name clearly carved out by hand in rough letters. There was a matching little footstone as well. It was another strong reminder of a parent's sorrow and love. At the foot of this little grave were posted small statues of guardian angels. Artificial flowers and a metal post with pictures of flowers and butterflies decorated the area around the headstone. The grave of the other little one, with the cement cross, was also decorated. There was a small guardian angel there, a few smaller crosses, a necklace, and more brightly colored artificial flowers.

These babies, with lives so short, were clearly loved and cherished. Fourteen years separated their little lives, but this they clearly shared — they were a blessing to their families, even if their stay on this earth was very brief. The love these families expressed through their efforts to beautify their children's graveyard resting spots were clearly deep, and their grief more devastating than could be shown by an outward show of flowers and other decorations. It seemed to me that their grief ran more deeply than the deep, dark current in the stream that ran through the valley below.

Each little child is special! Each is unique in his or her gifts and character. Every mother knows this. Some babies do not live beyond birth, but the love they bring into their parents' and grandparents' lives is exceptional. For reasons we do not understand on this side of eternity, God allows some babies to touch our lives only briefly. Others live long and hardy lives, and today, due to medical discoveries and even sometimes more access to better foods, we have more centenarians than ever before in history. In the end, if we acknowledge that God is our Father in Heaven, then we must leave the choice of life and death to Him. We must have faith that He knows more than we ever could about his design for each one of us. He knows best. Therefore, we must leave the decisions of life and death to Him: He is God, and we are not!

> I am the LORD, and there is no other, Besides Me there is no God . . . — ISAIAH 45:5a, b

Abortion Survivor Testimony

I have heard the testimonies of many abortion survivors. It takes only a quick search on the internet to come up with many names and testimonies of those whose mothers sought to end their little lives before they had a chance to be born. Miraculously, there are many stories about those who lived through chemical burnings in the womb. There are many other horrors to be heard, yet there are so many adults, who as little preborn babies, fought hard for life! I read about one man who lives with the use of only one arm, the result of a botched D&E abortion. In this type of abortion, a baby is torn limb by limb, one section at a time, while still in the womb. Many people struggle with daily existence because of their birth and pre-birth trauma. Even so, I have never heard one abortion survivor proclaim the wish that he or she had never lived!

The following is a letter given to me by a very good friend who found an ability to experience forgiveness in her own heart. She has given me permission to use it in hope that it will others. The names are changed.

3/1/17

My name is Mandy and I am an abortion survivor. I have often stated that I could have lived my life without ever having known the information in this story which I am about to share. However, as I recall the scripture (Romans 8:28): "And we know that all things work together for good to them that love God, to them who are the called according to his purpose."; I know that the information was called to my attention for a definite reason. It has become very clear to me that I am called to share this testimony for the purpose of helping others.

This story begins prior to my marriage or having a child of my own. One night, long ago, my sister shared with me information that I did not initially believe. I've tried to recall, exactly what brought up the topic of conversation, and the only thing I can think of, is that I must have been defending my parents. I recall telling my sister that there are many children that have had worse parents than we did. My sister then told me that my parents are not the wonderful people I believe them to be. She continued to explain to me, that when my Mother was pregnant with me, she tried to have me aborted three times!

Let me take a short aside here: I am the "baby" of the family; I have two older sisters, one ten years older than me, the other, sixteen years older. My sister Susan is ten years older than me, we have the same father and she is the sister that told me this story. My other sister, Brenda, is sixteen years older than me and does not have the same father as Susan and I. Actually, my mother never told Brenda who her father was. It is my understanding, from other family members, that Brenda's father was a married man. He had told my mother that he was going to leave his wife and children to marry her. This never happened and my mother had Brenda alone and unmarried; she never even told the man she was having the affair with, that she was pregnant by him. My mother's parents helped raise Brenda. My mother met my father and married him when Brenda was approximately 5 years old. My Father, William, legally adopted Brenda and gave her his name. As I think back on all of this, I guess many of Brenda's "antics" sort of add up, to a certain extent.

As I've already stated, Susan was 10 years older than me so she would have been 9 years old when our mom had the abortion attempts. I asked Susan why our parents would have done such a thing and how and why, with her being only 9 years old, she would have even known about it. Susan told me she was "there." Again, I asked her what did she mean that she was "there"? Susan told me she distinctly remembers going to the park with Daddy; she thought it was odd that they went to the park at night. She remembers Mom walking up a flight of stairs and wanting to go with her, but Dad said no, they were going to the park. Susan says that Dad was pushing her on a swing and crying. I've never seen my Father cry. I saw him get teared up once right before his heart surgery, but I've never seen him cry. Susan explained to me that after overhearing different family members speaking about this, through the years, she put two and two together. But again, the question was WHY? Susan told me that

Brenda had accused my Father to my Mother of "touching" her.

After I was given this information, I sort of discarded it, as I felt it was fabrication/imagination. Later, when I was married and expecting a child of my own, I shared this information with my husband. I was led to question other family members (my Aunts, my Mother's sisters), about the story Susan had shared with me. As I began to question other family members, I realized, due to their reactions (a lot of um, ahh, ums), that there must be something to this story. Both of my Moms sisters each told me that "that was a very difficult time in everyone's life and they didn't like to think about it, much less talk about it." I continued to question about my Mother's pregnancy with me and realized that the only way I would ever get a straight answer, was to speak with my Mother personally.

Shortly after my son was born, my Mother came to my home to visit with her grandson, William (I named my son after my Father.) The baby was asleep in the crib and that allowed time for my Mother and I to speak, over coffee, in the kitchen. I confronted my Mother, with the information that had been shared with me, years earlier. To my utter shock, my own Mother confirmed that the information was, indeed, correct. At this time, my Mother stated to me that: "I will not apologize for what I did, prior to you even being born, however, I want you to know, that the moment I saw you and held you in my arms, I loved you, and would have given my own life for you!" My Mother made a comment to the effect that "she always knew in her heart the day would come, although she'd hoped and prayed it wouldn't, that she would have to explain to me what she had attempted to do when she was pregnant with me; something about her sin finding her out."

As this tearful discussion continued, I asked my Mom if it was really true she tried this three different times. The answer was, yes. I remember being so very hurt and asking my Mom if maybe after the first time it didn't work, she might have thought the Lord was trying to tell her something. I'm reminded of Psalm 139: 13-16 "For thou hast possessed my reins: thou hast covered me in my mother's womb. I will praise thee; for I am fearfully and wonderfully made: marvelous are thy works; and that my soul knoweth right well. My substance was not hid from thee, when I was made in secret, and curiously wrought in the lowest parts of the earth. Thine eyes did see my substance, yet being unperfect; and in thy book all my members were written, which in continuance were fashioned, when as yet there was none of them." My Mother went on to explain to me that she did what she felt was right "under difficult circumstances" She took her daughter Brenda's word, over my Father's. She said she already had two children and couldn't see bringing another into this situation.

I defended my Father, although I was angry with him as well for allowing this to go on. I knew in my heart that the man I called Father was not capable of what he had been accused. I was absolutely correct! My Mother went on to explain that shortly after I was born, Brenda came to her and said she'd made up the whole story about Daddy "touching" her; she just did it for "attention"! As my Mom and I continued to talk, we realized that this was just the beginning of a long list of male family members that Brenda accused of doing things they didn't. I thank God that no marriages broke up over these stories (although difficult problems arose.) As if what was said and done when my Mom was pregnant with me wasn't enough, Brenda later accused my own husband of the same.

Although my Mom told me she would not apologize for something she considered to be right at the time and under the particular circumstances, I told her I did not fault her and that I forgave her. I was also able to forgive my sister

Brenda, but that took a bit longer. I know that my Mother believed I had forgiven her because she asked me to make her a promise that day. She made me promise that I would never let my Father know that I was aware of all of this; Mom said she was afraid it would kill him. I made and kept that promise to my Mother that day. I never spoke of this to my Father and actually, haven't really spoken to any others about it; until now.

As I think back on the day my Mother told me the truth about what happened during her pregnancy with me, I remember my infant son asleep in his crib and am reminded of Proverbs 17:6 "Children's children are the crown of old men: and the glory of children are their fathers." I often wonder what would have become of my parents, had I not been born (kind of like the Capra story "It's A Wonderful Life") My husband and I were the ones that took care of my parents and their families. Neither one of my sisters were of much assistance. We cared for my Father during his illness and we moved into my parent's home, after Daddy's death, to take care of my Mother. "Lo, children are an heritage of the Lord: and the fruit of the womb is his reward." Psalm 127:3

A Word regarding forgiveness (actually, I'll use God's Holy Word). "Forbearing one another, and forgiving one another, if any man have a quarrel against any: even as Christ forgave you, so also do ye." Colossians 3:13 and Matthew 6: 12 state: "And forgive us our debts, as we forgive our debtors. "In 2 Corinthians 12, the apostle Paul speaks about God's strength being made perfect in our weakness. It is only through the shed blood of Christ and His forgiveness, that I am able to forgive. Thank you Lord for your merciful grace and the power of your Holy Spirit.

The point of sharing this story. . . I am a living, breathing, walking, talking MIRACLE! I am here only by the grace of Almighty God and His divine intervention! I'm reminded of Psalm 71 and also of Psalm 91:4 "He shall cover thee with his *feathers, and under his wings shalt thou trust: his truth shall be thy shield and buckler." Oh, to have been able to see what was going on in the spirit realm those many years ago as I lay innocently and safely in my Mother's womb (to know what saint of God must have been praying for me, yet unborn); God was with me then and He is with me now. It is the Lord who guides me to speak out for LIFE! Choose life! The Lord allowed me to know these truths so they can be used for His honor and His glory!*

Did you know that blood has a voice? "And he (God) said, What hast thou done? the voice of thy brother's blood crieth unto me from the ground." Genesis 4:10 I know that the blood of murdered infants cries out to the Lord... for justice. Abortion affects more than just the mother and child involved; it's like a form of "ground zero" and the shock waves of destruction continually resonate throughout the lives of the remaining family members. Saints of God, His chosen, His elect; we must continually cry out to the Lord for these innocents. Jesus blessed the little children and told his disciples to "forbid them not, for of such is the kingdom of God." The Word tells us in John 10:10 that "Satan comes but for to steal, kill and destroy." We need to get by all the "fancy" words and phrases like women's health care, planned parenthood, fetus, abortion, terminate the pregnancy, etc . . . We need to seek and speak the truth of the matter; Satan is a liar, he is the father of all lies, and he is lying and murdering our children. We must bombard the throne of grace with our prayers, we must cry out to the Lord for His help and intervention. We must be willing to do His work and what He asks of us. He will guide us, He will give us the strength and the ideas, the holy boldness to do His will and His work. If the telling of this story might save just one precious baby. . .
Mandy

My Thoughts

In a short dream last year, God revealed to me that the writer of the preceding letter is a spiritual general in God's army. In my dream, she was dressed similarly to the officers in the Salvation Army, although she is not associated with that group. In the natural, she is a sweet wife of a pastor and volunteers a tremendous amount of her time helping a young family by babysitting for a family of four children, while the mom works. She receives no financial compensation, but we know her reward awaits her in Heaven! Only a woman with an incredible connection to God could have the patience and love necessary to be a surrogate grandmother to this family, and I am sure they are thankful for her. She also gives great assistance to her church. She is a beautiful testimony to the grace, mercy, and generosity of God!

Prayer to Deliver Our Land from the Sin of Abortion

I hope that you will pray along with me, or please add your own prayer, as the Holy Spirit leads!

Our Heavenly Father and LORD, we acknowledge You as the Creator of the universe and of each little baby.

LORD, Deliver us from the sin of abortion. Bring our nation to its knees in repentance. We cry out for justice for the unborn babies who are the work of Your creative powers. Bless us with hearts of humility and forbearance, that we will not ignore the cries of the unborn babies. We pray that we will not ignore the blatant disregard for human life by the workers of iniquity – the abortionists.

LORD, Deliver us from greed. Help us to be aware of the ulterior motives of those in the abortion industry.

LORD, Deliver us from bloody hands. Cleanse us as we repent of the deaths of your little children, whom You love.

LORD, Deliver us from negligence as we have largely ignored the loss of life all around us. Your precious gift of life is mocked in every corner of the nation as the abortionist's scissors, knives, and chemicals seek the death and destruction of our most precious gift – our nation's children.

LORD, Be with the mothers and fathers of these little ones and help them to see Your magnificence. Help them turn to You and Your guiding hand in their moments of need, rather than to the bloody hands of the abortionists.

LORD, Carry us through to a place of cleansing. Wash away our sins of greed, avarice, and murder. We praise you for Your mercy! Bring us to a place where our nation can experience Your loving forgiveness and mercy!

LORD, Bless us and keep us daily by Your side as You lovingly guide us to do Your work as Your servants. Help us to increase Your Kingdom on earth by helping us to show others the path to You and Your righteousness. Let Holiness be our direction, and You our Guide, as we prayerfully turn this nation back to You.

In the Name of Jesus Christ, our Savior, we pray all of this, Amen.

Let Your Light Shine

Thank you for embarking upon this journey with me as we explored what God has to say about the importance of life. I sincerely apologize and repent to God and my fellow man for allowing so much time to pass before fully revealing what God has told me to share. Life has been busying me in many directions, and I do not doubt that part of that, at least, has been spiritual warfare against the release of this book. This is information that Satan does not want to be revealed. Any work that glorifies the cross of Jesus and His resurrection and shares the Gospel message is a weapon against the power of sin. I have surrendered all to my LORD and Savior, and my prayer is that every person reading this will also do this. Will you join with me and others, and will you allow God to lead and guide you?

Lately, there has been an upsurge in organizations and individuals who are willing to stand up to the lies of the evil one. They are boldly pronouncing them as demonic and wrong. If you are among them, I thank God for you! If you are seeking answers, then I pray that you will finish this book with a clear picture of the truth. In the book of John, Jesus explains that the Holy Spirit of God guides us into all truth.[1] May the Holy Spirit inspire each one of us as we delve into His Word. Let us always be attentive to hear what the Spirit of God has to say about the issues of life and death in the United States today.

> For my mouth will utter truth; And wickedness is an abomination to my lips. — PROVERBS 8:7

We must submit to God and resist the enemy. We have authority over the kingdom of darkness only in the name of the LORD Jesus Christ. We must fear God, but not the devil. Fear feeds upon itself and grows because we allow it. All authority over the enemy is ours. We also cannot stress the love of God enough, as we minister to others. In his work, John Wesley said, "You have nothing to do but to save souls."[2]

My Prayers of Love for You

When Jesus gave the beggar, who was born blind, the ability to see he had to explain his healing to the Pharisees. He said, "He applied clay to my eyes, and I washed, and I see."[3] My prayer is that those reading this book who have been involved with or hurt by abortion will accept Jesus's healing. May the scripture verses be applied to your spiritual eyes, like the clay that Jesus applied, and may you wash your spiritual eyes and see the truth.

My prayer for everyone reading this book is for blessings and abundant life! Also, I pray the same for you that Paul prayed in Ephesians (that):

"He would grant you, according to the riches of His glory, to be strengthened with power through His Spirit in the inner man, so that Christ may dwell in your hearts through faith; and that you, being rooted and grounded in love, may be able to comprehend with all the saints what is the breadth and length and height and depth, and to know the love of Christ which surpasses knowledge, that you may be filled up to all the fullness of God." — Ephesians 3:16 -19

Letter to All Pastors and Church Leaders

Dear Pastor, Church Leader, and other Leaders of any Assembly, who desire to promote "Life,"

Please allow me to share with you the mission God gave me, which I have been called to after years of ministry as a pastor, evangelist, Christian radio host, and music minister.

Years ago, God placed a burden on my heart to be a voice for the preborn. Recently the Lord has led me to seek opportunities to speak to the larger Christian community regarding the sanctity of life and the Good News that Jesus

Christ is life-affirming, as well as loving and forgiving. I believe that He wants to both deliver the most vulnerable from death and bring healing to those suffering the guilt of abortion. My message is informative, highlights Bible truths, and is supportive, affirming love and forgiveness.

Although the exact numbers are unknown, it has been estimated one out of every four women had an abortion, with an equally large number of men affected also. Many identify as Christian. Abortion is often an uncomfortable and difficult issue for pastors to deal with, either from the pulpit or in counseling. I feel called to be of service to bring hope and healing to these hurting hearts.

During my years of ministry, I have worked with churches and church leaders from many denominations, including Presbyterian, United Methodist, Nazarene, and Pentecostal, as well as non-denominational and interdenominational fellowships. I believe that all Christians can work together to prevent violence and foster healing and reconciliation for our most vulnerable persons: the preborn.

If you feel that my ministry can be of help to you and your congregation, I am available to speak at regular services, address groups within the congregation (women's, men's, youth, and young adults), lead retreats (day-long or longer), and to consult with you as to how your congregation can address these needs and concerns. I am living by faith and do not charge fees, but love offerings are appreciated.

Please pray as to whether my ministry may be a blessing to you and your congregation. I will pray that God our Father will continue to bless you and your ministry. I look forward to talking with you.

Your sister in Christ,

Melanie Jean Garuffi

Bibliography

Preface

1. Jones, Lewis E., There Is Power in the Blood. 1949, Public Domain.

2. Philippians 4:13

3. Jeremiah 30:11

4. Ezra 9:42

5. Chronicles 7:14

6. Matthew 2:1-16

7. John 8:40

8. Matthew 27:19

9. 1 John 4:1

10. John 16:13

11. Matthew 4:17

12. Matthew 18:25

13. Gehman, Ph.D., S.T.D., Henry Snyder; Davis, John D., Ph.D., D. D., LL.D.,The Westminster Dictionary of the Bible., The Trustees of the Presbyterian Board of Publication and Sabbath-School Work, U.S.A.: The Westminster Press, 1944, Print, 62.

14. Matthew 5:13-17

15. 1 Peter 3:20

16. Unger, Merrill F. Unger's Bible Dictionary. Chicago, Illinois: Moody Press, 1970, Print, 2.

17. Revelation 4:11

18. Revelation 1:7

19. John 1:12; Galatians 3:26; Romans 8:17

20. Ephesians 2:2, KJV

Chapter One — God's Call

1. Thessalonians 5:17

2. Matthew 10:29

3. Ezra 9:4

4. Mark 12:3b

5. Hebrews 4:15

6. John 3:17

7. Matthew 25:40

8. 1 Kings 19:12

9. John 17:23

10. Ephesians 6:13-17

11. Romans 1:22

12. Acts 4:29

13. Hebrews 11:10

14. Ephesians 6:12

15. Job 38:4-7

16. Hebrews 13:2

17. Revelation 12:4

18. Isaiah 49:16

19. Matthew 6:13

20. Romans 12:12

21. 2 Corinthians 4:4

Chapter Two — An Evil King — The Spirit of Herod

1. Revelation 20:1-10

2. Mark 3:23-26

3. Jude 1:9

4. James 4:7

5. Ephesians 6:16

6. Revelation 5:5

7. Unger, Merrill F. Unger's Bible Dictionary. Chicago, Illinois: Moody Press, 1970. Print, 470

8. Unger, Merrill F. Unger's Bible Dictionary. Chicago, Illinois: Moody Press, 1970. Print, 470

9. Unger, Merrill F. Unger's Bible Dictionary. Chicago, Illinois: Moody Press, 1970. Print, 471

10. Douglass, J. D., M.A., B.D., S.T.M., Ph.D, ed. The New Bible Dictionary. Grand Rapids, Michigan: Wm. B. Eerdman's Publishing Co., 1962, Print, 522.

11. Unger, Merrill F. Unger's Bible Dictionary. Chicago, Illinois: Moody Press, 1970. Print, 471.

12. Gehman, Ph.D., S.T.D., Henry Snyder; Davis, John D., Ph.D., D. D., LL.D., The Westminster Dictionary of the Bible., The Trustees of the Presbyterian Board of Publication and Sabbath-School Work, U.S.A.: The Westminster Press, 1944, Print, 238.

13. Douglass, J. D., M.A., B.D., S.T.M., Ph.D, ed. The New Bible Dictionary. Grand Rapids, Michigan: Wm. B. Eerdman's Publishing Co., 1962, Print, 522.

14. Josephus, Flavius, The Complete Works of Josephus, Antiquities of the Jews, Trans. by Whiston, William A. M., Grand Rapids, MI, Kregal Publications, 1960, 1978, 1981, Print. (Book XVI, Ch. III, pg. 340; Ch. XI, pg. 355)

15. Josephus, Flavius, The Complete Works of Josephus, Antiquities of the Jews, Trans. by Whiston, William A. M., Grand Rapids, MI, Kregal Publications, 1960, 1978, 1981, Print. (Book XVI, Ch. III, pg. 340;)

16. Josephus, Flavius, The Complete Works of Josephus, Antiquities of the Jews, Trans. by Whiston, William A. M., Grand Rapids, MI, Kregal Publications, 1960, 1978, 1981. Print. Book XVI, Ch. III, 339; Ch. VII, 347.

17. Gehman, Ph.D., S.T.D., Henry Snyder; Davis, John D., Ph.D., D. D., LL.D., The Westminster Dictionary of the Bible., The Trustees of the Presbyterian Board of Publication and Sabbath-School Work, U.S.A.: The Westminster Press, 1944, Print, 238.

18. Matthew 14:1-12

19. Josephus, Flavius, The Complete Works of Josephus, Antiquities of the Jews, Trans. by Whiston, William A. M., Grand Rapids, MI, Kregal Publications, 1960, 1978, 1981, Print. Book XVII, Ch. VII, 365; Ch. VII, 347.

20. Josephus, Flavius, The Complete Works of Josephus, Antiquities of the Jews, Trans. by Whiston, William A. M., Grand Rapids, MI, Kregal Publications, 1960, 1978, 1981, Print. (Book XVII, Ch. VIII, pg. 367)

21. Unger, Merrill F. Unger's Bible Dictionary. Chicago, Illinois: Moody Press, 1970. Print, 471.

22. Ruth 4:13-22

23. Ruth 1:14,15

24. Luke 23:39-43

25. John 1:29 (KJV)

26. Revelation 19:16

27. Genesis 29:18

28. Zachariah 2:8

29. John 1:12

30. Romans 8:17

31. Hebrews 11:10, KJV

32. Douglass, J. D., M.A., B.D., S.T.M., Ph.D, ed. The New Bible Dictionary. Grand Rapids, Michigan: Wm. B. Eerdman's Publishing Co., 1962, Print, 1074.

33. John 1:1,14

Chapter Three — The Loss of the Promise of the Future

1. Genesis 1:28

2. Roe v. Wade, 410 U.S. 113 (1973)

3. Ruth 4:11

4. Genesis 24:60, KJV

5. Genesis 20:17-18

6. 1 Samuel 1:9-20

7. Genesis 1:28, KJV

8. Exodus 1:22

9. Exodus 1:12

10. Exodus 2:2

11. Exodus 1:17

12. Exodus 1:21

13. Genesis 1:26

14. John 17:3

15. Matthew 4:1-10

16. Revelation 19:16

17. 1 Peter 1:18-20

18. 1 Corinthians 3:19a, KJV

19. John 6:44

20. 1 Corinthians 5:6, KJV

21. Stevens, W. B., Farther Along, Date unknown. (Later published by Warren, Barney E., 1911) Public Domain.

22. Revelation 20:11-15

23. Proverbs 6:17

Chapter Four — The Value of Life

1. Isaiah 46:10

2. Genesis 11:1-9

3. Psalm 36:9

4. John 8:44

5. Genesis 3:20

6. John 3:17

7. Matthew 10:30

8. Genesis 6:4

9. Galatians 3:26

10. CDC, Reproductive Health, https.www.cdc.gov/reproductivehealth/data_states/abortion. htm Web. 27 May 2019 United States. Dept. of Health and Human Services. Centers for Disease Control and Prevention, Web. 22 July 2019

11. Proverbs 11:17

12. Genesis 1:26

13. Psalm 8:6

14. Genesis 1:27

Chapter Five — The Valley of Slaughter

1. Exodus 3:14, KJV

2. Ezekiel 23:37

3. Smith, Wm. LL.D.; Peloubet, Rev. F. N. & M. A., Revised & Ed., Teacher's Edition – Bible Dictionary, A Dictionary of the Bible: Chicago, Philadelphia, Chicago: The John C. Winston Co., Porter and Coates, 1884, Print (p. 710).

4. 1 Kings 11:7

5. 2 Kings 16:3; 2 Chronicles 28:3; 33:6

6. Smith, Wm. LL.D.; Peloubet, Rev. F. N. & M. A., Revised & Ed., Teacher's Edition – Bible Dictionary, A Dictionary of the Bible: Chicago, Philadelphia, Chicago: The John C. Winston Co., Porter and Coates, 1884. Print, 710.

7. Smith, Wm. LL.D.; Peloubet, Rev. F. N. & M. A., Revised & Ed., Teacher's Edition – Bible Dictionary, A Dictionary of the Bible: Chicago, Philadelphia, Chicago: The John C. Winston Co., Porter and Coates, 1884. Print, 241.

8. Smith, Wm. LL.D.; Peloubet, Rev. F. N. & M. A., Revised & Ed., Teacher's Edition – Bible Dictionary, A Dictionary of the

Bible: Chicago, Philadelphia, Chicago: The John C. Winston Co., Porter and Coates, 1884. Print, 250.

9. Unger, Merrill F. Unger's Bible Dictionary. Chicago, Illinois: Moody Press, 1970. Print, 413.

10. Colossians 1:16; Romans 8:38

11. Ephesians 6:12

12. 1 Kings 18:28

13. Genesis 12:1-5

14. Unger, Merrill F. Unger's Bible Dictionary. Chicago, Illinois: Moody Press, 1970. Print, 415.

15. Judges 8:33; 9:4

16. Unger, Merrill F. Unger's Bible Dictionary. Chicago, Illinois: Moody Press 1970. Print, 130.

17. Smith, Wm. LL.D.; Peloubet, Rev. F. N. & M. A., Revised & Ed., Teacher's Edition – Bible Dictionary, A Dictionary of the Bible: Chicago, Philadelphia, Chicago: The John C. Winston Co., Porter and Coates, 1884. Print, 413.

18. Psalm 96:9, KJV

19. Smith, Wm. LL.D.; Peloubet, Rev. F. N. & M. A., Revised & Ed., Teacher's Edition – Bible Dictionary, A Dictionary of the Bible: Chicago, Philadelphia, Chicago: The John C. Winston Co., Porter and Coates, 1884. Print, 60.

20. Smith, Wm. LL.D.; Peloubet, Rev. F. N. & M. A., Revised & Ed., Teacher's Edition – Bible Dictionary, A Dictionary of the Bible: Chicago, Philadelphia, Chicago: The John C. Winston Co., Porter and Coates, 1884. Print, 145.

21. Smith, Wm. LL.D.; Peloubet, Rev. F. N. & M. A., Revised & Ed., Teacher's Edition – Bible Dictionary, A Dictionary of the

Bible: Chicago, Philadelphia, Chicago: The John C. Winston Co., Porter and Coates, 1884. Print, 60.

22. 2 Kings 23:4-14

23. Genesis 31:19

24. Isaiah 14:12; Revelation 12:7-9

25. 2 Peter 2:4, Jude 1:6

26. Matthew 25:41

27. 1 Kings 1:19

28. 2 Chronicles 21:6

29. 2 Kings 11:1

30. 2 Kings 11:4-21

31. Smith, Wm. LL.D.; Peloubet, Rev. F. N. & M. A., Revised & Ed., Teacher's Edition – Bible Dictionary, A Dictionary of the Bible: Chicago, Philadelphia, Chicago: The John C. Winston Co., Porter and Coates, 1884. Print, 413 – 414.

32. 2 Kings 9:1-33

33. 2 Corinthians 11:14

34. Revelation 2:20

35. Luke 16:15

36. Mark 6:21-23

37. Douglass, J. D., M.A., B.D., S.T.M., Ph.D, ed. The New Bible Dictionary. Grand Rapids, Michigan: Wm. B. Eerdman's Publishing Co., 1962. Print, 1125.

38. Mark 6:25

39. CDC, Reproductive Health, cdc.gov/reproductivehealth/data_states/abortion.htm.web. 27 May 2019

40. CDC, Reproductive Health, cdc.gov/reproductivehealth/data_states/abortion.htm.web. 27

41. Jeremiah 19:6

42. Hebrews 13:5

43. 1 Peter 2:24

44. Ephesians 2:8, 9

Chapter Six — Spiritual Battle for the Heart of America

1. Genesis 1:28

2. Ephesians 5:25

3. Psalm 10:18

4. Isaiah 55:11

5. Hebrews 4:12

6. https.www.cdc.gov/reproductivehealth/data_states/abortion.htm Web. 27 May 2019 United States. Dept. of Health and Human Services. Centers for Disease Control and Prevention. Centers for Disease Control and Prevention, Web. 22 July 2019

7. Webster, Noah, "abortion" websters1913.com. Webster's 1913 Dictionary, 1913, Web. 11 July 2019.

8. Webster's New World Dictionary and Student Handbook, Elementary Edition, International Copyright Union, Pan-American Conventions of Montevideo, Mexico, Rio de Janeiro,

Buenos Aires and Havana: The World Publishing Company - The Southwestern Company, 1966. Print.

9. Exodus 20:13, KJV

10. Genesis 3:15

11. Matthew 19:30

12. Ephesians 2:2

13. Job 42:12

14. Miriam Webster online

15. Webster, Noah, "propaganda" websters1913.com. Webster's 1913 Dictionary, 1913, Web. 11 July 2019.

16. Isaiah 5:20

17. 1 Peter 5:8

18. Ephesians 5:25

19. John 8:44

20. Ephesians 2:2

21. 1 Timothy 4:1

Chapter Seven — Judgment

1. Psalm 7:11

2. Haggai 1:13; Matthew 28:20

3. Habakkuk 1:2

4. Webster, Noah, "propaganda" websters1913.com. Webster's 1913 Dictionary, 1913, Web. 11 July 2019

5. Revelation 3:16

6. Proverbs 6:16, 17

7. Romans 1:28

8. 1 Timothy 6:10

9. Luke 10:18

10. 1 John 4:18

11. Matthew 24:44

12. Psalm 33:9

13. Ecclesiastes 12:14

14. John 6:44

15. Ephesians 2:9

16. 1 John 4:16

17. Jeremiah 23:5; 1 John 2:1

18. Hebrews 13:8

19. John 1:29 KJV

Chapter Eight — Hope and Forgiveness

1. Genesis 19:37

2. Ezra 9:10-12

3. Matthew 1:5 and the Book of Ruth

4. Matthew 1:3; Luke 3:33; Genesis 38:6-30

5. Joshua 2:1, 2:3; 6:17-25; Matthew 1:5, Heb. 11:3

6. 2 Samuel 11:1-17; Matthew 1:6

7. 2 Corinthians 5:8

8. Philippians 1:22-24

9. Revelation 20:1-15

10. 1 Thessalonians 5:17, KJV

11. John 8:7

12. James. 1:17

13. 1 Corinthians 13:8

14. 1 Samuel 2:6

15. Matthew 12:31

16. Matthew 13:43

17. Matthew 4:17

18. Matthew 28:18

19. 1 Corinthians 15:3

20. 1 Corinthians 4-6

21. Romans 8:6

22. Luke 18:17, KJV

Chapter Nine — The Church — Light Dispels the Darkness

1. Matthew 25:41

2. Acts 19:15, KJV

3. 2 Corinthians 11:4

4. Leviticus 17:11

5. 1 John 4:18

6. Luke 1:39

7. Acts 11:1-18

8. Matthew 16:18

9. Matthew 28:18-20

10. 1 Peter 4:17, KJV

11. Matthew 13:41,42,49,50

12. Matthew 8:29; Romans 6:23; Jude 13; Revelation 20:7-10

13. 1 Peter 5:8

14. Judges 4:9

15. Judges 4:22

16. 1 Corinthians 6:9

17. 2 Corinthians 4:4

18. Joshua 24:15

19. Revelation 7:17

20. Colossians 3:11, KJV

21. Jesus Loves the Little Children, Public Domain.

22. Wesley, Charles, And Can It Be That I Should Gain? 1738, Public Domain.

23. 1 John 4:18

24. Joel 2:23

25. John 7:38,39

26. Isaiah 35:8

Chapter Ten — Winning the Victory

1. Baring-Gould, Sabine, Onward Christian Soldiers. 1865, Public Domain.

2. Romans 2:14,15

3. Ecclesiastes 2:14, KJV

4. Jeremiah 29:4-10

5. 2 Peter 3:9

6. John 3:17

7. Acts 5:29b

8. Ephesians 5:18

9. Matthew 5:5, KJV

10. Unger, Merrill F. Unger's Bible Dictionary. Chicago, Illinois: Moody Press, 1970. Print, 709.

11. Hebrews 10:25

12. Matthew 14:28-31

13. Matthew 7:12

14. 1 Corinthians 12:28, KJV

15. Ephesians 5:27

16. Revelation 1:6

17. Leviticus 20:7-8; 26

18. 1 Peter 1:9, KJV

19. James 3:11, KJV

20. Matthew 6:24

21. John 17:14,15

22. John 14:1

23. Isaiah 5:20

24. Revelation 3:14-22

25. John 16:13

Let Your Light Shine

1. John 16:13

2. Wesley, John; The Works of the Rev. John Wesley, A.M., First Complete Standard Edition, J. Emory, B. Waugh, pub., J. Collard, printer, 1831, Print.

3. John 9:15b

www.ingramcontent.com/pod-product-compliance
Lightning Source LLC
Chambersburg PA
CBHW060000100426
42740CB00010B/1350